Horace

HORACE

By Jacques Perret

Translated by Bertha Humez

NEW YORK UNIVERSITY PRESS   1964

14994

The original French edition of this
book appeared under the title Horace
and was published by Hatier, Paris.

WITTY, capable of indignation but almost impossible to ruffle, thoughtful but not profound, well-informed but scornful of pendantry, Horace is the best known and the least known of Roman poets. He has told us of the stars at his birth, his father's concern to have him properly schooled, his cowardice at Philippi, the little farm in the Sabine hills, the slender girls who, he keeps insisting, could not resist him, his affection for his friends, and his observance of the rituals of Dionysus. He has acknowledged the kindnesses of Maecenas, submitted his own theory of poetry to searching inquiry, denied that he has any influence in government circles, snubbed a major bore, deplored the delinquency of the younger generation, and kidded politicians, poets, legacy-hunters, name-droppers, madames, mad philosophers, artful blondes, and other stock characters-about-town. *Aere perennius, Graecia capta, parcus deorum cultor, aurea mediocritas, integer vitae,* and *curiosa felicitas* were household words for centuries; in some quarters they still are. His epistles are flawless gems in the most exquisite of verse; among them are real letters addressed to real people. His odes changed the course of literature. It is Horace more than any other writer to whom we owe the image of the easy-going, wise but not presumptuous, cosmopolitan Roman boulevardier, the Roman we would most prefer to sit next at dinner. Horace gives meaning to the term "urbane."

Yet this turns out to be a very lubricious character indeed.

v

The frames in which Horace has so carefully mounted his portrait are found on examination to be empty. The short, tubby poet, prematurely grey, is going to be transformed into a bird; into the most improbable of birds, in fact—a swan. The solemn hymns swing open to reveal Lalage scantily clad. The maidens whom he so ostentatiously violates are virgins still. The venom planted by his fangs has no sting. The queen of temptresses is Chloe—she plays the guitar.

Lest the reader be dazzled by Horace's charms, let him observe him through a screen or filter, a service which French scholarship is uniquely fitted to render. To the appraisal of an ancient writer the Gallic critic brings logic stripped of irrelevant sentiment and of superfluous posture. We are doubly fortunate in this essay: that it was written by Jacques Perret, professor of Latin at the Sorbonne, and that it was ably translated by Miss Humez. You will see Rome and the literary world of the Romans illuminated by new light; when you have finished you will feel that you know Horace better and that you hardly know him at all. You must not be disappointed, because this is the perennial fortune of those who would understand Horace.

Jotham Johnson

March, 1964

CONTENTS

Horace

1 · The Poet's Youth

WE KNOW the exact name of our poet from his works themselves. We know the place, the year, the month, and the day on which he was born. In fact, we know the hour almost to the exact minute; he has told us that, too, by referring to astronomical configurations which we can interpret with near certainty. Quintus Horatius Flaccus was born at Venusia (halfway between Beneventum, now Benevento, and Tarentum) on December 8 in the year 65 B.C. Libra had just emerged on the eastern horizon, where Scorpio was already visible (*Od.* II 17, 17); it was therefore about three o'clock in the morning. It is of some importance that we should know so many things about him immediately, from the very cradle; these tiny details, carefully saved and communicated (whereas most of the contemporaneous artists—Vergil, Propertius, Tibullus—are so secretive), this attention paid to everything that concerns him, are characteristic of a man who organized his whole life and his whole work around himself. In this respect, Horace is the extreme opposite of Vergil, so naturally ensconced in forgetfulness of self and indifference to his own person. Vergil is pure mind; Horace, man in his body. True, the two poets—they were approximately the same age—though launched in such different directions in life, were to become friends; they would work in the same city, they would conceive a certain enthusiasm for the same objects. Genius reconciles, and causes improbable confluences; but different natures remain different.

THE SON OF A FREEDMAN

Horace received at birth the *praenomen* of Quintus, which tells us absolutely nothing, and the *cognomen* of Flaccus, which does not tell us much. It was originally a nickname, doubtless having to do, we are told, with some physical blemish—softness, flabby muscles, or big soft ears. It seems strange to us that the Romans, though very conscious of the power exercised by names, were never afraid to assume ridiculous ones: Brutus, Verres, Scrofa, Ofella, Pansa—the list could go on at length. As these *cognomina* were often handed down from father to son, and as we never know under what circumstances they entered a family line for the first time, we shall refrain from coming to any conclusions about the physical appearance of any individual who bore such a name. Furthermore, it is probable that in a considerable number of cases people had ceased to think of the semantic value of something that had become a personal designation. In particular, we can be sure that at the time of Horace the *cognomen* of Flaccus no longer had any pejorative sense; it was borne in all walks of life and, around the Christian era, by four consuls. Perhaps we should even compare it to what would now be a fashionable first name.

The name of Horatius, on the other hand, must be explained. It is certain that Horace was named after his father. But since this father, as everyone knows, had been a slave, he himself cannot have taken, or received, this name before the time of his manumission; and at that point why the name of Horatius rather than any other? The simplest hypothesis is that Horace's father was the slave of a citizen whose name was Horatius, and that the latter, according to custom, gave him his own name when formally freeing him. Against this hypothesis the point has been made that the name Horatius, after having been brilliantly borne in the past by some semilegendary figures—the three brothers who conquered the Curiatii, Horatius Cocles, two fifth-century consuls—appears very rarely in the literature and inscriptions of the republican era. However, a letter of Cicero dated June 43 (*Fam.* XII 30, 7) refers to an Horatius more or less contemporaneous with our poet, and under the Empire the Horatii become more numerous again; one of them has even been found at Venusia (*CIL* IX 528). As L. Halkin has suggested, it is possible that the former *gens* died out, perhaps in the fourth or third century, and the name survived in families descended from its freedmen. These families, consisting entirely of individuals of modest rank, may have continued through several centuries in obscurity, leaving no trace in either literature or epigraphy. Perhaps in 291 B.C. when a colony was established at Venusia, or in 200 when the colony received a new contingent of Romans, one of these plebeian Horatii was among the new citizens of the town. This colonial could have been the ancestor of the inhabitant of Venusia who for a time numbered Horace's father among his slaves.

Another hypothesis has been advanced. Since the Venusians were registered in Rome as belonging to the Horatian tribe, perhaps this aspect of the question should be investigated. Horace's father could have been a public slave, a slave of the town of Venusia; he could have taken upon gaining his freedom the name of the urban tribe to which his new cocitizens belonged. To be a private slave or a public slave was not the same thing; the public slave had a superior legal and social position. He could, for example, marry a freedwoman; he could make a will governing the disposal of some of his earnings. Is it possible that Horace's father, when he was a slave, belonged to that privileged and more respected category?

Before we come to a conclusion, what weight should we give to the silence of Horace himself on the subject? If indeed this had been the situation of his father, should we not find it surprising that the poet, so ready to do honor to his father's memory, never found occasion to disclose the fact to us? I confess that I do not know. On the other side of the question, great attention should be paid to the observations set forth by Halkin upon the basis of considerable documentation; from them we must conclude that, at the present level of our knowledge, nothing authorizes us to suppose that at manumission public slaves took a name derived from that of the tribe to which their municipality belonged. The custom seems to have been that they took the name Publicius or a name derived

from that of the town to which they had belonged; in the case
of Horace's father, this would have been Venusius, an actual
name to which two inscriptions attest (*CIL* XII 181, 234).

Looking objectively at the life of our poet, one does not see
that the humility of his origins ever weighed heavily upon him.
As a young man he was raised in schools attended by the
children of the best families (*Sat.* I 6, 76–80). At 23 he was a
military tribune in command of a legion (*ibid.*, 48). He was to
become a friend of Maecenas, table companion of senators and
consular officials. He was a Roman knight. At the secular games
of the year 17, for the climax of the most solemn liturgy that
Rome had ever known, it was he who composed the hymn; it
was with words from his mouth that the flower of Roman
youth, the elect of the most glorious and most ancient families,
addressed themselves to the gods.

Yet, in spite of these undeniable successes, the memory of
the father who had been a slave obsessed him. "The son of a
freedman"—*libertino patre natum*—this famous hemistich returns in this particular form, to say nothing of other allusions,
four times in his works (*Sat.* I 6, 6, 45, 46; *Ep.* I 20, 20). It was
the envious, Horace tells us, who kept dinning this reproach in
his ears. Perhaps another man would not have heard them so
clearly; another, less preoccupied with the past, would have
made it easier for those around him to recall it less. He never
blushed for his beginnings; on the contrary, he wished to derive
some credit from them: "Add to my merits all that you take
away from my birth" (*Ep.* I 20, 22); but we would still prefer,
I think, that he should appear never to have felt bitter about
them. Now, it was often when he was sullen, tempted to withdraw into himself, tempted to consign his most tactful friends,
even Maecenas, to the devil, that these memories attacked him;
he remembered then that he had been born poor, that he had
never sought either honors or money; he proclaimed that he
would do well to go naked from the camp of the rich (*Od.* III
16, 18–24); he asserted that every man must measure himself
against his own standards and stay among his own people (*Ep.*
I 7, 40–98). All this does betray a certain embarrassment on his
part, some inner difficulties, on the subject of his past. If we
had been friends of Horace, we should have advised him, no

doubt, to be less complicated, less susceptible, less suspicious in
that quarter; today we marvel that he usually overcame what
our psychologists would call his complexes, that he was without
bitterness, without mental reservation—a man of indulgent wisdom, thoughtful friendship, and airy lyricism.

Moreover, to arrive at an exact idea of the meaning of references like *libertino patre natum*, we should not forget that statements of this kind are encountered in many contemporary
writers: Valerius Cato, one of the masters of the *neoteroi*, had
written a poem *Indignatio*, in which he upheld his *ingenuitas*
against those who claimed that he had been born a slave. In
the preceding generation, Sevius Nicanor set forth his exact
legal position in one of his satires: a citizen, but a freedman,
retaining two *cognomina* from his past. Orbilius, Horace's
teacher, had had to uphold in his *Peri alogon* his claim to
equestrian rank, which had apparently been challenged. All this
literature, on a subject that we are likely to discuss today only
with administrative authorities, is understandable in a city upset
for so many years by prohibitions, confiscations, and a thousand
arbitrary measures that flung members of hitherto honored
families into beggary while raising former slaves, and even slaves
themselves, to positions of dignity. Rome did not have an equivalent to our civil registers; if circumstances were propitious, the
field was open to the most presumptuous pretensions and the
least-founded allegations. In short, it was up to each man to
declare who he was. Finally, we must not forget that when
Horace kept stating that he was the son of a freedman, he was
also stating, perhaps necessarily, that he himself had been born
free.

As is natural, it was from his earliest childhood at Venusia,
in a town where everyone had known his father or his parents
when they were slaves, that Horace's feelings received their
most serious wounds; perhaps it was the scars of those days that
he bore. With an ironic emphasis he recalled his little school-
mates: "noble children of noble centurions" (*Sat.* I 6, 72–73).
From a distance of twenty years they no doubt appeared
thoroughly ridiculous, awkward, and provincial; at the time,
however, they were intimidating and formidable, and doubtless
it was they who from the height of their nobility—descended

as they were from citizens and minor officials—despised the son
of a slave, come to join them in their studies.

One can readily believe that this unpleasant situation—which
was certainly not confined to the schoolroom—had something
to do with the decision to leave Venusia forever. Horace tells
us that his father resolved upon this for pedagogical reasons:
in Rome he wanted to find better schools and better teachers,
ones more worthy of his offspring (*Sat.* I 6, 72–78). Yes, to be
sure. But the former slave also felt that in changing cities he
would be leaving his past behind and would be able to begin
to create the life of a truly free man for his child, in the great
capital where the family would be known only in its new walk
of life.

What traces remained in the poet's soul and works of
Venusia, which he probably left at about the age of ten? Nothing of the town itself, which must have been fairly grim after
the consecutive destructions and colonizations of Hannibal's
war and the later war of the Allies. By the year 83, the centurions whose grandchildren had left such a poor taste in the
mouth of their schoolmate had probably received from Sylla
the privileged status of veterans. Doubtless mutual sulkiness
characterized the relations of these conquerors and the old population. And meanwhile the town began to slip into torpor
after the Appian Way was detoured from it by a more com-
fortable route between Beneventum and Brundisium—the route
that in the year 38 would be described in *Satire* I 5. Horace
recalled only the stern administration of Flavius, the municipal
magister.

We should remember, furthermore, that before coming to
Rome Horace's father cultivated a small tract of land (*Sat.* I
6, 71): our poet grew up on some rural farm; his clearest childhood memories were of countryside and fresh air (*Od.* III 4,
9–20). He would always retain the image of the high towns,
like nests on the tops of the hills, and the dark woods where
there were bears; below, great flat white horizons, dust rising
from the Apulian soil at the gusts of the Atabulus; the two
citadels, one brilliant, the other somber even in the sunlight,
Garganus and Voltur; far off, the Adriatic with its terrible rages.
In certain exaggerated aspects of his character, the poet liked

to see the severe and sharply contrasting climate of his native land; he felt that Calabria had its own Muses, its own Pierides conferring immortality (*Od.* IV 8, 20). Comparing him to Vergil, thinking of the mists rising from the Mincius and of the vague, vast landscapes of the *Aeneid*, we feel more vividly the clean, sharp vision of Horace, a poet truly predestined to Atticism and to brilliance of form.

Horace's family as it moved from Venusia to Rome should not be pictured as a train of poor refugees. In Rome young Horace would go to the best schools, those attended by the best people. His bearing, the slaves that accompanied him, gave the impression that "a rich inheritance was covering his expenses" (*Sat.* I 6, 76–80). This ease of manner was not acquired in a day. It must have dated from the Venusia period, and perhaps we have an indication of it in the famous horoscope of *Ode* II 17. In the nativity of Horace we find, in fact, the constellation Capricorn. Now, according to ideas then prevailing, this constellation, at inferior culmination at the moment of his birth, seems to have had an influence on him only in that on that particular day, as our modern astronomers have established, it was the locus of Mercury, which was then in quadrature. In fact, we know that Horace always considered himself a "man of Mercury," and he never reminded his readers of the fact more explicitly than in that very ode (ll. 29–30). His exact knowledge of the planetary configuration existing at his birth leads one to suppose that his nativity was established by immediate and direct observation. For, although it is always easy to calculate a zodiacal horoscope in retrospect—it is necessary only to know the day and the hour of birth—it is quite another problem, and one that the ancients were apparently incapable of solving, to determine some years later the exact position of a planet, especially of a planet as mobile as Mercury. We therefore conclude that Horace's parents, the moment he was born, were interested enough and well enough off to have his complete horoscope drawn up; they used a technician who was competent, hence expensive; they already felt the beginnings of aspirations and ambitions for their newborn child.

Horace tells us that his father had been a *coactor* (*Sat.* I 6, 86). We do not know whether he was already practicing this

profession in the Venusia period. In any case, it must have been
this profession that supplied the needs and expenses of the
family in Rome. The *coactor* is essentially a receiver, a collector
or banker of funds. This term, which finally came to mean
specifically a collector of duties and public taxes, at that time
had a broader meaning. Probably a magistrate, an administrator,
or publican could give a *coactor* the responsibility of collecting
public debts. But this was not his major activity, which was
rather, as Horace's text makes clear, closely associated with that
of the crier (*praeco*), and centered around the organization of
public auctions; the *praeco*, like our auctioneer, directed the
sale and oversaw the placing of bids; the *coactor* received the
funds from the purchaser and delivered to him the personal
property involved in the transaction. The *coactor's* own income,
closely regulated by law, was a percentage of the sums that
passed through his hands. He was thus more or less well off
in proportion as he handled more or fewer transactions. But
on the whole we must not think of the family as a humble one.
Records have been found at Pompeii of one Caecilius Jucundus,
a "banker," whose activities seem to have been very much those
that we suspect were a *coactor's*. We can therefore be sure that
fairly large sums of money passed through his hands each day;
and we should probably visualize a *coactor* in Pompeii as a man
of the middle class, in an average setting—like the director of
a bank branch in one of our French prefectures. It appears
conceivable from the text of the *Satires* that Horace's father
may have become fairly wealthy, perhaps after modest beginnings. But we must bear in mind that his manumission, and
hence the beginning of the career he pursued for his living,
occurred before the birth of his son.

From his studies in Rome Horace remembered one of his
teachers, Orbilius, and the blows received from him (*Ep.* II 1,
69). This picturesque detail, recalled with a smile, must not
cause us to visualize some sort of ridiculous thrasher. Besides, it
would be difficult to understand why Horace's father, who had
come to Rome expressly to find better teachers, should have
confided his son to any poor wretch. In fact, L. Orbilius Pupillus
was one of the most important pedagogs and grammarians of
the age. His social rank was, furthermore, enough to set him

apart from the majority of his colleagues: he was a Roman knight. A native of Beneventum, of which he was the pride, he had been accorded the honor of a statue during his lifetime. This was a rare distinction, inconceivable if he had been nothing but a poor devil of a schoolteacher; in fact, it probably expressed the gratitude of his fellow-citizens for an opulent liberality on his part. At the time when Horace may have been his student, he had been in Rome for ten or fifteen years. He was well past sixty and was venting his spleen in a work on human idiocy called *Peri alogon,* feuding with the "antisophists," attacking the important people of the city in his satires, and complaining of his (doubtless relative) poverty.

It would be surprising if such a personality had not had thoroughly backward ideas of teaching, that is of literature. Horace remembered that Orbilius had made him study Livius Andronicus (*Ep.* II 1, 69–71), the oldest of the Latin poets. Even if it was not the Latin *Odyssey* in Saturnian verses that was studied but rather, as it seems, some of the old author's tragedies, which would have been much more accessible to a school boy of the first century, such teaching demonstrates beyond doubt that the teacher had a strong predilection for the ancients. We do seem to discern a real prejudice in that direction on the part of Orbilius from the obscure lines that in some manuscripts precede the customary text of *Satire* I 10. I tend to consider these lines authentic; after the demonstration of Eduard Fraenkel it is at least certain that they were written in the first century before our era, and they speak of a pedagog with a ready whip, of the most learned of the grammarian-knights (and all that suggests Orbilius); this person had apparently hoped to develop in his pupils the taste for "taking up the defense of the Ancients against the scorn of today." Such preoccupations, at that time, in the contemporary literary atmosphere, are quite believable. Ten years or so later we find the equivalent in Cicero's *Brutus,* when the great orator, to the astonishment of his auditors, becomes a panegyrist of the art of Cato the Elder (63–69).

Horace, therefore, received from Orbilius from his early adolescence an education that was, as we would say today, very much "oriented." Contemporary literary polemics entered the classroom to give vigor, or an unexpected spice, to the scholarly teaching itself. Later, our poet frequented circles of a very different doctrine; in the quarrel of the ancients and the moderns he placed himself firmly on the side of the moderns. Let us not imagine that the bad memory of a few blows of the stick had much to do with this; it is too evident how the theses he supported were rooted in a general conception of art. But it is surely of some significance that literary problems were presented to him early in his life in the form of a necessary choice between present and past.

It appears that our thoughts should turn to Orbilius again to resolve one of the enigmas of Horace's career: he who had such a tendency to quarrel with the ancients made himself, in his *Satires*, the disciple of one of them, of that Lucilius who had some of the faults most odious to the moderns. Where did he become acquainted with Lucilius? At school, probably. In maturity a man often perceives that he resembles to some extent the teachers, even the parents, whom he had formerly believed he detested. Was Orbilius himself—apparently an admirer of Lucilius, if we are not mistaken about his literary predilections— not a sort of image of Lucilius, a provincial knight, an old man forever engaged in altercations? It would be some accomplishment on his part if Horace only learned in a real, concrete way from his company that Lucilius existed.

Another discovery of the same period is that of Homer, especially the *Iliad:* "I had the good fortune to be raised in Rome and to learn there what harm the rage of Achilles did to the Greeks" (*Ep.* II 2, 41–42). For a young schoolboy it was obviously an inevitable meeting, and one of the most beautiful he could have experienced: with or without Orbilius, Horace would in any case have known and admired Homer. But we should take note of two traits from which we will readily recognize the peculiar circumstances of that discovery. For our poet, Homer was always an "ancient," afflicted with the faults of the ancients: in spite of the praise found in the *Epistle* to the Pisos (ll. 140–52) (which was perhaps a little conventional or forced—Horace had at that time other axes to grind), Horace's reaction is dominated, from the artistic point of view, by reservations. Homer is uneven (*Sat.* I 10, 52), soporific (*AP.*

359), a wine drinker (*Ep.* I 19, 6). This last trait has a precise literary significance, for it contrasts a disorderly inspiration, an overflowing work, with the artistically constructed and usually brief poem of a water drinker.

Homer is not a demanding artist, but a moralist without equal. It was in this spirit that the aging Horace reread and commented on him in *Epistle* I 2; but it was also in this spirit, as we have seen, that Homer had been presented to him in school. The traditional, even reactionary, attitudes of Orbilius were no doubt, as is so often the case on the scholarly level, associated with a fixed code of morality.

Thus we understand better why Horace studied with Orbilius. For an inexperienced father, who desired to do everything right and was anxious not to see his son corrupted by the big city, this teacher, who perhaps also came recommended by certain provincial rumors (Beneventum was not far from Venusia), obviously offered all guarantees.

Horace did not, however, study exclusively with Orbilius; a student does not stay forever with a grammarian. In fact, in one satire (I 6, 82), there is mention of *doctores* (in the plural) whom the young man frequented. No doubt the teaching that they provided was more advanced and more important in the orientation of his life and the formation of his habits. No doubt it was because of this that Horace's father was careful to know them personally; not, of course, that he regularly accompanied the big pupil to school, but that he would take advantage of some public lecture or of a visit to inquire about the progress of his son's work. The natural order of studies led from grammarian to rhetorician to philosopher. Of these three, the second (of which there may have been more than one) left no distinct trace in the memories that Horace gives us of his youth; and it is also the influence of the second that is the least perceptible in all the work of the poet; there is no Latin author in whom one finds less rhetoric than in him. Perhaps these studies, if he undertook them, did not interest him. There is also the family situation to consider. One day, certainly, as we will show, Horace would see before him the possibility of a political career and would refuse it. But around the decade of 50, when the young man had not yet revealed his powers, such a future was assuredly impossible to foresee. What was evident at that time was that Horace was the son of a freedman; and a freedman, if he was wise, did not think in terms of directing his son into an honorary career. And if that was the case, what use would eloquence be? It was much rather in business, in banking or financial administration, that the young man seemed to have a future. No one would have disapproved if he too had become a collector or an auctioneer (*Sat.* I 6, 86). If he was going to do better than that, it seemed that at least he must do so in the same line. In fact, he must have spent his childhood in an atmosphere in which figures and bank accounts were often under discussion (*Ep.* I 1, 52–56; *AP.* 325–32), as the favorite subject of conversation of young and old. When, after his misfortunes, he had to undertake to earn his own living, he naturally thought of becoming a *scriba quaestorius,* which would be similar to a modern clerkship in the ministry of finance.

Thus it is possible that, on this particular point of relative indifference to rhetoric, Horace's origins had a bearing on the orientation of his intellectual development. In the same sense, we should note that from his years in Rome he retained no recollections of political life. Should we surmise that he may have known and heard Cicero or Pompey, of whom he never speaks, or Caesar himself? At one point, in 43–42, he would become engaged in politics and would even take up arms, but apparently for reasons—friendship, philosophical ardor—in which real politics did not take first place. As for the rest of his life, he would remain absolutely indifferent to the subject, remembering without the faintest embarrassment the fact that he himself had changed sides, incapable at the beginning of a new civil war of seeing any difference between the opposing parties, always taking the side of friendship, and remaining, so far as he could, friends with everybody, Pollio and Messalla as well as Maecenas. Here, too, compare the attitude of Vergil, a supporter of Caesar from his infancy, ready from the year 40 on to recognize Octavius as a god, an Augustan to the core. Perhaps as a result of a lack in his early education, Horace had a kind of blindness to the importance, the grandeur, and the necessity of choice in politics.

A young man does not spend all his time in school; but we

have difficulty discovering what milieus Horace frequented before his voyage to Greece. Rostagni has conjectured that he haunted Epicurean circles, but the allusions to or borrowings from Epicureanism found in his entire *oeuvre* teach us very little, for nothing tells us that he did not acquire his knowledge at a much later date. It would be more important to be able to identify Horace with the little group recalled by Philodemus: Vergil, Horace, L. Varius Rufus, and Quintilius Varus, whom we like to think of as friends, disciples of the Epicurean Siro in the years immediately preceding the death of Caesar. But the papyrus that preserves this list for us is in a miserable state; in the case of Horace, the assumption of his name is based upon only the three Greek letters *tie*. In the following years, Horace's assiduity at the lessons of the academicians and the circles, centered around Brutus, that he frequented in Athens in the company of Bibulus or of Cicero's son seem to have been foreign, if not hostile, to Epicureanism. Furthermore, one may well wonder whether Horace's father, while he had his son under his eye, would have appreciated his frequenting these men of ill fame.

I would more readily believe that at that period Horace spent most of his time with the people among whom his father lived. It may have been then that he observed at firsthand that urban lower and middle bourgeoisie from which he would so soon be snatched by his role of poet and the fortune that came too rapidly. More than one picturesque character must have gravitated toward a *coactor*; Horace often described this society with good humor. The happy man, the man without desires, the wise man who is the envy of the preoccupied rich, for him took on the unforgettable features of the crier Volteius Mena: "a man of small fortune but without reproach, a man known for his ability to work and rest each at its own time, to earn and to enjoy, living happily among men of his own rank, with a house, and the games and the Field of Mars when his work was over" (*Ep.* I 7, 55–59).

Then there were his talks with his old papa, so valiant, so good, whom he would soon leave and never see again. We must believe the poet when he says that these memories were the seat of his moral life. He has left us a considerable sampling of

these words from father to son, in which observation of the
conduct of others gave rise to a morality of common sense. In
these thirty verses (*Sat.* I 4, 103-38) there is much more than
is disclosed by a rapid reading. For anyone other than his son,
Horace's father would perhaps have been merely a worthy man
anxious to turn an adolescent aside from debauchery and extrav-
agance. But the essential point—and it is the essential point that
a powerful personality and a heedful heart would be likely to
retain—was that such morality, instead of being presented as a
dogma, as nearly all the moral codes of antiquity were, was
experimental, an invitation to think about concrete and individual situations. And besides, it contained a duality between a
sociological moral code—provisional, Descartes would say—the
moral code of the *antiqui*, which would be valid so long as one
was still the prisoner of youth and inexperience, and, for later
on, the definitive morality—"you will swim without a raft"—
where personal values become of primary importance.

Indeed, during his whole life Horace was to bend his efforts
toward discovering *his* morality, a morality valid for him; and
that morality would have to accomplish the difficult end of
bringing into harmony and regulating the diversity of his nature
and his desire for freedom.

THE SOLDIER OF BRUTUS

It was apparently in the spring of the year 45 that young
Horace undertook the voyage to Greece which seems to have
been the crowning event of every liberal education of the time.
The date can be reasonably deduced from a letter in March 45
of Cicero (*Att.* XII 32), in which the orator deals with the
departure of his son for Athens; we learn incidentally that L.
Calpurnius Bibulus (third son of Marcus, the unfortunate
consul of 59) and M. Valerius Messalla Corvinus were leaving
too. Now Cicero's son was born in 65, the same year as Horace,
and Messalla in 64. It is fairly natural to group Horace with
others of his age, all the more since later on we find him linked
with Messalla (*Sat.* I 10, 85; *Od.* III 21) as well as with Bibulus
(*Sat.* I 10, 86). By that time Athens was merely a university
city, living on its teachers and students (*Ep.* II 2, 81-82). But
while Horace's fellow-disciples divided their time between

rhetoricians and philosophers, perhaps even besetting the former especially, Horace, decidedly indifferent to eloquence, provided himself with a cultural formation based upon philosophy: "Good Athens added something to my culture; yes, she inspired in me the desire to distinguish between a straight line and a curved line and to search for truth in the midst of the groves of Academe" (*Ep.* II 2, 43–45). That last indication is important: the academy, which Horace therefore attended by choice, was at that time the least dogmatic and the least sectarian of all the schools. Without renouncing its own weapon, a redoubtable criticism that preached in general the suspension of judgment, the *épochè*, it aspired to assemble the most reasonable hypotheses of the ancient academy, those of Peripateticism and Stoicism; it was able to welcome minds that were very jealous of their independence and to develop them in their own directions. The Scholarch whose courses Horace took, Aristos of Ascolon, who had succeeded his brother, the famous Antiochos, around 67, was then nearing the end of his life. He was an affable old man who had been a friend of Cicero (*Att.* V 10, 5; *Tusc.* V 22) and Brutus' teacher (Plutarch, *Brutus*, 2). In the *Tusculanes*, debating against Cicero, he defended the argument that the happiness or unhappiness of a wise man does not depend entirely upon his strength and virtue. Horace must have been pleased with views of this kind, in which reason took account, without dogmatism or passion, of all the elements of reality.

Should we place at Athens the awakening of the poetic vocation in the young student? He himself has told us (*Sat.* I 10, 31) that he had once composed Greek verses. In any case it is sure that in Athens he could find aids to his cultural development that were unknown in Rome. Until Asinius Pollio and then Augustus opened the first public libraries, it must not have been too easy, especially for a young man without any particular connections, to have access to the work of certain poets, like Pindar, Archilochus, or the poets of Lesbos, whose works do not seem to have been the habitual reading of many Romans.

During the summer of the year 44, Brutus, the murderer of Caesar, now convinced that any understanding with Antony would be impossible, had left Italy for Athens. Cassius came

to join him there for a few days, to the plaudits of an enthusiastic people, who put up a statue to the two near to those of
Harmodios and Aristogiton, the murderers of Pisistratus. It is
not precisely known why Brutus had chosen Athens as the site
of his exile. He lived there at first as an ordinary private person,
assiduously attending the philosophical lectures of Cratippus
and Theomnestes. However, whether because he had had the
intention from the start but had dissimulated it from prudence,
or whether his courage, often somewhat feeble, had been stimulated by the atmosphere of Athens, with its memories of demo-
cratic traditions and its young people greedy for adventure, he
finished by gathering around him the elements of an army,
which the students of Athens helped to frame. Cicero the
Younger became a legate in it, and Horace, a military tribune.
By the end of 44, Brutus was able to count on the loyalty of all
the troops stationed in the Balkan peninsula. The year 43 and
the first six months of 42 were passed in consolidating the
defenses of Illyria, then making sure of all of Asia in order to
equip a great republican army there with arms and materiel.

It is very probable that in the seventh *Satire* of Book I we
can follow Horace participating, as a member of Brutus' circle,
in the mobilization of the Asian forces. The *Satire* is a picturesque evocation of a debate before Brutus' tribunal by two
enraged litigants. The scene must have taken place at Claz-
omenae (l. 5), during the very early months of 42; one can
deduce as much, in fact, from the fact that Rupilius Rex is
called an outlaw, and from the information that we have on the
movements of Brutus at the time. Horace does not, it is true,
say specifically that he was there in person. Yet it seems that if
we were not to suppose so, the recital, already a little thin,
would lose much of its savor. And above all, if the poet did not
wish us to infer that he had been a witness of the affair, how
could he be so clumsy as to tell us at the beginning that it has
already been the talk of one and all?

An active participation in the operations of 43 and those of
the first months of 42 is the only possible explanation, furthermore, of how so young and apparently inexperienced a man,
without any family background to recommend him, should have

been able to distinguish himself sufficiently to be promoted to the rank of military tribune and receive the command of a legion. Besides, Horace was always somewhat vain of his service. In an ode (*Od.* II 7, 1) he evokes the great perils that he valiantly faced; later (*Ep.* I 20, 23) he seems to be telling us that "in war as in peace, he deserved the esteem of the first men of the city." This is at least the most natural reading of the line that is sometimes translated, "I have deserved the esteem of those who were, in war or in peace, the first men of the city."

We should like to know what made young Horace decide to enlist and fight so actively under Brutus' banner. The reasons he has given us—danger (cf. *Sat.* I 6, 45–64), the boiling waters of political passion (*Ep.* II 2, 47)—are certainly not all. Other things entered into it: the influence of his comrades, the desire of an isolated man, the son of a freedman, to attach himself to others; and the desire not to let the moment slip by in which loyalty in the face of danger might lead to a definitive social ennoblement. To these we should add philosophical ardor and love of liberty. In Athens, in that particular year of 43, such a passion was bound to lead to political involvement. But it was above all an effect of prevailing circumstances; and that is why later, when he had become a friend of Maecenas and an intimate of Augustus, Horace never had the feeling of having gone back on any of his convictions.

Other variables may have had an influence. Horace, thanks to the energy and enterprising spirit of his father, had grown up in the midst of an industrious and property-owning middle class. His father had a little farm in Apulia. His work as *coactor* put him in daily contact with businessmen. Now, it appears that these social elements were hostile to Caesar and received the news of his death with considerable satisfaction. "There are transports of joy in all the towns," wrote Cicero from Fundi on April 12, 44 (*Att.* XIV 6, 2). "I can hardly describe their rapture; they rush up to me from all sides to hear me tell about it." Apulia, which was still an area of small property owners (Varr. *RR.* I 29, 2), must have shared in the jubilation. So many grandiose plans, so many wars, and the upkeep of so many armies meant for them, as they well knew, expropriations and crushing levies. And indeed, once Caesar was dead, the inheritors of his spirit, Mark Antony and his brother, once more (April 44) renewed their connection with the disastrous tradition of agrarian laws. Here again there is an obvious difference between Horace and Vergil. Vergil sympathized with grand ideas; he was always on the side of the grandiose, and therefore on the side of Caesar, and certainly no personal incident such as the loss of a property would have been able to sway his convictions. Horace had more individual density, more sensuous attachments, and more wariness of theories; naturally he would be conservative. It is true enough that one day (*Sat.* II 2, 133) he would invite us to admire the wisdom of old Ofellus, finally resigned to the expropriations of which he had been a victim and cultivating as a wage-earner the land that had been his. This is the wisdom of an old man. Even supposing that Horace had made it his, at the moment when he speaks for Ofellus he had reestablished himself. We may be permitted to doubt that fifteen years earlier, on the eve of losing everything, the young man had the same reflections.

Horace's enlistment in Brutus' army and the opportunity that, to all appearances, he found there to exhibit his qualities of courage and loyalty mark an important point in the poet's life: in 43 or 42, the freedman's son became a Roman knight. Admission in this order seems to have been automatic immediately upon his appointment as military tribune. At that time, officers of this rank were chosen exclusively from the two highest orders of the state, from young men of senatorial family or from the knights. It was probably not often that a freedman's son was admitted to these privileged orders. But the circumstances are enough of an explanation of why Brutus had recourse to an action that was not forbidden by either written or social authority. When Caesar, in 45, had wanted to replenish the decimated Senate, he had called in among the newcomers several sons of freedmen, perhaps reestablishing in so doing a tradition that was said to go back (Liv. IX 46, 10) to the famous Appius Claudius Caecus, the censor of the fourth century. Furthermore, we know by name two contemporaries of Horace of whom we are told that they, although sons of freedmen like the poet, had attained the equestrian rank; one survives for us only in an epigraphic text (*CIL* XIV 2298); the other, Vedius Pollio, had so dazzled his contemporaries with his eccentricities that they were still stimulating the imagination of Seneca (*De ira,* III 40) and Pliny the Elder (*Nh.* IX 77). In Horace's case, the two necessary conditions for enrollment in the equestrian rank may well have been met in the ordinary way. One was the possession of a sufficient fortune, 400,000 sesterces. But the very presence of Horace in Athens and his frequenting of its gilded youth give us enough information on the degree of his comfort. When he wrote later (*Sat.* II 1, 75) that he was below Lucilius (also a knight) in both rating and natural gifts, we should not conclude that his fortune was lower than the minimum for a knight, but only that he was not as rich as Lucilius. The other condition was the support of an authorized magistrate acting as censor. But by that time there was no longer an organized system of censorship. Perhaps it was felt that that formality had gone out with the preconsular *imperium,* with which Brutus had been invested since January 43 for Macedonia, Illyricum, and Greece.

Biographies of Horace have not always paid sufficient attention to this event, which was surely one of the most important of his career, and without which many details of his later work would be inexplicable. Would we understand as well the insistence with which Horace keeps reminding us, in all circumstances and in all periods of his life, that he has no political ambition and prefers the liberty of his retreat above everything else, if because of his social position such an ambition, whether he wanted it or not, had been denied him? But if he was a knight everything makes sense, for to be a knight was to be a potential senator. Under those circumstances it is easier to understand the jealousy, curiosity, and ill will aroused by his relations with Maecenas. Horace was in a position to push himself further forward; but he was wise enough, after that promotion at twenty-two or twenty-three, to be satisfied. The career that he did not desire was that of Tillius, who was criticized for his stupid ambition (*Sat.* I 6) and who got himself into the Senate (1. 25) and even into a praetorship (1. 108) in spite of being the son of a freedman (l. 41). On the other hand, we may note that Horace embraced both the pride and the sensitivity of the equestrian rank in which he had the natural good sense to remain. Vulnerable to what can seem to us from a distance to be class prejudice, he considered it a scandal when a freedman was made a knight and dared to enter the theater section reserved for that rank (*Epod.* 4, 16). To have a clear idea of the nature of his relations with the powerful of this world whom he so assiduously frequented, particularly with Maecenas, it is also useful to visualize his social rank, not forgetting his beautiful purple-bordered toga, which was just like those of the equestrian and consular friends who came to visit him.

The drive of the republicans was broken at Philippi (October 42). Like nearly all civil wars, the affair was ill undertaken but inevitable, and could not end without many deaths; but at the end it was not as sterile as the vanquished may have thought. "The sacrifice of Brutus," writes G. Ferrero,

was not in vain. At the final moment he must have said to himself that the grand, classical idea of the Republic was dead. . . . He could hardly guess who would take up that idea again and would be able to adapt it to the new conditions in the world. But that man [he is speaking of Octavius] was not far from him; he had fought at Philippi, but in the other camp.

Under such circumstances, it is well that there are such heroes as Brutus and Cato's son. But it would be a disaster for everyone if all the vanquished were swallowed up in collective suicide. Those who survive and rally are still useful to the cause when it has fought and lost. If they remain worthy of it, they will contribute toward giving it some measure of the victory.

We know that Horace survived Philippi. It would not occur to anyone to hold this against him if he had not appeared himself to recall the affair in frivolous terms. I am speaking of *Ode* II 7, dedicated to a certain Pompeius, whom we do not know:

Oh you who were often led with me to the final peril, when we were serving under the leadership of Brutus . . . with you I knew Philippi and the rapid flight, when I ingloriously left behind my little shield (*relicta non bene parmula*), when valor had been broken and menacing countenances had touched an unworthy soil with their chins. As for me, I was carried off terrified by agile Mercury past the enemy . . .; and you the sea took back into its churning waters, and carried you off toward war again.

The imagination of the moderns has been much taken with the story of the shield. But first let us try to see what Horace himself thought of it, and if possible what he thought would be thought of it. In this regard the context is eloquent. The ode is addressed to an incorrigible: to a man who, after Philippi, continued the war against the conquerors of that day, no doubt at sea with Sextus Pompeius. It starts by recalling the dangers that they had often faced together, even to the edge of death. Is it conceivable that before such a man, and after evoking such memories, Horace would joke about an incident that, in the common judgment, would dishonor him?

We do not really know what happened. Horace may have been taken prisoner, either after a chase or in the camp where the conquered had tried briefly to regroup; or he may have completely escaped the enemy. He does not tell us, as he is often accused of doing, that he threw down his shield; he "left it ingloriously," which does not exclude his having been taken fully armed or his having been forced, alas! to leave his lovely equipment in the solitude of a hiding place. The text of the ode is, furthermore, less clear than it seems. As has been accurately pointed out, the interpretation that attaches to Horace the words about the abandoned shield hangs upon the placement of a single comma. If we attach those words to "when valor had been broken" instead of to "I knew Philippi," then it is no longer Horace (who would have fled and finally escaped, like Pompey) but his companions, who, taken prisoners, have had to give up their arms to the conqueror; "an unworthy soil" and "ingloriously" would belong to the same syntactical group, in opposition to "menacing countenances." The ambiguity, which astonished us, was perhaps prevented for the ancient reader in the easiest way possible, without his even being aware of a risk, by the use of the word *parmula*. Suppose we read this word not as a humorous diminutive but as a technical term. If this type of shield was, to the common knowledge, used by simple soldiers and never by officers, it cannot have occurred

to anyone then to attach to Horace himself the words that
less informed readers would later hold against him.

However, the war finished for Horace, he never had any
personal reason to complain of the conquerors; furthermore, he
never thought of doing so. Let us not imagine that the man
who came back to Italy at the end of the year 42 or at the
beginning of 41 was embittered, or disillusioned, or a social
stray, and above all let us not interpret what he was about to
write by pushing him in that direction. Certainly on his return
to Rome Horace was poor, but his participation in the civil
war on the side of the vanquished apparently had nothing to
do with the fact. His father was dead. The *coactor's* appointment with its substantial income had naturally passed into
other hands; the house may have been sold; and it is possible
that the property at Venusia had been confiscated (*Ep.* II 2,
50–51). But this would not have been because the owner was
a republican; we know from the writings of the time—the
Bucolics, Propertius' autobiography, Horace's own story of
Ofellus (*Sat.* II 2)—and of course from the corroborating evidence of the historians, that these spoliations for the benefit of
demobilized soldiers struck at everyone indiscriminately. These
are important facts. They serve to explain how easily Horace
may have readapted himself psychologically and politically to
the city that must not have been, all in all, very different from
the one which he had left three or four years earlier.

Thus he almost immediately found honorable employment,
worthy of the equestrian rank which he kept without challenge.
The *Vita* tells us that he obtained—that is, that he bought—
an appointment as *scriba quaestorius,* and this information
seems to be confirmed by a passage of Horace himself (*Sat.* II
6, 36 sq.) in which we see scribes requesting the poet to intervene with Maecenas to help them in bringing about a matter
of interest to the whole body.

The *scriba quaestorius* was supposed to be an aide to the
quaestor, that is, of a magistrate charged with financial responsibilities; and it is easy to suppose that the former friends of
Horace's father had not been indifferent to the future of his

son. But it is clear from the literature that at that time the work no longer consisted solely, as it had formerly, of doing the *quaestor's* bookkeeping; the *scribae* were now assisting the magistrates on a much higher level. The prestige of the career is established; epigraphy makes it clear that in Horace's time more and more Roman knights were engaged in it. In the provinces, the *scribae* were part of the staff of the magistrate, *praetor*, or proconsul. They were members of his *comites:* Albinovanus Celsus, the addressee of *Epistle* I 8, was *comes et scriba Neronis,* or companion and secretary of Tiberius, at the time of his mission in Armenia in 21; he was obviously a young man with a great future. There is no reason to believe that Horace ever resigned his post as *scriba.* In 31-30 we see him involved with the interests of the body. The offer that he received from Augustus (apparently around the year 25) to fulfill this function for him is more readily understandable if we assume that the poet was still engaged in the career. No doubt it was possible, if one wished, to lighten the material obligations of the role; thus one could, as epigraphy seems to suggest, keep the title of *scriba* for one's life without having to undertake much writing. At the time of *Satire* I 6 (which is probably about the year 36), Horace was a man of much leisure (ll. 110-31).

However, although these functions were not without a future, and there is no evidence that he ever looked upon them with distaste—indeed, he recalled them with some pleasure, even pride (*Sat.* II 6, 36-39)—they did not fulfill his whole potential. He could not forget his years in Athens, his friends of that time, literature, and poetry. He hastened to get his footing again in that universe that had so quickly disappeared. Besides, all of that—a nostalgia for pleasant relationships and a nostalgia for the land of the Muses—went together. We are speaking of one of those privileged moments in history when for some years love of poetry constitutes a social bond and causes the unlikeliest people to meet. What had until then been the occupation of only certain specialists who were personally unknown even when their works had become well known—what, outside of this circle, had still, even for the most enlightened, not yet become more than a simple momentary amusement—had become something important: the poet was sought out, feted, spoiled; and everyone more or less, in all situations, sacrificed to poetry. This was the moment when Scipio Aemilianus and Laelius played, like big children, with Terence, and thought that they too would write comedies. We knew the same thing in France at the end of our civil wars, at the beginning of the great age: Richelieu prided himself on his writing.

In Rome, in the decade that separated Philippi (October 42) and Actium (September 2, 31), a great reign was in preparation, although no one knew it yet; and as in the first half of the seventeenth century the historian discovers an astonishing array of men of blood and iron and of thunderous plots and counterplots, men fresh out of combat and quite ready to return to it—a Messalla, a Pollio, a Maecenas, a Bibulus—all bending with tenderness and an all-consuming interest over the cradle of the renascent Muses. All this passed quickly, because the years passed, fixing each in his true life: here men of politics, there the two or three great geniuses who make a great age. At that time, whatever glory they were to acquire elsewhere, in literature these zealous men seem to have been merely rather naïve amateurs whom it is impossible to take entirely seriously. It is not because of his poetry that Maecenas cuts so honorable a figure in the eyes of posterity. But while those happy years lasted there was a unique opportunity for a true poet to escape being enclosed all his life in literary circles. Somewhat as in those periods when beautiful women like to be celebrated in verse, poetry was then a way of becoming the friend of noble and admired men whom one wished to frequent and whom there was hardly any other way of approaching.

When Horace wrote to Florus that "audacious poverty pushed him into making verses" (*paupertas impulit audax versus ut facierem*) (*Ep.* II 2, 51–52), it is necessary to understand properly: the meter—the break after *audax*—indicates sufficiently that we have a joke here, which consists precisely in the fact that the composition of poems is certainly the least expected and least adequate means to which one may turn to wrench oneself out of poverty. The text signifies, as F. Villeneuve has rightly interpreted it, that in the audacity of poverty the young man found the necessary courage to face up to the labors of poetic composition, whereas at the time that he wrote the epistle (about the year 19), now an old man living to less stringent rhythms, to address himself to the task again would have required an effort that he was no longer willing to make. Horace was never a famished parasite who had to earn his dinner by an epigram or—as has even been suggested—by sordid maneuvers of defamation and blackmail; he was an independent man, a Roman knight, temporarily ruined by events, who had doubtless done nothing that was not perfectly honorable. He was "poor," certainly. But let us not forget that the "poor man," in Horace's vocabulary, is that field mouse who is so plump, so well nourished, so happy in his hole (*paupere cavo, Sat.* II 6, 80), and at the same time so pleased to have good relations and to do a little courting of adventure.

From a distance, nothing is more difficult than to grasp the essence of the life of those little literary circles, which must have had as large a place in Horace's beginnings as in those of Vergil; first because everything evolved so fast: groups formed and dissolved; and then because it is very hard for us not to mix up different times, and interpret a certain moment or movement in the light of what would come of it later in a more durable form; and then because very different ties may have united the members of these groups. It was rare, notably, that a literary group did not have a political color; but political situations and attachments also evolved very quickly in that period, and certain poetics would be united with certain politics only by an occasional and readily breakable link. It is no less difficult for us to see how a given story grew out of the story that had preceded it; in these circles there were elder, younger, and belated members, there were old quarrels which dragged on inexplicably and into which the novices flung themselves with ardor. After two thousand years we must give up trying to know exactly who was grouped around Pollio, who were the members of Messalla's circle or Maecenas', and whether Maecenas had one at all. Were the same faces seen in more than one place, were there exclusives? Horace, in any case, seems to have been received everywhere with pleasure; he was an intimate of Maecenas, he celebrated Pollio and Messalla; he was a personal friend of Vergil, whom we situate at that time with Pollio, and of

Tibullus, who was the glory of the circle around Messalla. We are not very much better informed about all that than we would be about the poetry of the first years of the seventeenth century if we had no one but Molière or Boileau to clarify matters. Horace himself gives us many names, but we have nothing precise to connect with them, and often are not sure that the personages were not imaginary. And besides, the poets did not live in a surrounding composed solely of other poets; or rather they belonged to a whole intellectual environment which was very diverse; we catch glimpses of philosophers like the Stoic Crispinus, who was also a poet, then of balladeers, entertainment entrepreneurs who in spite of their profession prided themselves on arbitrating the contests of the poets, and beyond them still others—a whole mixed world, a demi-monde, it is said, of dancers, flutists, and mimes, in which Horace is supposed to have moved, and which certainly amused him.

We have arrived at the moment in which Maecenas will enter the life of our poet; a great event for both of them, which seems to have had a hesitant beginning. Vergil and Varius introduced Horace; Maecenas courteously welcomed the newcomer. Eight months passed; he seemed to have forgotten him. One day he summoned the poet back and asked him in the future to be his friend (*Sat.* I 6, 54–62).

The chronology of these meetings is unfortunately uncertain, not that there is any lack of texts but that the texts seem difficult to bring into agreement. According to *Satire* II 6, 40–42, it would seem that Horace became Maecenas' friend at the beginning of 37; but on the other hand, a trip to Brindisium recounted in *Satire* I 5 makes an assumption of the friendship, and if one refers to general history—for the trip was of a diplomatic character—it is difficult not to date it in the autumn of 38. I tend to believe, together with certain philologists of the last century, that another interpretation can be given to the lines of *Satire* II 6. This interpretation would give us an extra year. Under these conditions, the friendship of Maecenas and Horace would have dated from a decisive meeting that can be fixed no more exactly than sometime in the first six months of 38. For a focal point we might think of Maecenas' birthday, which fell on April 13, and would certainly have been an occasion for gathering many people together.

The first introduction of Horace and Maecenas would then have taken place eight months earlier, toward the end of the summer of 39. If we remember Horace's recent political past—and in addressing himself to Maecenas, an official, he could hardly detach himself from it completely—no moment could have been more favorable, with the atmosphere of gaiety and concord in which the peace of Misenum was concluded. Of course the agreements entered into by Antony and Octavius on the one hand and Sextus Pompeius on the other would not institute an eternal peace; in the spring of 38 they would be an issue again. But at that moment people did not know this, or tried not to think about it; it was, after all, the first time since the murder of Caesar, indeed since the beginning of the war between Caesar and Pompey, that the chiefs of the opposing parties were meeting without being either under arms or in the unequal relationship of victor and vanquished. The agreements also had a personal significance for many Romans, for since the catastrophe of Philippi the bravest republicans (who had been on the side of Pompey during the preceding years) had regrouped around Sextus; this had, for example, been the story of Horace's friend Pompeius, his companion in misfortune at Philippi, to whom *Ode* II 7 is dedicated. The reconciliation between Sextus and the triumvirs could thus be the opportunity for many who had fought in Brutus' armies to make their final peace with the present masters of Rome. It is thus that Cicero's son then returned to the city, perhaps benefiting from the very general amnesty of which the historians tell us.

We should like to be able to visualize that first meeting between Horace and Maecenas, and to know what it already took for granted:

It was not chance that gave you to me. One day the excellent Vergil, and after him Varius, told you what I was (*dixere quid essem*). When I came before you then, in some painfully offered phrases—for the reserve that ties the tongue kept me from saying more—I did not boast of being the son of an illustrious father or of circling my properties on a Saturian horse, but I explained what I was. You answered me, according to your custom, with few words;

I departed; you summoned me eight months later and invited me to become one of your friends. [*Sat.* I 6, 54–62]

Our first impression is that the meeting lacked warmth, with Horace extremely ill at ease and Maecenas indifferent; we are somewhat surprised to find that the conversation seems to have turned on the family connections and financial condition of the poet. But let us take care not to look upon the tale above as if it were the proceedings of the meeting. These memories are presented from the perspective of the whole sixth *Satire*, Horace's apology against those who suspected him of having entered Maecenas' friendship by surprise and of nourishing misplaced ambitions. It is therefore important to demonstrate that nothing happened in haste or in the first flush of a favorable impression, and to insist upon the fact that at no time did Horace play a trick on Maecenas or try to hide any truth from him. Once this is recognized, we perceive that these lines, dominated by a self-justifying motive, contain even less useful information than appeared on first reading; in the end there remains little more than the names of the actors of the scene, and above all of the promoters of the meeting, Vergil and Varius, which is extremely important in itself.

It was certainly poetry that brought these three poets together; as we see in *Satire* I 4, Horace, at a time when he was not yet in contact with Maecenas, already assiduously frequented the world of the poets. Bad poets, if we believe what he says of them—but it is apparently the satirical form that imposes this qualification on him. He had no reason whatever not to meet good ones as well. It does seem unlikely to us that Vergil should have felt an immediate rapport with the inspiration to which the first *Satires* owe their birth. But Horace was never—and this must have been even more evident when one could meet him in person—the man of one or another of his works. He was not every day the acrid persecutor of Rufillus and Gargonius. Those who approached him must have been receptive, too, to that pleasantness, that refinement of sentiment, and to that light humor which was already apparent or would soon manifest itself in some of the pieces that he collected later in his *Epodes*. Above all—and for young poets these questions were of capital importance—Horace's literary position with regard

to the poetical schools and their quarrels was exactly that of
Vergil and Varius: all three, as we already know of Vergil and
Varius and will shortly learn at leisure of Horace, were thorough
"Alexandrians," *neoteroi*, partisans of the short poem, of difficult art, of the laborious file, great enemies of eloquence, and
somewhat disdainful of anything that did not bear the fairly
clear stamp of Greek art. It is surely not by chance that the
detestable poet Mevius was simultaneously scoffed at by Vergil
(*Buc.* 3, 90) and Horace (*Epod.* 10).

More specifically, it is possible that we can establish precise
occasions for meetings between Vergil and Horace, although
we need not attach too much importance to these facts. In the
spring of 40, a companion from the Athens years, a comrade in
arms at Philippi, and an always loyal friend of Horace (cf. *Od.*
III 21), M. Valerius Messalla Corvinus, returned to Rome.
After the defeat of the republicans he had rallied to Antony.
But Antony sent him to be with Octavius, "lending" him with
the idea of having an ambassador and observer at the side of
his formidable ally. This situation, of an Antony sympathizer
placed with Octavius, was at the same time more or less exactly
that of Pollio, one of Vergil's protectors; in the tenth *Satire*,
Horace would later link (l. 85) the names of these two men,
whom he considered to be, apart from Maecenas, the most
eminent of his noble friends. Pollio and Messalla were also both
poets, and the second, who like Horace wrote in both Greek
and Latin, while limiting himself to the bucolic idyl and am-
orous verse, cultivated a mixed style that sometimes appears in
the *Odes* of Horace, and that was probably pleasing to the poet
of the *Eclogues*. Vergil and Pollio, on the one hand, and Messalla and Horace, on the other—we even find all four of them
grouped together around a curious affair that at the time must
have excited the curiosity of the Romans. In the autumn of the
year 40, Herod the Great, recently installed by Caesar on the
throne of the Jews, was in Rome on business. It was Messalla
who championed his cause; but he must also have frequented
the home of Pollio, and it has often been supposed that a
certain Biblical coloring in the fourth *Bucolic*, writtten at that
time and dedicated to Pollio, could be attributed to the influence of prophecies advanced or brought out of the shadows

for the king's coming. One of the most striking themes of the
celebrated *Eclogue* is that of innocence and harmony reestablished even in the animal kingdom: "And the flocks shall no
longer fear the great lions" (l. 22) makes us think of Isaiah
(11: 6–7); but it is also striking that no other verse of the sixteenth *Epode* comes closer to the Vergilian model than precisely
the one (l. 33) where Horace takes up the same prophetic
motif.

Whatever the truth was about Herod, it is fairly apparent
that Messalla and Pollio had more than one interest in common;
the habitués of the two houses, or of the two circles, must have
seen a good deal of each other. In the particular case of Horace
and Vergil, there was a common desire to reanimate poetry
according to the formulas of a demanding art; and they were
the same age. This is probably enough to make us understand
fairly easily how they met. It has sometimes been conjectured
that Horace, still unknown and somewhat younger, had tried
to arouse Vergil's interest by ostensibly finding his inspiration
in the *Bucolics*. It is true that the influence of the *Bucolics* is
perceptible in a very great number of the *Epodes*; but some of
the *Epodes* in question, like the sixteenth, were written much
later. Furthermore, the *Bucolics* themselves were not published
until 38, or perhaps even 37. It would be necessary to assume
that at least some of them were already known, even in literary
spheres far outside of the circle of Vergil's friends. It would
also be necessary to assume that some of the *Epodes* characterized by a Vergilian tone were written at a rather late date. Of
course none of this is impossible. However, it seems much
more likely that Horace's imitations belong to a later period. If
they have some significance in the history of his personal relations with Vergil, they bear witness to his affection and gratitude, not to a desire to attract attention to himself.

Thus we see the sort of psychological climate in which
Horace's introduction to Maecenas may have taken place, probably with considerably more grace and simplicity than is suggested by the lines of the sixth *Satire*. Maecenas, who like
Pollio and Messalla was both a poet and a great lord, was re-
quested to interest himself, like them, in Horace, just as certain
other lords already took an interest, as friends and poets, in

Horace or in Vergil. Above all we must not imagine—it would have been particularly improbable at that date—that Vergil presented Horace to Octavius' minister as a poet of promise who might later sing the praises of the great prince or add luster to his great reign. None of these men was a soothsayer. Who could then sense in Horace the poet of the *Odes* and the *Carmen saeculare?* On the contrary, the distaste that for so long held him paralyzed before all poetry of an epic or panegyric type, his inability ever to become a court poet—this trait, already recognizable in him, was one of those that dominated his character.

Maecenas was a friend of poetry; and it was in this capacity, we can be sure, that he interested himself in poets. Furthermore, he too was a poet; some fragments have survived that permit us to judge him for ourselves. Most moderns have no great opinion of his work; it was complicated poetry, much given to rare forms, perhaps novel in meter, and precious in the extreme. Of course we must not forget that ancient learning was always intrigued by the peculiar, and may well have preserved for us precisely those works of this delicate poet that represented his riskiest refinements. Suppose that Horace himself were known to us only through such a winnowing: what kind of idea should we have of his art? Once this rectification is made, it no longer seems likely that there was such a disparity as is often imagined between Maecenas' literary tastes and those of Vergil and Horace. Whatever the inequality of their genius, the three poets were "on the same side," held the same ideal of professionalism in art, and were exposed to the derision of the same literary enemies.

One fact has perhaps contributed to the illusory idea held by the moderns that Maecenas and Horace had no literary tastes in common, so that their relationship must have been at the beginning only that of suitor and patron: in his writings, Horace never evoked the Muses as a bond between his friend and himself: never did he praise Maecenas' verses. This incontestable fact can, however, be explained in many ways, and without any need to interpret Horace's silence as a discreet reprobation. In the judgment of the ancients, the only noble forms were the epic and the play. Light poetry, which was what Maecenas cultivated, was created for friends and shunned publicity. But the essential point may be that the two men, born to understand each other so profoundly, very soon ceased to see in the friend anything other than the friendship itself. That purity of sentiment, that calm and penetrating joy born from sharing the least things "because it was he, because it was I," as our Montaigne said, have been expressed in few texts as happily as in a few lines of *Satire* II 6. Stupid people of the times believed that Horace and Maecenas were constructing nefarious political plots; our philologists are amazed not to see Horace taking Maecenas to task for his poor taste, or they interpret his silence in the most sinister way possible: that the two friends, happy to be peacefully together, talked of nothing but the weather. R. A. Schröder has written an admirable page on the understanding between these two "princes": Maecenas, who claimed, and doubtless finally believed—perhaps even with truth—that he was the issue of a royal family; and Horace, of an indubitably humble origin, were both strangers to the ambitions of those who fall between the two levels; one, because he knew that he had been born superior to everything, so that neither senatorial dignity nor a magistrature represented a plus for him; and the other, because entering upon such a career would oblige him to make efforts contrary to his nature. The royalty of the nobleman and the royalty of the "poor" man both arose from independence and were founded upon the awareness of an inner dignity and fullness to which possessions could add nothing, and which resided entirely in their beings.

It was the autumn of 39. Now begins a period in Horace's life in which the study of the man becomes principally the study of his works. In that literary activity, which was beginning to bear permanent fruit, we can distinguish four periods: the *Satires* and *Epodes* would occupy the poet from 39 to 29; the *Odes* (Books I–III) from 31 to 23; the *Epistles* (Book I and *Epistle* to Florus II 2) from 23 to 19. A last period was that of isolated works, the *Carmen saeculare* in 17, the *Epistle* to Augustus (*Ep.* II 1) in about 15, the fourth book of *Odes* in 14, the *Epistle* to the Pisos, or *Ars poetica*, around 10. Horace died on November 27, 8.

2 · Epodes and Satires

THERE IS a very simple way of explaining literary works, which is to see them as the spontaneous fruit of a personal temperament. La Fontaine was a fable maker, hence he produced fables as an apple tree produces apples; Lamartine had an elegiacal and musing temperament, hence the *Méditations;* Racine was "tender," Vigny haughty; and with a satirical and lyric temperament, Horace naturally had to write the *Satires,* the *Epodes,* and the *Odes.* Of course to conceive of the genesis of literary works in this way minimizes the distance that exists between a given characteristic of sensitivity or intelligence and the form through which this characteristic finds a way of expressing itself. Juvenal tells us, it is true, that it was indignation that dictated his verses to him: *facit indignatio versum.* However, no matter how carefully one examines this statement, it is still difficult to see how indignation would have sufficed to make him regularly find under his pen the long and short syllables whose alternation constitutes lines of verse. Make no mistake: indignation, and even the desire to communicate his indignation, were not the only forces at work. Racine's tenderness dictates tragedies in five acts, Lamartine's dictates lyric poems; and if one argues from that difference the deduction that probably the two had two different kinds of tenderness, I wonder if one does not become the dupe of too easy a method: abstracting the work and its author from their whole environment, planting them face to face in an ideal solitude, and then explaining the work by a picture of the author that is derived from the work.

Around the writer, and at the very center of the inspiration that makes him a writer, we must reestablish the presence of a literary universe. To conceive of writing tragedies, one must live in a sphere where tragedies are written; to have the idea of expressing oneself in writing, one must know that this is possible and be concerned with what others have written. It is not the obligation of each poet to invent poetry, or the satire, or the ode; he receives them, as he received words themselves in his childhood. In a nonliterary civilization, he would not have written; living in another literary atmosphere, the same man would have written something else; brought up among the mute, we would never have spoken. In these beginnings of the literary activity of a Horace whose personality was already beginning to emerge a little, the instigation, the first jog, must have come from events or circumstances of a literary nature, situations which influenced him and to which he reacted by choosing to write.

It was true among the ancients, as it is today, that a literary vocation takes cognizance and possession of itself only in the heart of a literary universe. The future poet dreams of himself as already established in that universe, face to face with those forerunners and rivals upon whose heels he is now pressing, aroused to competition by the admiration or repulsion that they awaken in him. But today these sentiments can remain the secret of the poet, who will say nothing of them in his poems. His readers, furthermore, do not ask him to give an account of his feelings; they only hope that he will produce fine works, works of value that have authority in themselves; all the rest is history, which some day will probably interest informed scholars but is felt to be external to creation itself. In antiquity such was not the case. People did not enjoy taking a work as an absolute, a monad. On the contrary, they wanted to be able to fit it into a sort of aesthetic cosmos, and to find other works corresponding, or analogous, or antithetical, to it. They expected every poet to make his intentions known in this respect and to flourish a banner. Everybody had to say what he had meant to do: Vergil lets us know that he is writing after Theocritus, Hesiod, and Homer; Propertius tells us that he wishes to see Callimachus' laurels green again. The poets were not merely expressing devotion to remote ancestors, or rather they did not feel the ancestors to be so remote: they lived in the conviction that in each age analogous situations are reborn, so that the evocation of a master of the past often has significant value, even its true significance, in relation to the situations of the day.

For the period that occupies us, Horace, we know, wanted to enter posterity by hoisting the pennants of Lucilius and Archilochus to his mainmast. This is a very valuable indication that we must not lose sight of, for it is an indispensable complement to the insights that we may gain by attempting to reconstruct the poet's psychology:

My own pleasure is to assemble words into a metrical line in the fashion of Lucilius. He used to confide his secrets to his writings as if to faithful companions; in misfortune as well as in success he never sought other recourse; so that the life of the old man is fully deployed there, traced as if on a votive tablet. I follow his example. [*Sat.* II 1, 28–34]

And, "I was the first to make known at Latium the iambics of Paros, imitating the rhythms and spirit of Archilochus, not the subjects nor the words which pursued Lycambes" (*Ep.* I 19, 23–25). Thus our research is oriented: Lucilius for the *Satires*, Archilochus for the *Epodes*. The problem now is to learn what these names meant for the poet and how he chose his masters.

It is doubtful that either of them conquered him at the outset, so that he was moved by an immediate and overwhelming attraction. The case of Lucilius is striking: Horace, who professed to be his disciple and assiduously studied and imitated him, from the first *Satires* on, also criticized him so sharply, at the same time and in the same pieces, that he had to justify himself against the reproach of malevolence (*Sat.* I 4, 1–13; 10, 1–71). Here is a thoroughly complicated situation. With regard to Archilochus, the texts are less abundant. We will note, nonetheless, that in the very passage where he claimed to be Archilochus' follower, Horace set the exact limits of his imitation: it had to do with the metrical form of the poems (*numeros*) and their inspiration (*animos*); but the subjects (*res*), what we might rather call the themes, of this poetry did not particularly concern him. Besides, can we really conceive of a poet even in antiquity who would make a prodigious leap six hundred years out of his own world to find a model? Why that particular one among so many others? Was it the result of a divine sympathy that could erase centuries to unite two spirits? No; it is precisely the essence of the heritage from Archilochus that Horace repudiates.

One can, of course, use an illustrious and very ancient name as an ornament or a tool, to state one's identity or to defend oneself; but it is always in one's contact with living and contemporaneous surroundings that one is stimulated to be and to be aware of being. It is all very well for Sainte-Beuve to tell us that romanticism is a continuation of the lyricism of the sixteenth century; his poetry is still "against Delille" rather than "for Ronsard." Or, rather, he uses Ronsard only as a club with which to crush Delille, and as a prestigious ally lending him authority for experiments that are purely personal to Sainte-Beuve and that he undertakes only as a result of contemporary problems. We must not imagine Horace receiving the illumination of Archilochus in Greece, returning from Greece with a copy of Archilochus under his arm, and resolving to be the Archilochus of the Romans. These reveries, into which the best minds can sometimes be drawn, may give rise to striking images and create perspectives in which a poem, for example the sixteenth *Epode*, will glitter with an almost supernatural brilliance. They are not the less false for that, for they give us a Horace whom it is impossible to reconcile with the one who is unquestionably revealed by so many other poems of the same time. The very works that the reveries most brilliantly illuminate are thus shown in a false light.

We shall return later to Lucilius and Archilochus. But in resolving the problem of Horace's literary vocation we must not give these two names more than an initial role. We shall have to return to them, for we shall then learn how Horace came to them. But first we must consider how Horace lived, how he set his sights, how he created a poet's identity for himself in relation to the literary environment that surrounded him, which he more or less frequented, and whose applause or jeers encouraged or irritated him. It is on the level of his immediate sympathies and antipathies that we have the possibility of glimpsing a beginning.

Epodes and Satires 37

LITERARY SPHERES

From the *Satires* it is easy to make up portraits of bad poets:
there are the man who dictates, "on one foot," two hundred
lines an hour, the blabbermouth, the lazy man who shrinks from
the painful struggle of composition, the feverish mind whose
inspiration brings to mind the boiling of a torrent, the grapho-
maniac whose life is passed in covering so many scrolls and
parchments with his verses that in the end they will have to
be bundled together and piled up to make his funeral pyre;
another spreads out like a muddy river of troubled waters that
discourage thirst; one is jagged, another is distended; the verses
of the third evoke the panting of a bellows. The ambition of all
these wretches is to write a great deal, as much as possible: "But
here is Crispinus challenging me, betting a hundred to one:
Take some tablets, please; I will take some too; let them give
us a place, a time, and some witnesses; let us see which of us
can write more" (*Sat.* I 4, 13–16). They assiduously seek out
admirers. They pester people at the forum, in the baths. They
recite their poems at women on their way back from the public
ovens or from the wells. What joy if they are able to enchant
a bookseller, or make sure, through gastronomical favors, of
gaining the support of influential babblers, so that at last they
may see their works in the sweaty hands of the commoners!

On the contrary, and the gods be thanked, Horace's mind is
sterile and small. He produces only rarely and a little at a time.
He has no desire to become a classic whose verses are read aloud
in school. He is not interested in the crowd and refuses to give
public readings. What he is able to write is for his friends only,
and even then his friends must take pleasure in hearing it, he
must be urged, and the company and the moment must be favorable. "Do not put yourself out to be admired by the crowd:
be satisfied with a small number of readers" (*Sat.* I 10, 72–74).
What he likes are verses that are artistically constructed (*factos,
Sat.* I 10, 58), flowing (*euntis mollius, ibid.*), and polished with
a file (*limatior, ibid.,* 75). The poet must be able to erase a
great deal, to strike out, and to subject himself to the minute
work that makes him scratch his head and bite his nails to
the quick. He must be terse, so that the thought moves freely

along and does not bog down in words. Tartness is allowable from time to time, but usually playfulness, the tone of a companionable man, together with the firm intent of always staying well within his own limitations (*parcentis viribus atque extenuantis eas consulto, ibid.,* 13–14). The crowd of old poets (*poetarum seniorum turba*) were ignorant of all this, but it is required of all men of reason whose destiny has caused them to live in our time (*ibid.,* 67–68). "Turn your stylus over often to erase, if you wish to write works that will be worthy of being reread."

Devil take the sellers of literature, the grammarians, the schoolteachers, the public amusers; the only audience worth writing for is the right people. Even the mime Arbuscula despised the whistles of the stalls, being content to please the knights alone. It was for Maecenas, Vergil, Pollio, and Messalla that Horace meant to write.

We have seen that our poet was rather severe toward the old Latin authors. His admiration, in the medium he had made his own, was reserved for the Greeks, the masters of the ancient comedy. Everything good about Lucilius was derived from the same source; when he was not able to imitate them closely he was generally less felicitous, and it was this lack of a sufficiently close Greek model that was the real excuse for his awkwardnesses. Horace hoped to be happier because he knew the Greeks better and imitated them more assiduously. When he went to his Sabine farm, it was not scrolls of the *Satires* of Lucilius that he took with him, it was Plato, Menander, Eupolis, and Archilochus (*Sat.* II 3, 11–12). Everyone knows the precept from the *Ars poetica* (ll. 268–69): "Go to the Greek models, and leaf through them over and over night and day." The conviction that inspired it was already present in the very beginnings of Horace's career. Therefore it is not reservations about Hellenism that we should see in our poet's aversion to the use of both Greek and Latin words in a single work. On the contrary, this base confusion, inconceivable in a Greek work, is one of the most disgraceful inventions of the old Latin poets.

The texts that we have been discussing are taken from the first book of the *Satires,* especially numbers 4 and 10. The second book grows out of the same aesthetic principles. We learn through Damasippus that Horace spent his time in scratching over his poems, never deciding to make a fair copy, writing perhaps three or four pieces a year, always discontented with the conditions under which he worked, always surrounded by books (*Sat.* II 3, 1–12). We know also that certain critics accused him of having too ambitious, perhaps too literary, an idea of the satire, and pushing the form beyond the limits of its laws; others regretted that his productions did not have more muscle or more "nerve" (*Sat.* II 1, 1–4). The accusations are apparently contradictory; at least Horace enjoyed placing them in contradiction to each other by playing on the word *acer*, which he took in the sense of roughness. In fact, what they upbraided him for was exactly that artistic writing, that finesse, that subtlety that were so dear to him.

All these traits contribute toward delineating a literary physiognomy that it is not difficult to decipher in the light of the poetical controversies and disputes of the time. Horace is on the side of what we call Roman Alexandrianism, on the side of the disciples of Catullus and Calvus, those scrupulous authors of rare and exquisite works, who held prolixity, facility, and self-satisfaction in great contempt.

That Suffenus . . . writes many more verses than anybody. I really believe he has ten thousand and more, all copied out in full. . . . When you read them, he strikes you as a goatsherd or a ditchdigger . . . coarser than the coarsest book, never so happy as when he has written a poem, so much does he like and admire himself. [Catullus, 22]

And again: "While Hortensius writes five hundred thousand lines in a single year, the *Zmyrna* of my dear Cinna" was nine years in the making; and *Zmyrna* will survive through centuries, while the *Annals* of Volusius will be forgotten tomorrow. "May the little masterpieces (*parva monumenta*) of my friend be always dear to my heart! Let the people savor the bombastic works of Antimachus" (Catullus, 95). "Let the people," because such works were in fact fashionable and were to be found (like those of Fannius, Horace's enemy, later on) in the booksellers' boxes (Catullus, 14); they were the books that were recommended by those dunces of schoolmasters (*ibid.*).

Thus the themes and even the vocabulary of the literary

polemics of Catullus and Horace were identical. It is particularly noticeable that Volusius' derided work belongs to the old Roman epic, a genre that Horace also disdained in the person of Furius. In the same way, Antimachus was an epic poet whose work, riddled with the epigrams of Callimachus, became the symbol of everything detested by those who were on the side of exquisite and refined poetry. It is clear that these resemblances are by no means the result of chance. In the Rome of 60 and thereabouts, as in the Rome of 35, there were two ways of seeing literature, and opinions were divided accordingly. Catullus and Horace were on the same side. In the generation preceding Horace's, believers in the aesthetic against which the poet of the *Satires* aimed his arrows could be found in the caricatures of Catullus. To find them elsewhere at the same time we should have to turn to Cicero, that indefatigable praiser of the old Roman poets, who was always eager to defend them a little peevishly against the disdain of the *cantores Euphorionis* (*Tusc.* III 45) and likely to be reserved toward the Greeks because he wanted to believe that Rome could find the equivalent of their masterpieces in its own literature. Furthermore, Cicero liked to mix Greek and Latin words together in his joking letters. He always praised abundance. He always severely judged persons of pretended refinement whose exquisite elegances prevented them from reaching and touching the public. If we listen to his criticism of the doctrinaires of the opposite school, we will find the themes and even the very words that we meet in Horace, with the single difference that the identical objects praised by the one are blamed by the other:

Calvus had a more careful and refined way of talking . . . but he observed and criticized himself too much. His eloquence, too reduced [*attenuata,* cf. Hor. *Sat.* I 10, 14 *extenuantis*] by this excessive scrupulousness, may have conveyed something to connoisseurs and careful listeners, but it passed over the heads of the forum and the crowd. . . . Why reserve praise for dryness of style, thinness, poverty [*inopiam,* cf. Hor. *Sat.* I 4, 17 *inopis*], just because it is burnished, polished, elegant? . . . How does it happen that when these orators speak they are deserted not only by the curious, which is humiliating enough in itself, but even by their client's friends, who have come to be of help? [*Brutus,* 283–89]

The two camps even differ in their judgments of persons: This Calvus, who seems to annoy Cicero somewhat, is the poet and orator whom Catullus puts on a pedestal; and among the friends of Cicero or those whom he most admired can be found Hortensius, mocked by Catullus for his prolixity, and Varro, whose *Menippeae* systematically combine the vocabularies of Greek and Latin. It is the great quarrel of Asianism versus Atticism. The Asiatics were Hortensius, Varro, and to a large measure Cicero himself. The Atticists were Catullus, Calvus, Cinna. Horace liked and condemned all that the Atticists had liked and condemned.

The quarrel in which Horace launched himself as a resolute partisan went all the way back beyond Catullus and his friends to the great dispute initiated in Alexandria in the third century by Callimachus and Apollonius of Rhodes. Callimachus' side held to a *dictum* to which Horace would have subscribed: "Big book, big foolishness." It held especially to the profession of faith that closed the wise verses of the *Hymn to Apollo* (ll. 105–13):

Envy glides to Apollo's ear: I like only, she says, the poet whose song is like the great sea. But Apollo pushes her away with his foot and speaks: The course of the Assyrian river is also powerful, but it carries in its waves much sullied earth and mud. Deos' priestesses do not bring to her the water of every comer, but only that which gushes, clean and limpid, from the sacred springs, a few drops of supreme purity.

We have already seen this muddy river, this ravaging flood, in Horace, promoted to the rank of a literary symbol. In the *Response to the Telchines*, we find again the defense of an exigent art which fabricates works that are rare, condensed, and exquisite, destined only for connoisseurs.

I have not concluded a long continuous poem, singing kings or heroes in numerous thousands of lines; my little book is of a few words, as if it were a child's, and my years are counted up in many decades. Yes, I know that I am a poet of short poetry, but the birth seed is more powerful than the immense oak. Go find ill fortune, baneful children of Evil Envy; measure my poetical knowledge with the yardstick of art, not with a surveyor's chain. My Apollo has told me: Incense offered to me, O poet, must be heavy; but the Muse must be light. I sing for those who like the sharp song of the grasshopper. Let another go bray with the donkeys; as for me, may I always be the graceful being, the being with wings.

Or again (*Epigr.* 28): "I hate the cyclical poem"—here is a

relation of the *Annales Volusii* disdained by Catullus, a brother
of the *scriptor cyclicus* of the *Ars poetica*—"I want none of the
road on which the crowd drags its feet; I do not drink at the
common spring; everything that is public repels me."

In the light of these texts, Horace, once he is situated in relation to the literary disputes of his time, seems less aberrant,
less unclassifiable than is sometimes claimed—to the point of
making him a real prodigy. It is especially not true that at a
time "when Vergil was still imitating Theocritus" Horace had
already repudiated the "smallnesses" of Alexandrianism and
now dreamed only of restoring a great classical literature. No,
Horace was on the side of the "new poets," those called the
neoteroi. And it was not only the most salient aspects of the
doctrine that he professed; he also used the images, the very
words to which the members of the school unanimously rallied.
We may guess that in the Athens years his admiration for
Brutus, hero of liberty, may have taken equal pleasure in the
literary prestige of one of the most illustrious representatives of
the "Attic" tendency. We especially understand how he came
to be the friend of Varius and Vergil, of Pollio, who was
Alexandrian in poetry and "Attic" in eloquence, and of Messalla,
an "Attic" himself. We understand his speaking kindly of
Valerius Cato (*Sat.* I 10 introd.), and his submitting his writings to the judgment of C. Valgius Rufus (*Sat.* I 10, 82), the
subtle singer of the handsome Mystes, an admirer of Cinna and
of his famous poem, and of course an "Attic" too. Finally, we
understand much better how Vergil and Varius could have had
the idea that Horace and Maecenas might be congenial on the
literary plane as well. For Maecenas too was an admirer and
imitator of the poetry of Catullus. He adopted his metrical discoveries, his original turns of syntax, and sometimes even his
vocabulary. It is surely significant that in the two poems that
he dedicated to Horace, one (fr. 2 Morel) picks up the rare
word *Tunnica* (equals Bithynian, cf. Catullus, 31, 5) and the
other (fr. 3 Morel) imitates the famous opening: "If I did not
love you more than my eyes, my sweetest Calvus," and continues
too, as Catullus did, with a pleasantry.

All this seems self-evident. Yet in going through the studies
on Horace one discovers that this interpretation of the facts has

not gained universal support. We often read that Horace was the enemy of the *neoteroi*, that he was on the side of the classics, and that his position in the literary disputes was more or less that of Cicero. But the texts that we have cited and compared still stand, and they cannot be gainsaid. The error of the critics who place our poet in the camp opposed to the one in which he really fought is explained, I believe, as the result of a prejudice and of a poor understanding of two texts. On the prejudice, there is little to be said; it has an essentially pedagogical origin, and it consists of imagining Horace to be the legislator of the Roman Parnassus and seeing him in this role through the eyes of seventeenth- and eighteenth-century European classicism. The French are particularly exposed to this danger to the extent that they have first made acquaintance with Horace through Boileau.

As to the two precise facts that might make Horace appear to be an adversary of the *neoteroi*, the first consists in the fact that the *Satires* frequently ridiculed a poet by the name of Furius, the author, apparently, of an epic whose action took place at least partly in the Alps and on the Rhine. Acron identifies this Furius as Furius Bibaculus, one of the *neoteroi* most in the public eye; this sole fact, nothing more, would seem to suffice in the opinion of many moderns to settle Horace's position toward the literary schools. The identification of the grotesque Furius with the famous friend of Catullus has nonetheless been frequently contested, and to me it appears untenable. How could a "new poet" have launched himself—we know how the school felt on this point—with an epic that seems to have contained at least eleven books? How could Bibaculus, an implacable enemy of Caesar and Augustus, have composed a work whose subject appears to have been a war against the peoples of the north? How can we attribute to a poet from Catullus' circle hexameters like:

> *Pressatur pede pes mucro mucrone uiro uir*

or

> *Quod genus hoc hominum Saturno sancte create.*

The structure of these lines makes one think more readily of Ennius or one of his close imitators. And indeed we know

through Cicero (*Brutus* 132) of the existence, at the end of
the second century, of a poet named Furius from Antium, to
whom Q. Catulus had dedicated a history of his consulate.
Now, we recall that the most striking event of that consulate
had been a war against the Cimbri. The relationship between
Catulus and Furius of Antium recalls that of Cicero and
Archias: the political man furnishes a poet friend with the
documents from which to make an epic in his praise. The bad
poet mocked by Horace is thus not a representative of Roman
Alexandrianism, but, quite the contrary, one of those "ancients"
whom the Alexandrians, and Horace more than any other, always judged so severely.

The second text that is incorrectly adduced to define the
literary positions of Horace concludes a eulogy of the authors
of Greek comedy. These, according to our poet, are wholly
unknown "both to the handsome Hermogenes and to that
monkey *nil praeter Calvum et doctus cantare Catullum*" (*Sat.*
I 10, 19)—which is usually translated "who does not know how
to sing anything but Calvus and Catullus." Thus, they claim,
Horace must have seen the admirers, perhaps the imitators, of
Calvus and Catullus as nothing more than monkeys incapable
of appreciating real literary greatness. This interpretation, however, raises serious difficulties in the very context itself. The
"monkey" does not know and disdains Greek poets. This attitude does not seem to go with a Catullian. The "monkey"
belongs to the literary coterie of Hermogenes, and Hermogenes
has the same tastes as "the crowd" (*Sat.* I 4, 72); he is a friend
of Fannius (*Sat.* I 10, 80), who is a successful poet (*Sat.* I 4,
21). These tastes are hardly those to be expected in the refined
and somewhat haughty followers of Catullus. Finally, the polemics of the tenth *Satire* seem to associate Hermogenes with
those who defended the ancients and were indignant at Horace's
strictures on them: another feature that hardly suits one of the
neoteroi. But everything would straighten out if *cantere*, instead
of being interpreted in the sense of "sing," were taken in the
sense of the French word "chansonner," to mock, as in the other
text of the *Satires* where the verb is used (*Sat.* II 1, 46). Denigrating parody flourished in that period; there was a parody of
Catullus' *Phaselus* (*Catalepton* 10), and an obscene version of

Lesbia's Sparrow (cf. Martial, XI 6); the *Bucolics*, too, were
ridiculed, a certain Numitorius parodying the first line as
follows: "Tityrus, if your toga is warm, why the shelter of a
beech?" One of the loveliest passages that Vergil took from
Aratos for his *Georgics* is also mistreated, in a thoroughly disagreeable fashion (Quintilian, VIII 3, 47). Is it by chance that
these buffoons seem to us to have specifically chosen the works
of the Alexandrian poets for their activities? And if the bizarre
name of Numitorius, no doubt a pseudonym, evokes a respected
name of the old Roman past, a character from Ennius, who
has come back to make fun of the futile and complicated poetry
of the moderns? In all ages it is easiest to raise a laugh by
making fun of a new, aristocratic, and refined poetry. The
"monkey" detested by Horace was no doubt one of those taste-
less humorists.

In literary history as well as in general history, the reestablish-
ment of the truth is often obscured by the false light of evidence
that appears decisive, so that by merely referring to it in a few
words one can appear to refute any reasonable contestation.
In the present case, it does not seem to me to be a good method
to prefer an isolated, and debatable, text to the whole body
of texts that present Horace to us with such unanimity as a
supporter of the doctrine of the *neoteroi.*

Now that we begin to see which living poets engaged Horace's
sympathies, we must try to see him in relation to his enemies,
especially that Hermogenes whose name comes back so often
in the *Satires* and who seems to have aroused such a lively
aversion in the poet. Hermogenes was not a poet: he was a
satiric "singer" (*Sat.* I 3, 129). But he read the poets' books,
and entertained poets at his table, and Horace found it worth-
while to say loudly that one did not care whether or not one
was read by him (*Sat.* I 4, 72). We see that he reigned over a
band of girl singers and actresses, his pupils (*Sat.* I 2, 91). In
the preceding generation, the care and feeding of this motley
troop had been taken care of by another Tigellius, perhaps his
father (*Sat.* I 2, 1–4), also a "singer." Rather than as "singers"
in the modern sense of the word, the two Tigellii appear to
have been heads of a troop (cf. *Ars poetica*, 155), professional
entertainers, impresarios, organizers of those collective amuse-

ments that always had so important a place in the life of the
Romans. It is thus understandable that Hermogenes could be
courted by poets who wanted an engagement, and that it might
be important for a poet to be received at his table, since being
there might guarantee him a reputation. Hermogenes read the
poets, but not to improve himself (*Sat.* I 10, 18), for he was
not a cultured man. He read the poets from whom he hoped
to derive something to use in composing his entertainments.
To renounce being read by Hermogenes was to renounce being
known by the masses (*Sat.* I 4, 72). Hermogenes was the natural protector of the old poets of the repertoire, such as Ennius
and Accius, who gave him a living; he defended Laberius and
the ones who made people laugh (*Sat.* I 10, 6). In all the aspects
of his character and activity, he could not but be odious to
Horace.

We are sometimes astonished that our poet grew so heated
over a man whom he succeeded only too well in making low
and ridiculous in our eyes. But our surprise is anachronistic.
Neither of the Tigellii was socially insignificant. Tigellius the
Elder had been Caesar's friend, and it is a little painful to see
poor old Cicero, even at the height of his career, worried lest
he had temporarily displeased this favorite. Having been
Caesar's friend, he went on to be Octavius' (*Sat.* I 3, 5). We
see in Suetonius that the latter, even when he had become
Augustus, was careful never to seem to despise popular entertainments. Besides, he had no reason whatever to be sympa-
thetic in the beginning toward those aristocratic poets who had
riddled his father with epigrams. In the generation preceding
Horace's, there had already been hatred between Calvus (hence
the *neoteroi*) and Tigellius the Elder. In those unstable years
when everything, even literary quarrels, ran the risk of degen-
erating into political controversy, it is likely that the favor of
the powerful tended to fall on those who supported the traditional literature and had the favor of the public. It is true that
Augustus would finally choose between Horace and Hermogenes, and would select Horace. But for this Horace would have
to awaken to a sense of responsibility with which the *neoteroi*,
at least in their poems, had not concerned themselves; and
after writing the Roman *Odes* and the *Carmen saeculare* he

would have begun to think about what a Roman popular theater could be. In the year 35, he had not yet reached that point.

From the literary point of view, the hostility of an Hermogenes was not a negligible matter: his performances and his skill with people naturally gave him a sort of monopoly on the diffusion of poetic works. And not only works of drama. We are told that Vergil's *Bucolics* were presented in the theater. We know that this was the case with Ovid's poems, and that in the same category the *Annales* of Ennius were still being received with general enthusiasm in the time of Aulus Gellius (XVIII 5). To be hired for a public presentation in this way was glory, in a city where the less restrained poets went, for lack of anything better, and declaimed their poems in the public baths. Horace refused to falsify his art by making the compromises that would have opened his way to popular fame. He contrasted his elegant "games" with the texts that were chosen for theatrical performance and which first had to please the stage professionals (*Sat.* I 10, 37–38). He liked to believe that real poetry—read, that of the *neoteroi*—had all the powers against it, for we see schoolmasters and grammarians grouped around Hermogenes: poetry was already the butt of that conspiracy, which poets have so often denounced, of the university, the academy, public powers, and today the popular theater and the big publishers.

It has sometimes been supposed that the old *collegium scribarum histrionumque*, created in the time of Livius Andronicus, flourishing in the time of Accius, and still active, as we can deduce from an anecdote of Valerius Maximus (III 7, 11), in the year 90, might have been striving in the time of Horace to rule over Roman letters. In that case it could have been to break up this monopoly that the *neoteroi* instituted the tradition of what we would call public readings, which were, on the contrary, private readings, given before invited guests, but without the necessity of getting anyone's permission. We know that the initiative came from Pollio, whom we have already placed on the side of Horace, Maecenas, Vergil, and Catullus in the literary quarrels of the time.

Horace's links with Roman Alexandrianism give us the key to the *Epodes*. Even if we were able to compare them to the poems of Archilochus, this extra information would change nothing in the observations that we are now in a position to make, and which make it evident that there is a kinship of inspiration and manner between the *Epodes* and the *libellus* of Catullus. In any case, we should believe Horace himself on the subject: *numeros animosque secutus Archilochi, non res (Ep. I 19, 24–25)*. That is, Archilochus was his model for his meters, and perhaps for the arrangement of the pieces in the collection. He also acted as a warning against a certain pugnacity. But the subjects (*res*) are not his. They are those of Hellenistic poetry. The characteristic sharpness of iambics is called upon for minute incidents: the sending of a garlic cheese (*Epod.* 3), the departure of an annoying person on a trip (*Epod.* 10), the wily attacks of an imaginary enemy (*Epod.* 6), the indiscretions of an old coquette (*Epod.* 8 and 12). A papyrus from Strasbourg has given us a few fragments of a Greek epode perhaps attributable to Archilochus: the poet hopes that one of his enemies will be shipwrecked on the Thracian coast and enslaved by savages. Horace may have remembered this poem in writing the tenth *Epode*, since he too writes of a shipwreck. But whereas the Greek author pursued "a former comrade, treacherous to the friendship that he had sworn," Horace seems to have nothing more against Mevius than his evil smell (l. 2): we are now on a joking plane. I hesitate very much to interpret *Epodes* 8 and 12 as an echo of the invective of Archilochus against his former betrothed. But it seems to me no less imprudent to interpret it as personal poetry, representing memories or confessions on the part of our poet. The sources of this theme, to which Horace returned several times in the *Odes* (I 25; III 15; IV 13), are rather to be sought in epigrams, such as those in the *Palatine Anthology* (XI 66–74). Elsewhere, Horace tries to frighten us with stories of witches (*Epod.* 5 and 17); recollections of the eighth *Bucolic* are apparent in these pieces, whose subject itself is entirely modern. The second *Epode* is an elegy on the pleasures of the country; it has a perhaps more Tibullian or Vergilian flavor, with a very adroit structure of turns of phrase inspired by or taken from the *Bucolics*. Horace excuses himself again for the laziness of which Maecenas accuses him, which makes him keep postponing the publication of his *Epodes*; it is because he is the slave of love and so much occupied in that quarter. Does not Maecenas, who presses him, also know the power of Cupid (*Epod.* 14)? Here, he inveighs against the faithless Neaera (*Epod.* 15); there, he deplores the slavery in which love holds him, and his powerlessness to compose his *versiculi* (*Epod.* 11). Really, where are we to find the spirit of Archilochus? We are with Catullus, the Catullus of the banterings, the *nugae*. There is a bit of edge sometimes, as in Catullus too; but the whole is gay.

Together with these exercises, which hold our attention chiefly by their virtuosity and ingenuity, we are not surprised to find pieces where the truest and most simply expressed emotion unquestionably shows through. But this mixture too is characteristic of the Catullian tradition. We do not doubt the sincerity of the affection expressed by the first *Epode*: It is the year 31, war has broken out again, and Maecenas is about to risk all at Octavius' side. Horace will not abandon his friend, and will share all his perils. The same anguish is the inspiration of the thirteenth *Epode*, in my opinion the most beautiful of the whole collection: "For the rest, do not speak of it; perhaps a god, by a generous reversal, will put things back in order again."

The modern reader is perhaps even more deeply touched by the burning ardor that appears to devour the poet at the sight of public scandals: the civil war, constantly breaking out again, is the worst of all (*Epod.* 4, 7, 9, 16). But that inspiration too is present in the collection of Catullus: numbers 29 and 52, in the same iambic rhythm, remind us vividly of the fourth *Epode*, and one can, I think, plausibly visualize a perhaps less partisan Catullus, confronted by events as grave as those of the years 42–30, writing the equivalent of the other national *Epodes*. This is not to diminish the originality of Horace. But it is important not to look upon these justly famous pieces as having been created in a vacuum, or as successes whose equivalents are to be found only in the archaic Greece of Archilochus or Solon. The fourth *Eclogue* is no apocalyptic oriental fragment that has somehow fallen into the country of Tityrus and Galatea, and neither are the seventh and sixteenth *Epodes*, especially, to be understood except as surrounded by all the other *Epodes* and as written by the same poet. It is then apparent that the personal quality of Horace's soul was what made masterpieces of them, pieces that certainly no one else could have written. Yet these poems do not ring false under the pen of the author whom we are beginning to know, and who is evolving in the midst of the "new poets."

If, in short, the *Epodes* are a natural result of that time and that environment, it is surely much more difficult to see along what roads Horace was moving toward the writing of his *Satires*: how the idea came to him of imitating Lucilius, and later of openly proclaiming himself his disciple. I believe that it is useful to distinguish between these two aspects of the problem: we will perhaps find a way of glimpsing the evolution, the future, of our poet.

Horace was a professed Lucilian. The attitude was singular: it was almost unprecedented for a Latin author to be the avowed follower of another Latin writer. Terence claimed to imitate not the comedies of Plautus, but rather those of Menander or of Apollodorus; Ennius addressed himself to Homer and disdained Naevius; the "new poets" imitated Callimachus and Philetas; Horace himself would later be careful to connect his *Odes* with Alcaeus and his iambics with Archilochus. Of course, the avowal of these models did not in any way limit the liberty of the poet; in the *Georgics*, Vergil ostensibly followed Hesiod, but it was Aratos whom he imitated the most closely, without naming him; Cicero reproached Ennius for his ingratitude toward Naevius (*Brutus* 76); and in defending himself for imitating Naevius and Plautus, Terence had to affirm—but who would believe him?—that he did not know of the existence of the pieces in question (*Eun.* 33). Thus, and naturally, the Roman writers took inspiration indiscriminately from all their predecessors, whether Greek or Latin; but when it came to confessing to an influence, they made a choice, guided by the preferences of their schools, and above all never admitted to anything owed to their compatriots. Rather than Lucilius, why did Horace not claim to imitate the poets of the ancient comedy, of whom he seems to have thought for a short time (*Sat.* I 4, 1; II 3, 11–12), or the Greek moralists of the line of Theognis or Cercidas, with whom his work certainly has much in common? He would still have been Horace, and nothing would have prevented him from taking inspiration from Lucilius as well.

The reference to Lucilius seems even more surprising in view of Horace's literary tastes. It is paradoxical to see our poet taking his contemporary adversaries to task for faults that are precisely those of the model he has chosen: Crispinus was an inexhaustible improviser, but Lucilius wrote two hundred lines "on one foot" (*Sat.* I 4, 9). It is paradoxical to see that in the current polemics, Horace, the disciple and continuator of Lucilius, was on one side, while the admirers and defenders of Lucilius were on the other. This mixed attitude was evident to Horace's enemies, who accused him of denigrating his master, and it must have caused equal concern to his friends. It is sometimes thought that they took fright at his Lucilian boldness, which was supposedly incompatible with the peace of the city. Surely not; the Romans were not so thin-skinned, and we see Maecenas himself urging Horace to get on with the composition of his iambics. Horace's friends were, rather, surprised at his choosing a pitifully inartistic old soul as a model, and feared that the association would corrupt our poet's taste. From the beginning of the second book of *Satires*, Horace had to defend himself against the same accusations of carelessness and facility that he himself had addressed not long before to Lucilius: "They claim that they could spill out a thousand lines like mine in a day" (*Sat.* II 1, 3–4). The criticism must have struck home, for he makes another illusion to it in the *Ars poetica* (ll. 240–42).

Furthermore, in reading the *Satires* as a whole one cannot escape the impression that Horace hesitated a long time before openly declaring himself to be a disciple of Lucilius. In the terms of *Satire* I 4, Lucilius was "wholly a product" of the ancient comedy of the Greeks; he did nothing but imitate those authors, with the small difference that he wrote very badly; and it is Eupolis, Cratinus, and Aristophanes whom Horace, passing over Lucilius, likes to call to witness to lend him authority for the freedom of his languge. There is not a word to indicate that he regards Lucilius as his master. The end of the piece, as we know, recalls the youthful Horace's conversations with his father: it is from them that he has his liking for the role of the observer and for freedom of speech. Between the wisdom of his father and the literary cachet of the poets of the ancient comedy, Lucilius is passed over.

In *Satire* I 10, it is no longer Lucilius that our poet attacks, but rather his inept admirers. No longer is it argued that Lucilius is totally the product of the Greeks; on the contrary, the Greeks had no idea of that literary genre, *Graecis intacti carminis* (l. 66), so that we must be particularly indulgent toward the Roman innovator. But even here Horace does not exactly present himself as an imitator of Lucilius; he says that he has only taken up a genre again that had long fallen into disuse (ll. 46–49). Not until the second book of the *Satires* do we finally find the definitive statement: "My pleasure is to write in the style of Lucilius. . . . It is he who is my model"—*Sequor hunc* (*Sat.* II 1, 34).

Thus there is no doubt that an evolution has taken place. Perhaps it sheds some light on the story of those eight lines that are still rather hard on the old poet, and that some manuscripts place at the beginning of *Satire* I 10. We might easily conclude that Horace himself removed them when his first book was reprinted.

What can be the final reason for Horace to have admitted himself to be a disciple of Lucilius, of whom he had spoken so ill in the beginning? A firm answer is impossible, because we do not know enough of the details of the controversies in which Horace did battle. He tells us that he was reproached for having spoken ill of Lucilius; but given the habits of the ancients, how can we fail to believe that the same accusations were made against his *furta*, his plagiarisms? Rather than to indulge in dangerous epilogues on this count, he probably thought it better to enroll himself bravely in Lucilius' line, as others enrolled in the train of one Greek or another. It is also possible that with the passing years things fell into their proper places, and he acquired a clearer picture of the ties that bound him to Lucilius and wished to acknowledge them.

In any case, one thing is certain: he deeply loved and admired Lucilius. The texts that we have just reviewed arose largely from literary strategy; they give us only a very partial and very distorted idea of Horace's relationship to the work of his predecessor. Even on the basis of the wretched scraps that are all that remains of Lucilius today, the kinship of the two poets is striking. The kinship of two minds: but also, on the part of Horace, the will to imitate, to pour his work and even his personality into the mold that Lucilius had created.

This careful fidelity is even more striking in a literary genre that takes its life, as the Lucilian-Horatian satire did, largely from personal experiences and anecdotes undergone by the writer. Before Horace wrote of his trip to Brundisium (*Sat. I* 5), Lucilius had had occasion to write of a trip from Rome to Sicily in Book III of his *Satires*. It is very natural that Lucilius' tale should have given Horace the idea of putting an analogous episode into verse; but what is really surprising is that the most specific anecdotes of Horace's trip are already found in that of Lucilius. The mischievous servant girl in Trivicum and the false hopes that she roused in poor Horace had already appeared on Lucilius' road: here she was a Syrian innkeeper, as ardent as a young mare, and she too no doubt first tempted her guests and then left them hungry, since one line recalls the punishment of Tantalus and another seems to imply an accident analogous to the one that concluded Horace's unlucky adventure. Are we to suppose that this story, purely personal to Horace, is only a play without substance, invented for the purpose of recalling Lucilius? It is much more striking to find in Lucilius an episode in which all Horace's companions participated, and which for this reason it would have been much more difficult for the poet to invent entirely from his own imagination: Lucilius appears to have been present at the dispute of the two clowns Sarmentus and Messius Cicirrus: more, the sallies of the two antagonists are the same that Horace used: where Horace speaks of a unicorn, the jester met by Lucilius mentioned the tooth of the rhinoceros; in Horace, one of the adversaries seems to be deformed on a whole side of his face; in Lucilius, a century earlier, he had only one eye. No doubt these similarities could be explained to a degree if we assumed that the two voyagers actually attended the same performance, a local entertainment unvarying in its costumes, disguises, and repartee; but it is, nonetheless, striking to see Lucilius guiding the attention of his distant disciple and concentrating it on matters that had caught his attention, while the rest more or less shades off, passes, and perhaps is not even noticed.

In *Satire* I 7, which, as we have seen, has undeniable ties with Horace's own life, it is again a memory of Lucilius that stimulated the poet's curiosity, sharpened his eye, and caused him to amuse himself with a trifle which otherwise might not even have caught his attention. The trial of Persius and Repilius lives again like a reflection of the trial of T. Albucius and Q. Mucius in the second book of Lucilius: the same confused circumstances coming up against the complications of provincial administration, the same judicial setting, the same burlesque invective, and in the end, a jest that seems to conclude the dispute with laughter. Again: it is in almost the same terms that the two poets apologize for telling a story that has often been told before—"known to every barber," says Horace, and Lucilius, *fandam atque auditam iterabimus famam*.

But the most manifest mark of his admiration is seen in the form that Horace adopted from the outset. Only Lucilius can have suggested the idea to him of writing his *Satires* in hexameters. At his side Varro had used a polymetry for his *Menippeae* that was perfectly suited to the sallies and unexpected touches of his invention and composition. The Greek works that may have inspired Lucilius himself and whose tone is more similar to Horace's satire were not in hexameters: Callimachus and Herondas used iambics or scazons, and both Callimachus and Cercidas used a polymetry based upon iambics. The hexameter does appear in Timon's *Silloi*, but because he was parodying the epic form; that particular source is the inspiration, in both Lucilius and Horace (*Sat.* II 5), of some amusing pieces, which are, however, of a somewhat marginal sort. The Greek prehistory of the satire, as Horace wished to see it (*Sat.* I 4, 1), would belong rather to dramatic poetry, that is, to a style of verse from which hexameters were excluded on principle. It is also notable that Lucilius started by writing his satires in iambic, trochaic, and mixed meters, and came to the hexameter only later. In the Catullian atmosphere in which Horace lived, the most natural thing would have been for him to write his amusing scenes and witty stories—as Catullus did, and he himself did in his *Epodes*—in iambics, Phalaecians, or elegiac distichs.

The use of the hexameter is thus a notable trait among those that show Horace's intention of being faithful to Lucilius. But he did more: he, who was so concerned with formal perfection, took up and modernized—that is, somewhat regularized—the chaotic and nearly lawless verse line of his predecessor. This is not to say merely that he took up the hexameter of olden days, which had not yet undergone the retouching of the *neoteroi*, though this would have been much in itself; but the hexameter of his *Satires* is ruder and more disheveled than that of Lucretius and Ennius. It is impossible to think that the vivacity of the tone is enough to explain all the irregularities that are visible, wandering caesuras and rasping elisions. Here there is a will to Lucilianism that is the more notable in that Horace must have realized that he would be accused of writing badly. He had taken his stand (*Sat.* I 4, 40–62) and did not concern himself over the all too foreseeable criticism (*Sat.* II 1, 1–4), since from one end to the other of the two books the versification remains identical in style.

How bonds had been formed between the young man and the old poet that were capable of resisting literary fashions, the incomprehension—that is certain—of his dearest friends, the irritation that he must have felt toward the others who, though very different from him, also claimed Lucilius as master—this is what it is very important for us to know in order to be able to have a true picture of the stages in our poet's formation.

Perhaps we should turn to even older experiences, experiences that were already memories. We have spoken of the teaching of Orbilius as a possible influence. But again: The surroundings in which Horace lived in his childhood, in the time of his father, before the trip to Greece of 45, must have borne little resemblance to the one in which we find him between 40 and 30, nor can Horace's father have resembled a reader or a character or a friend of Catullus. That provincial wisdom, echoes of which his son has transmitted to us, must have more warmly received a writer whom reasonable old people—Horace's father belonged to Cicero's generation—still read with pleasure and felt to be in harmony with their sentiments. The young man, who had not yet had any reason to rebel, must have bathed in that wisdom. From this the contradictory and passionate character of Horace's judgments on Lucilius might be fairly well explained as having to do with a part of himself or of his past that he could not, or did not, wish to deny and yet against which he struggled. The harshness of some phrases is no doubt only the other side of a tormented attachment.

Yet, at the time when he was writing the *Satires*, Lucilius, from whom he should now have been feeling himself separated by his new requirements of formal perfection, must have been more to him than a memory of childhood. For Horace to have sought out this attachment when everyone around him was claiming to be the successor of some Greek, he must have seen in Lucilius some merit that was not to be found elsewhere. And perhaps, in light of what we know of his life and work, in light of the few remaining fragments of the old poet, we can distinguish two particular points of agreement.

The poetry of Lucilius corresponds to a certain social structure and to a certain art of living that are not common. It is made to give form, consistency, and ornament to the life of a society of friends: it seeks to awaken an affectionate echo in a small group; it does not address itself to the masses. We have already clearly seen that the same was true of Horace, and we have attributed that aversion to the masses to a certain aesthetic esotericism. But now it is important to be precise. In fact, Horace's true milieu was not a literary circle. His friends were not all poets, and even with those who were also poets he was not sure that it was not more the friend, the man, that he sought out. Octavius, Aristius Fuscus, the two Visci, Messalla's brother, Bibulus, Furnius—none of these, though perhaps they were occasional poets, seems to have made himself illustrious by his muse, and we have already noted that in the *Satires* we are never present at any conversation or literary discussion between Horace and his friends. Our poet would later make fun of those circles of literary men where mutual compliments were paid, one member being a Callimachus and another an Alcaeus (*Ep.* II 2, 87–101). Could it be, then, that he was looking beyond the literary cloisters, toward universal man?

Certainly not. He felt no less aversion for the masses; he had a horror of the infatuations into which uncultured men hurl themselves. Above all he was reserved, feeling that he could give the best of himself only to beings who knew him personally and felt friendship for him. It is significant that *Satire* I 3, in praise of indulgence and gentleness, is entirely devoted to the way in which one must live among friends. We all know that this preoccupation with friendship is found constantly in Horace at all stages of his life, in the amusements of the *Satires*, in the most settled reflections of the *Epistles*, even in lyric exaltation. It reflects, we can be sure, one of the essential traits of his personality.

Now Horace found that character trait in Lucilius himself, manifesting itself in situations where our poet could recognize himself as well. Horace's quarrels with the official poets who were at the same time the entertainers of the masses, his dispute with Hermogenes—one hundred years earlier these had been the fencing matches between Lucilius and the great Accius, then president of the college of poets; as early as the time of Lucilius the grammarians had entered the dispute, and on the wrong side. Far from these peevish bands, far from the ignorant crowd, far from the indifferent, too, Lucilius had found in a circle of friends an atmosphere in which he could expand. Scipio Aemilianus and his friends anticipated the circle of Maecenas. Now as then, the center of the little group was a statesman in love with poetry, who, now as then, wrote poetry himself. Beside this great man was Lucilius, was Horace, both knights, both materially independent, equally unconcerned with any advancement or personal political career.

Lucilius' poetry had for the most part been what Horace himself so much enjoyed writing: he was the chronicler of the little group, recording conversations and amusing remarks, recounting a trip, a dinner, an anecdote that made people laugh, a dispute that made people talk. Horace had no reason to interpret Lucilius through the intermediary of Juvenal. These satires, which the rhetorician of Antony's time saw as the work of a madman continually brandishing a hot iron and impassioned with the desire for the triumph of an implacable virtue, were interpreted by Horace, with common sense, as the rather

free and easily exaggerated expressions that settled and congenial
men exchange naturally about others when they know that they
are among friends. Neither Horace nor Cicero thought that
violence and bitterness were the distinctive traits of Lucilius.
Quite the contrary, they appreciated entirely opposite qualities
in him: grace, playfulness, politeness, urbanity—the very qualities that, together with a touch of verbal fancifulness, make up
the charm of friendship.

The other trait by which Lucilius must have held Horace's
attention and imposed himself on him as a unique model is the
ease with which he places himself on stage and talks of himself.
"As if to faithful friends, he confided his most secret thoughts
to his books . . . so that the whole life of the old man is spread
out there, traced as on a votive tablet" (*Sat.* II 1, 30–34). Now,
as we already know and will see more and more, Horace's principal merit as a writer is to have dared, and then to have been
able, to be interested in himself. The rather flitting diversity of
his work, apparently divided up among so many influences—
satires after Lucilius, iambics after Archilochus, odes after
Alcaeus or Sappho (which are so diverse themselves, ranging
from bacchic chant to paraenesis or mythological tale)—all this
pulls together only around a person, who tells of himself and
proposes himself.

He found, then, in Lucilius, the assurance that one could
build a literary work around one's own person. Perhaps no
Greek author would have encouraged him in that direction.
The individual always seemed minor to the Greeks, at best good
for an epigram of a few lines, and with the further requirement
that the anecdote or confession be stylized and generalized by
its formal setting, since the true individual cannot be captured
by words. The Latins had to innovate in order to overturn this
double barrier. They had to become bold enough to place themselves frankly on the plane of the individual. They had to invent
literary forms that would give them a little ease and the opportunity for sufficiently broad development. They had to free
themselves from the slavery of the great forms, and believe that
a feeble person, neither a legendary hero nor an historical personage, who had known only the adventures and life known by
everyone, nonetheless deserved to hold the attention of the

reader. They had to create for this new kind of painting a style that would be less extended and dense, so that from the perspective of tradition it would appear relaxed. Starting with the epigram and those very short pieces of which we have excellent samples from Rome itself in Catullus and in Horace's *Epodes*, they created poems that were much longer and somewhat floating at times, the satire and the elegy: the beginnings of what would later become the novel, progress in catching individual and common situations by means of an art conceived originally for the empyrean.

The development of the elegy in the generation to which Horace, Gallus, and Propertius belonged is some demonstration of the force of the current that was then carrying young poets toward the search in literature for possibilities of individual expression. But the elegy from its birth was confined to the limited area of the dramas of the life of the heart, where the descriptive style lent itself best to effects of generalization which tended to efface individual features. Horace did not have a taste for making elegies. Life, his own life, seemed to him to have much more richness and diversity than an elegy could grasp. So it is quite possible that in seeking for an equivalent, a model who in the past might have had the same desire to put his whole self into his work and to make himself entirely present there, he found no one but Lucilius. In the Lucilian satire, the chronicle of a group of friends, the delineation of an individual life, he saw himself prefigured.

Besides, the more assiduously he frequented the old poet, the more he probably discovered in him, and in areas where at first one would have been least likely to seek them, the possibilities of a true agreement. In spite of Lucilius' carelessness, his judgments on art and his intentions conformed to those of Horace: opposition to tragic grandioseness, disdain of the effects that impress the common people, simultaneous rejection of the judgment of the uncultured man and that of the professional man of letters, writing destined for literate friends, the claim that he was not a poet, the profession of literary modesty. But at the same time, and as a correlative to this disclaimer of genius, importance was given to judgment and taste in the arrangement of a poem: it was not Horace, it was Lucilius who made fun of some bloated verses of Ennius; it was Lucilius who prescribed "that the finale and conclusion should be worthy of the beginning of the work" and who reminded his reader that "taste consists in knowing how to choose, to delete, and to put everything in its place." Lucilius, according to Pliny, had been the founder of literary criticism in Rome: *qui primus condidit stili nasum (NH. praef.* 7; cf. Hor. *Sat.* I 4, 8 *emunctae naris*). Thus when Horace criticized Lucilius, he may have felt that he was doing so in the very name of the principles formerly laid down by the old master; if he had lived in a more polished age, Lucilius would have taken more trouble over his works.

THE PHILOSOPHERS

Horace's satire is not only the chronicle of a group of friends or the journal of an individual sensibility. Another element is stated there, which seems to have had only a very minor place in Lucilius, and the presence of which will carry great weight in the further evolution of the genre. Moral problems often constitute the very weft of Horace's work; in fact, one wonders whether the Horatian satire, under a Lucilian disguise, may not well have been the literary launching of that Hellenizing and popular wisdom that was spreading widely in the Roman world at precisely that time, through the intermediary of innumerable manuals and the voices of preachers.

These moralists, orators, or writers, often appear as actors in Horace's *Satires*; the poet somewhat gives us the impression of having used them as a puppeteer uses his dolls, giving them voices without showing his own face. He took great care not to be confused with them, and this betrays both an undeniable aversion and a certain feeling of kinship. "But that's enough. Not wishing you to suspect me of having been stealing from Crispinus' boxes, I won't add another word" (*Sat.* I 1, 120–21). In fact, when he gives the floor either to Crispinus, an impudent slave's thinking-master (*Sat.* II 7), or to one Stertinius (*Sat.* II 3), who seems to have been a Stoic, it is not always easy to see wherein he finds them ridiculous, and why their words might not be his. One cannot escape the impression that Horace, perfectly at ease in using his own identity to tell the story of a meeting with a bore, a trip to Brindisium, or a ridiculous meal, to express the joys that he finds in his little property, or to break lances with his detractors or defend the rights of satire, finds it more difficult to moralize directly, and more seemly to moralize under the name of someone else, sometimes mocking even those to whom he lends his own words.

It is not possible to believe, in fact, that when he put philosophers and dogmatics on his stage his one thought was to ridicule pretentious and long-winded men professing a mad wisdom. If Crispinus or Stertinius had not seemed to him to have more to them than the bore of *Satire* I 9 or the ridiculous host of *Satire* II 8, he would probably not have devoted so much care to them. *Satire* II 3 in particular, with its 326 lines, would be nothing but a painful and fatiguing exercise. It has been noticed, besides, that Horace seems to have brought to Stertinius' sermon some contributions of an origin that cannot escape the reader. Beneath the mask of the gesticulating puppet that he controlled, he wanted his own presence to be guessed. Thus, it is obviously not Stertinius but Horace, native of Venusia, who tells through the mouth of his philosopher the story of a compatriot, Servius Oppidius, a property owner at Canusium.

How, furthermore, could he see only laughable stupidity in the affirmations of a morality that was substantially his own? We can compare particularly the criticism of avarice lent to Stertinius (*Sat.* II 3, 82–167) to the one formulated in his own name in the first book of *Satires* (*Sat.* I 1, 23–100). As P. Lejay has observed, in both places the subject is taken up in the same way, and the developments correspond: the miser who enjoys knowing himself to be rich (*Sat.* I 1, 61–67; II 3, 84–96); the miser who refuses to spend anything because of fear of the future (*Sat.* I 1, 69–100; II 3, 104–26); the miser who never tires of accumulating wealth (*Sat.* I 1, 28–40; II 3, 126–41); mention of the "great heap," *acervus*, from which the miser hesitates to take anything (*Sat.* I 1, 41–44; II 3, 111–14), and of the family disorders brought about by avarice (*Sat.* I 1, 80–91; II 3, 131–41). Singular similarities appear even in details: the mention of the last illness of the miser (*Sat.* I 1, 80–85; II 3, 142–57), the allusion to the legend of Clytemnestra (*Sat.* I 1, 100; II 3, 132–41). It is not even possible to say that what Horace wrote in his own name is more amusing or more pointed:

in the two passages that we are comparing nothing is as good as the story of the death of Opimius, and it is told by Stertinius (*Sat.* II 3, 142–57); when Horace takes responsibility for the discourse, there are fewer extreme exaggerations (100,000 bushels of grain in *Sat.* I 1, 45; 300,000 jars of wine in *Sat.* II 3, 116); but in the two cases the mobility of the development, the leaps of thought, are the same.

Thus he takes as mouthpieces precisely those whom he mocks; for even when it is ridiculous, criticism of human folly is serious and has its effect; and that effect carries a little further than a too naïve philosopher imagines, for in many ways it also reaches —without being the less valid for that—the person of the formulator.

In this creation of a subtle equilibrium, our poet evidently takes his inspiration from Plato, whom he has indicated to us himself as one of his bedside books (*Sat.* II 3, 11), and whose presence is very perceptible, especially in the second book of the *Satires*. The technique of the reported conversation alone is significant of this connection: in *Satire* II 7, Davus reports to Horace the words that Crispinus' porter has picked up from the mouth of his master; and in *Parmenides* Cephalus relates a conversation that had been narrated to him by Antiphon, who had it from Pythodorus. But there are many other echoes, as Fraenkel has just recently demonstrated: "Whence comes, where goes Catius?" (*Sat.* II 4, 1) is like "Where are you going like that, where are you coming from, my dear Phaedrus?" (*Phaedr.* 227a). And the parallelism goes on: Catius, desirous to fix in his memory a marvelous lesson he has just received (it is a matter of culinary recipes), reminds us of Phaedrus striving, in a walk at the foot of the Long Walls, to retain and hold forever the marvelous speech of Lysias; elsewhere (*Sat.* II 2, 2) the words of Ofellus are introduced by Horace as those of Phaedrus are in the *Symposium*. Now it is one of the most characteristic traits of the Platonic art—and even method—to attribute to a third person certain arguments in which the philosopher does not involve himself; it is up to the reader to judge what he must take completely seriously and as belonging to the doctrine. The great myth of the Republic is a story told by Er the Armenian; it is Diotima who gives the praise of love;

but again, in contexts where apparently malice and seriousness are mixed, is the speech of Aristophanes in the *Symposium* only a comic exaggeration? Or has Plato confided to even that hiccuping mouth some of his dearest ideas? Are the funeral oration of Menexenus and the speech of Lysias in Phaedrus presented for our admiration or to make us smile? For both, surely, if we are wise. In the rhetoricians' terminology, this device was known under the name of *dissimulatio*. Socrates was supposed to have been its inventor and master. It was a way of respecting the freedom of the interlocutor by making him understand immediately the contrary of what one seemed to be saying to him. Nothing, the theoreticians assure us, was more appropriate to the *sermo*, that is, to that familiar conversation whose free flow was precisely what Horace's *Satires* wished to imitate.

It is this absence of "irony," as we would say in our own language, that so sharply repels Horace in the dogmatic characters whom he sets on stage. He would no doubt have forgiven them their paradoxes, laughable and profound at the same time —the equality of offenses, the royalty of the wise man. But in daily life they were brutal, ill-advised, and untimely. Their morality, deduced from inaccessible principles, was applied and imposed in an authoritarian manner, never changing for anyone. It would not be astonishing if they came to the point of haranguing the crowd, for to everyone they had the same thing to say. The individualistic Horace, the man of good company, had a horror of that lack of discrimination, that leveling; and he remembered his enemies, the bad poets, who recited their poems in the public squares or the baths.

Yet these zealots were not negligible men. Horace had more than one idea in common with them. On the moral plane, he was a disciple of their masters, not of Lucilius. For the old poet who was the Scipios' friend, virtue seems to have consisted of facing up honorably to the obligations that social rank brings with it; and when he was forced to express himself on the subject, it was the formulas of Roman tradition that came from his pen: "First must come the interests of the fatherland, then those of one's parents, then one's own" (ll. 1337–8). Horace's wisdom had more to do with Greek thought: an ideal of a balance of powers and of happiness. Lucilius advises us to appreciate wealth and honors at their true value; for Horace, it is best to live on little and in seclusion (*Sat.* II 2, 110).

There is no school of philosophy whose claims upon Horace's soul have not been advanced in the last hundred years. These uncertainties may be explained in several ways. There is, to begin with, Horace's strong personality, to which the idea probably never occurred that he ought to belong to a particular school and adopt all its arguments for the reason that one of them appeared to him to be true. He may have taken up an Epicurean thesis, or he might in certain cases readily use Stoic terminology, without being either a Stoic or an Epicurean. Philosophies were not for him systems of life; they brought him materials (arguments, images, vocabulary), and he freely made a personal choice among them to resolve the problems that seemed most important to him, to try to correct illusions that he felt to be dangerous. Besides, the very materials that he kept often present themselves to us without very clear signs of their origins: careless of metaphysics, he interested himself almost exclusively in those problems of practical morality on which, as a matter of fact, all the schools were in agreement. The fundamental argument of *Satire* I 2 is that in the matter of sexual needs it is easy to satisfy nature without inconvenience of any kind; trouble begins only when one starts making refinements, by seeking out complications arising only from vanity or from an unregulated imagination. Lucretius, as we know, said exactly the same thing. But so many arguments that were constantly reiterated by the Cynics aimed at the establishment of the same doctrine: let us think of Diogenes, when he abandoned a carefully made vessel to content himself with a simple bowl, and then threw away his bowl when he perceived that the cup of his hand was enough to scoop up water. Nor is there any more reason to attach Horace to Epicureanism or to Cynicism. Philosophical agreement on the plane of practical morality was not only a Roman phenomenon: Bion himself had been the disciple simultaneously of the Cyrenaics and the Cynics; the hedonism of the one and the asceticism of the other recommended the same conduct of life.

I do not see what Horace can be said to have received specifically from Epicureanism. Dogmatism is the most striking trait of the sect, and Horace abominated it. Certainly he was an excellent friend, but it is clear that one can have a sense of friendship without being an Epicurean. One would be more inclined to call him a Stoic (except for the metaphysics), since Stertinius, whom, as we have seen, he uses as a mouthpiece, was a Stoic. We may recall that in the last years of the Republic many followers of Caesar, and Caesar himself, tended toward Epicureanism, while their adversaries—Cicero, Cato, Brutus— were Stoics or near-Stoics. Horace may have frequented some Epicureans, but his original attachments and the environment in which he was formed are not on that side. In any case, to speak of Stoicism is not to say anything very precise. Must the wise man participate in public affairs? Here is certainly a practical problem, and precisely one with which Horace was much preoccupied. Now the Stoics are divided on this point. In any case, the ease, the joyous simplicity with which, from that time on, we see our poet bearing himself toward all the pleasures of life, should not make us think that he would have been ill at ease in a Stoic climate. Stoicism is not asceticism, it is a doctrine of liberty and of self-possession. Let us reread Stertinius' speech: in speaking of *luxuria* (*Sat.* II 3, 224–80), the philosopher criticizes only its extravagances: the man fettered by the bonds of a mad passion, the bon vivant who dines only on nightingales, the irresponsible man who gives all his goods to the poor. None of all that has any bearing on the honest libations and easy love affairs with which Horace brightened his life. Pleasure for the Stoic is not an evil, it is a matter of indifference; and, finally, in that very respect the Stoic feels freer, more at ease, than the consequential Epicurean, fettered as he is by his pleasure-centered morality, constantly compelled to observe himself narrowly in order to know what pleases him most, a faithful calculator of the arithmetic of pleasures, taking his pleasure so terribly, so fastidiously seriously.

We should like to know how Horace's moral culture came into being: what he had read. The *Dialogues* of Plato, we can be certain. Lucretius too, whose developments he sometimes reproduced word for word, notably in *Satire* I 3, on the impossibility of cutting out anger, on the origins of civilization, and on the illusions of lovers. One can hardly doubt that he read

the works of Crispinus, the poet-Stoic. Perhaps he found in
Cicero's *Paradoxes* some of the exaggerated expressions that he
amused himself with. But he himself draws our attention to
another quarter still, when he designates his satires by the name
of "Bionian conversations" (*Ep.* II 2, 60). Perhaps in fact he
found from Bion and his imitators, in addition to a philosophy,
a certain way of approaching and treating philosophical problems. Since we are speaking here of writers whose works have
disappeared, we can arrive only at general and plausible con-
jectures.

Bion of Borysthenes lived in the first half of the third century
B.C. An auditor, first of the Academy, then of Crates the Cynic
(Diogenes' successor), then of Theodorus the Atheist, a disciple
for a short time of Theophrastus, from whom he learned the
art of portraiture—he does seem to prefigure the Horatian
eclecticism. Handling parody in a masterful fashion, having
recourse to all styles, disdaining neither invective nor obscenity,
spiritedly interrogating the reader or auditor—for he readily
spoke in public—caring little for logical construction, he had
the reputation of being the author of a considerable number of
maxims and anecdotes of edifying intent. Also attributed to him
were some "diatribes," that is, familiar speeches, which Horace,
again, may have read. The echoes that have come down to us
through Stobaeus hardly correspond to what we are told of
their original verve; they are no doubt only résumés.

Menippus of Gadara, a Syrian contemporary of Bion, was
on the side of the Cynics. Certainly Horace knew him well,
as the inspirer of Varro's *Menippeae* and of Lucilius himself,
since the *Assembly of the Gods* that opens the old master's
collection seems to be an early transposition of a piece by
Menippus. One of the essential themes of Menippus' work is
derision of dogmatic philosophies, which he causes to refute
each other by playing up their contradictions. His effort in this
has a goal parallel to Bion's: to establish a common morality
practically independent of all metaphysics. But Menippus is not
a preacher; he is a writer with a clownish and unbridled imagination. It is perhaps he who invented the "Dialogues of the
Dead," revived from the Homeric *Nekyia*: schoolmasters and
philosophers, called upon to explain themselves, file past before

Tiresias. Horace's *Satire* II 5 may take its setting from Menippus. Perhaps we should interpret the ridiculous meal at Nasidienus' house (*Sat.* II 8) as a Menippean echo of the great tradition of philosophical banquets. With Ariston of Chios, perhaps a little younger than Bion and Menippus, we are probably in the company of a Peripatetic. Cicero's *De Senectute* adapts one of his treatises. The influence of the school appears in him through his taste for portraiture. We cannot exclude the possibility that the initial idea of so personal a work as the *Satire* on the bore (*Sat.* I 9) owes something to that literature.

These comparisons have their importance. They help us to a better knowledge of the intellectual milieu in which Horace's moral thought developed. It is nevertheless very significant that we are unable ever to establish a certainty of dependence between the *Satires* and any of these works. Horace read these authors, but he did not consider them his masters; he interested himself in the problems that they debated, but he did not have the feeling that he was to continue or renew them. There is nothing in common between these general affinities and the close bond of fidelity that united him with the person and works of Lucilius. There is also nothing in common between that interest in doctrines felt by Horace the moralist, here always careful to make sure of his freedom, and the joyous, militant adherence that the same Horace, Horace the poet, brought to the literary program of his friends, the *neoteroi*.

3 · The Three Books of Odes

HORACE published the second book of *Satires* at the end of 30 B.C. and, doubtless more or less simultaneously, the volume of *Epodes*. This date represents a kind of break in his poetic activity: he would never again write iambics, and seven years would pass before he started again to write pieces in hexameters. This renunciation of the forms of satire and of familiar conversation is all the more strange in that it followed by only a few months the dialogue with Trebatius (*Sat.* II 1), in which the poet had affirmed so amusingly and decidedly that satiric writing was necessary to his happiness, indeed to his health.

Fraenkel has supposed that Horace had ended by recognizing the limitations of satire and had exhausted its resources; one cannot go on indefinitely jeering at misers. But here we fear that it is the learned philologist who is too forcibly limiting the possibilities of the form. Does it not appear, on the contrary, that in the second book, by inventing new forms and realistic, humorous, purely fantastical dialogues, by demonstrating an accumulated mastery of storytelling, and by allowing himself the whole universe of philosophic intercourse, Horace had on the contrary, and for good and all, torn satire away from the dangers of monotony? The charm and interest of the *Epistles* would show later how much that was new he could still bring to the genre.

It has also been supposed that Horace, after painful beginnings devoted to invective, had calmed himself and grown wiser in the course of a happier life. But this is to create a fallacious contrast between these two periods of his career. Certain outbursts in the *Satires* and the *Epodes*, meant only to make us smile, have been taken far too seriously. People have not taken note of the fact that from the first book of *Satires* Horace presents himself to us as a man who is gay (*Sat.* I 4, 104), thoroughly independent (I 6, 94–131), living as happy as a king (I 3, 142), in the midst of friends who like him well (I 4, 135–36). As for the material security that he enjoyed in the ensuing period while he wrote his *Odes*, there is of course no reason to doubt it; but are we to suppose that from one day to the next he ceased knowing envious men and having literary enemies, and meeting imbeciles, and being offended by the manifestations of vice? Naturally not. It is in the period of the *Odes* that he confesses to us that he is unstable and choleric (*Od.* III 9, 22–23), with faults that have accompanied him all his life (*Ep.* I 20, 25: *irasci celerem*). And besides, to stop writing satires is not to start writing odes, and it is this last, positive, point that it is most important for us to understand.

It seems to me to be nearer to the truth to connect Horace's new orientation to the great events that began in the year 31, his contemporaries very quickly recognizing their exceptional dimensions: the final return of civil peace, the unification of the Roman world, the opening of a new age, the promise of universal peace. Vergil and Propertius were surely not the only ones to realize that the battle of Actium had been an event without parallel. Such a feeling may have precipitated the end of a whole labor that had been going on within Horace, perhaps without his knowledge. It is not that the satiric genre necessarily appeared incongruous under the new regime. Octavius in 29 was not an aging Louis XIV, and in Rome who could be seriously worried about the publication of these playful and, all in all, inconsequential pieces? If Maecenas, Octavius, and some others (*Sat.* II 1, 2) pressed their friend to linger no longer on that road, it is because satire, as Horace himself kept saying, cannot be other than a minor genre. And that was not all, for, after all, the epigrams and certain bursts of iambic invective, which seem to have been more favorably received, were too; but these "conversations," burdened with the weight of the Lucilian tradition, bound to an anachronistic technique of versification,

could only appear as a defiance to art: "One could write a
thousand lines like those in a day" (*Sat.* II 1, 3–4). Certainly
it had been amusing to do them. But should Horace not do
better? And now that all things seemed to be taking new directions, now that on all sides there was nothing that was not big,
was it not the moment to think about it?

That is what they meant when they asked him to celebrate
"the work of Caesar," that is, of Octavius. Horace returned
many times to these solicitations, and, always desirous of re-
serving his liberty, he purposely gave them, not without humor,
an exaggerated form: How, poor feeble creature that I am, am I
to sing of war and battles? Certainly there can have been no
question of it; but who of his friends can have had illusions
on this point? Rereading the beginning of *Satire* II 1, one sees
clearly what they expected of him, the poet-moralist: the exaltation of just those virtues of strength and justice by which Octavius had made himself the saviour of the world; the evocation
of the new age, a happy age, freed of war and fear. How could
such a program fail to charm Horace? In the end he responded
well to the expectations of his friends. And they were right to
counsel him as they did, begging him to follow, among all the
bents that could tempt so mobile a mind, precisely that one.

But intention is never enough; even less for an artist than for
other men. It is necessary to find a structure, a form. Horace
certainly knew the literature of verse elegies. He did not even
disdain them as inspiration. But one cannot go on indefinitely
making panegyrics; their form is too rigid. In the career of a man
who lives by poetry, the panegyric can only be an incident.
Something else must be found.

It seems natural *a posteriori* that Horace, in his quest for a
new form, should have decided to put his faith in the lyric. But
that idea could perhaps not occur to those who advised him, and
if he arrived there it was only as the result of one of those progressively maturing acts whereby an original intuition develops
into a creative act. It is true that in the circles in which he lived,
lyric poetry was better received than satire; it lent itself to the
most exquisite refinements, to happy inventions of words and
rhythms. But in the state to which it had come in those days,

in the hands of Catullus' disciples and of the Roman Alexandrians and their Greek models, who could think that it could support with its exquisite grace the great works that they wished to see created?

Here let us set aside our habitual modes of thinking. For a man of the twentieth century, lyric poetry is the supreme, perhaps the only poetry. In the time of Horace such was not the case. Lyric poetry then was the epigram, the short, briskly turned piece, the vehicle of a fleeting impression or a commonplace dressed in an unusual manner. More than any other genre it was tied to bookish statutes, to conventicles of literary men; it did not seem capable of giving a voice to a nation.

Horace's stroke of genius was to believe that in his hands the lyric could become again what it had once been, or rather what it was almost mythically supposed that it had once been, in the Greece of olden days, in the time of Pindar and Alcaeus; a kind of poetry that had not existed in the world for three or four hundred years, and that would be capable of the greatest things —a universal mode of expression (*Od.* I 32; II 13, 21–40). The experience acquired in the preceding years, the reading done for the *Epodes*, then served him in very good stead. Having started originally with the intention of creating poetry of a Hellenistic type, he had now and then gone back as far as the great ancestors—something that probably few of his contemporaries did. Above all, he was able to feel in common with them, not merely to turn to them for certain features or an image that could be easily transposed into poetry of a modern type: he had recognized that in their ancientness they presented an extraordinary newness for the world of modern poetry. Little by little, in the company of the old masters, as the gigantic opposing forces that were to clash at the battle of Actium were growing up in the world around him, he was raising his tone. The work that shows this most characteristically is obviously the sixth *Epode*, a halfunsuccessful poem supported inadequately by its form but holding the highest promise.

One must wonder why a poet who believed himself capable of taking up the burden of universal lyricism chose Alcaeus as his model rather than Archilochus, Pindar, or the founders of the elegy, Solon, Theognis, or Tyrtaius, so close to him in so

many ways. We are speaking here essentially of versification and
rhythm, for he was obviously receptive to inspiration from any
source. At the most it can be said that it was in Alcaeus that
he believed he found the most variety and the greatest suppleness, a merit that would be particularly important to a genius
as mobile as his own. Nonetheless this choice—it is significant
that in a decisive text (*Ep.* I 19, 28) he did not separate Sappho
from Alcaeus—means this above all: he did not believe it possible to adapt the Pindaric form, and he repudiated the distich,
putting his faith in four-line stanzas.

On the Pindaric form, he himself gave us his reasons: "Pindar
is carried along in rhythms freed from law" (*Od.* IV 2, 11–12).
What he means by that is that in Pindar the elements that
correspond to one another are too far apart and too diverse for
their structure and their repetition to be readily perceptible and
give the feeling of rhythm. We know that a stanza of Pindar
often contains about a hundred syllables. Perhaps, by a sufficient
effort, the mind might manage to dominate these long series if
they were formed by a small number of readily grasped combi-
nations of elements, but such is not the case: every time, in each
piece, the poet uses the greatest freedom of structure. To those
accustomed to metrics with firmer demarcations, it is the very
negation of all versification. Thus we are not astonished to learn
that Cicero felt choral lyric poems to be a sort of solemn decla-
mation, sustained by rhythmic dominants but without any true
organization—in a word, very similar to prose (*Orator* 183).
Because it was not sufficiently perceptible, the metric design,
although it was a vigorous one, was unrecognized or misunder-
stood; some commentators of Pindar who were more or less
contemporaries of Horace, and the famous Didymus himself,
proposed textual amendments that the meter unquestionably
does not permit.

Another possibility would have been for Horace to write
distichs. He had tested out their range of expressiveness in his
Epodes. Was he afraid that they would be confused with
elegiacs? Or did he perhaps, as we shall see shortly, have an idea
of the lyric sentence that was incompatible with the form of the
distich? It is significant to observe that in the *Odes* there is
practically no poem written in this manner. The poet almost

always intended that his lines be taken in fours: even when the typography of our editions proposes distichs to us, we are forced to see them as elements of four-line groups constructed as integrally as in a poem written in Sapphic or Alcaic stanzas.

The four-line stanza is thus the master form in Horace, nearly the sole vehicle for all the lyricism of the *Odes*. Ordinarily it does not occur to us to be surprised at this, or even to notice it, so accustomed are we to that rhythmic structure. But it is only since Horace that we have been accustomed to it, or rather it is Horace who accustomed us. The unforeseeable character of that re-creation, indeed creation, of a poetic form stands out clearly in the light of historical facts: between the great poets of Lesbos of the sixth century B.C. and Horace, we know no one who used the Alcaic stanza, and the situation is not very different for the Sapphic stanza, because in that 500-year interval only Catullus appears with two short poems. During that whole period, lyric poetry moved either in distichs or in compositions in which a single type of line was repeated.

This reserve, even disdain, on the part of the poets on meeting a form that seems so happily appropriate for lyricism is undoubtedly to be explained essentially by sociological reasons: the stanza, with its regular repetitions, very closely resembled the forms of popular poetry. Alcaeus and Sappho, for all their genius, had been songwriters. Alcaeus' song is even, essentially, a drinking song, and the poet keeps that character for it even in pieces where his inspiration is patriotic or broadly human. One of the oldest odes of Horace, and one of those doubtless nearest to the Alcaean type, celebrates in the framework of a "symposium" the death and defeat of Cleopatra by beginning with *Nunc est bibendum* (*Od.* I 37). Now, however important convivial drinking was in antiquity—think of the *Symposium* of Plato—from literary as well as philosophical and political points of view, we can still understand well enough that the existence of drinking songs can have marked strophic lyricism in a somewhat unfortunate way and contributed toward fixing its place at the outer limits of good writing. Catullus' practice is rather significant of that attitude. If we except his two Sapphic poems, he had recourse to the regular stanza only once: in the epithalamium for Manlius and Junia (61), a poem that he wished to make as close as possible to real wedding songs, with jokes and double meanings. When the time came to write a serious epithalamium, he composed it in hexameters (62), and it is of little importance that a one-line refrain reappears in it from time to time; the units between which it is inserted have now four lines, now five, seven, eight, nine, or ten. One would say that the poet had intentionally avoided the creation of true stanzas. In Alexandrian literature, what resembles stanzas the most is the bucolic couplet, in Theocritus and his imitators and Vergil; but there again is a genre that consciously recalls the forms of popular poetry.

We can see that in adopting the four-line stanza to give a form to all the varieties of lyricism, Horace was undertaking to play a difficult game against the habits and traditions by which his contemporaries lived. Can we say that he won? Yes, so far as his personal success was concerned. If he wished to found a tradition, no. There were swarms of imitators of Vergil, but people hesitated long to take up the heritage of Horace. On this subject nothing is more instructive than the oratorical precautions to which Statius felt obliged to have recourse before slipping one poem in Sapphic stanzas and another in Alcaic stanzas (IV 5 and 7) into his *Silvae*, although the two were merely amiable imitations and did not pretend to any other merit. Pliny, when the muse inspired him, wrote after Catullus, in Phalaecians. Seneca inserts a few odes into his tragedies; but even then how noticeable it is that the fundamental line of the Sapphic stanza, the hendecasyllable, is used by preference outside of the stanza framework, in continuous series! Horace would have his real continuators only much later, in Christian hymnology: Ambrose and Prudentius were the ones who finally sealed the alliance of lyricism and the stanza. Like Horace, they were able to give it credit and to believe it capable of supporting the most sublime inspirations.

By observing *a posteriori* what Horace was able to draw out of the stanza form, and by resituating his success in the literary environment in which he lived, we can perhaps glimpse the problem of expression that he hoped to solve by having recourse to that forgotten instrument. From the beginning, the problem of poetic language had, with good reason, obsessed the Latins.

The Greeks did not have to worry about it, because with them, since Homer, poetry had always used a special vocabulary and special dialects, so that it was impossible to misconstrue its intent. But in Rome, where the poets did not have comparable resources at their disposal, they finally had to convince themselves that poetry, in order to mark its special difference and its special distance from prose, must above all conceive of other ways to group words and build sentences. We know of the Catullian discovery in the area of word groups: the splitting up of words belonging together syntactically became a principle, from which the line gained a nervousness and dynamism that no one until then, in either Greece or Rome, had thought possible. By that single invention Ennius and Lucretius, with all their genius, were relegated to the prehistory of Roman poetry.

But after Catullus the problem of the Roman sentence was still entire. Catullus was not a man to interest himself in it: a genius of lightning flashes, of cat strokes, of stiletto stabs, he needed only the simplest sentences. Around the 30's, those who were thinking of taking up the tradition of great poetry again, with more extended works and with the possibility of introducing a rather complex intellectual apparatus into them, had behind them nothing but the example of Lucretius: a great sentence capable of infinite amplitude, but too visibly based upon the great oratorical sentence of the same period that Cicero, in his area, was working to establish. It was precisely this recourse to the techniques of prose that poets now repudiated. But then how were they to manage? How, without having recourse to rhetoric, could they sustain the continuity and organization of a development?

Together with the Vergilian formula, which as we know consists of the establishment of a very subtle counterpoint between sentence and line, the Horatian stanza constitutes, I believe, a solution to that vital problem. What characterizes the Eolian stanza is, in fact, the very strict structure of its metric scheme. This is a grave danger in inexpert hands, and it is precisely here that popular poetry fails: the rhythm tends to devour everything. But let us imagine that tyrannical form in the hands of a really powerful poet who has something to say: it will be able to support a rhetorical density under which a poem treated

in a looser metrical structure would have given up its soul—
that is, would have turned toward prose. The syntax can become organic and complex, hence near to that of prose, without
causing the impression of the whole to become prosaic: to avert
this fall from grace a mere nothing will suffice, a few overflow
lines from one stanza to the next, the distribution of syntactical
anaphoras in different places in consecutive stanzas. The stanza,
for its part, by its structure alone lends itself naturally to characteristic effects that are sometimes very powerful, which it will
be the good poet's chief difficulty to keep under control. But
if he wishes at certain moments to yoke together—instead of
playing against each other—the effects of syntactical rhythm and
of strophic rhythm, he will be able, with the simplest words,
to produce effects of overwhelming violence; and yet, always,
the verse goes on its way, carried along by the repetitions of the
rhythm and those of long sentences which are no longer
prosaic. It is that struggle between two rude and despotic adversaries, the stanza on the one hand and the great complex
sentence on the other, that creates the tumultuous roughness
of the great poems of Horace. The reader feels and sees coming
or retreating the moment when the two currents will become
one. Then it is truly the lyric eagle, the thunderbird who plunges
down among us.

Horace does not always Pindarize; among the *Odes* there are
many short pieces, light, "fugitive" poems in which this struggle
does not have to take place, and where it seems that we are
nearer to song. The power of cohesion that inheres in the
strophic form was then often used to organize, like pearls on a
sinuous mounting, sequences of words that in the absence of a
metric bond would only form a chaotic and barbarous mass—a
sowing of words, as it has been called. The more rigorous the
form of a poem, the more the poem lends itself to supporting
rare verbal audacities. Horace, therefore, pushed the regularity
of his stanzas to the extreme. Elisions are reduced to a minimum, the caesura is fixed at a determined place, and in lines
that his models allowed themselves to start freely with an iamb
or a spondee or a troche, he no longer allows anything for the
first foot but a spondee. Is the result impoverished? academic?
Obviously not. If one passes beyond the narrow perspective of

the metrician, it quickly becomes clear that this framework is used to sustain the lightest verbal fancies and to bring into harmony and grace the most ingenious outrageousness.

Our poet paid close attention to the particular qualities of the various stanzas he used: The first poems of Book I illustrate them all one by one (*Od.* I 2–9). This is perhaps a naïve idea and one that would tempt us to smile if we were not able to see in it the pride of the good workman, that of the creator who wants us to know all his marvels immediately, to make us put our confidence in him. But the two stanzas that return most often in Horace are the Alcaic stanza (37 poems) and the Sapphic stanza (26 poems). The two forms, certainly much older than Alcaeus and Sappho, each of whom used both, received their names from Alexandrian erudition, and perhaps in a rather arbitrary way. In any case, a label, even when it is fortuitous, is never without its consequences: the reference to Alcaeus or Sappho, man or woman, strength or grace, violence or gentleness, was to contribute toward a differentiation between the two stanzas. Horace was visibly interested in the problem of using them appropriately; he links the Sapphic stanza to the religious hymn (I 2, 10, 12, 30; III 14, 18, 22) and the mythological tale (III 11, 27); the Alcaic stanza calls up struggles and triumphs, whether the poet is celebrating the final defeat of the Orientals (I 37) or the laborious restoration of Rome by Augustus (III 1–6). This contrasting use of the two stanzas can be felt particularly in certain pairs that the poet himself invites us to constitute: the *Carmen saeculare* dedicates to the gods its nineteen Sapphic stanzas grouped 9 + 9 + 1; in *Ode* IV–4, of the same length and the same composition, Drusus' triumphs in war are celebrated in Alcaic stanzas. The ten first *Odes* of the second book are alternately Sapphic and Alcaic, but in such a way that five times two successive poems in different rhythms treat an analogous theme: it is often very apparent that the Alcaic ode is more lively, more alert, more pathetic, while in the Sapphic ode the inspiration is more serene and the sentiments are more temperate or more controlled.

What seems to me to be the meter of these odes, or rather the way in which Horace understood it, does not assort ill with these observations. The Alcaic stanza is all diversity and contrast:

The facts are particularly clear in the last two lines: the third has an ascending rhythm, that is, the weak stresses precede the strong ones, and the line usually ends on a prolonged long syllable; the fourth has a descending rhythm, particularly rapid in its first part. The laborious slowness of the third, with its seven long syllables, also makes the rapidity of the fourth stand out. Within each of the first two lines, the same rhythmic and quantitative contrast is found on either side of a dieresis powerfully braced both before and after by two strong stresses. It is equally important that the four lines have nearly the same number of syllables; because of this it is not very difficult to link two consecutive stanzas syntactically.

The Sapphic stanza is both more continuous and more closed in upon itself:

The shortness of the fourth line gives this stanza's ending a very striking relief. Each stanza tends to constitute a whole. This form is particularly appropriate for making the reader feel the successive moments and the respiration, so to speak, of lyricism. Each unit suggests a flight, an elevation that concludes each time on a meditative accent. As for the first three lines, they undoubtedly contain, like the first two of the Alcaic stanza, a rhythmic reversal: here the rhythm descends first, then ascends, but this reversal, instead of taking place on either side of a strongly marked frontier, is brought about by a transition element: there is no collision between strong stresses of opposing rhythms, and correlatively the metric articulation, here a caesura, is much less noticeable and has a certain mobility. What is a violent contrast in the Alcaic stanza has become here nothing more than an undulation.

Between the Alcaic and Sapphic stanzas, those dominated by the Asclepiadean

$$- \; - \; - \; \cup \; \cup \; - \; // \; - \; \cup \; \cup \; - \; \cup \; -$$

(Sixteen poems) occupy an intermediary position. This line reminds one very much of the Alcaic hendecasyllable, with its strong dieresis flanked by two marked stresses. Yet the effect of contrast is less marked here; for if the second hemistich (identical to that of the Alcaic) is of a distinctly descending rhythm, the first hemistich does not, from this point of view, have a very definite design. In fact, the Asclepiadean is often used in poems of a smoother, less sublime inspiration. Compared to the Sapphic line, it is more lively: it springs up, it rebounds, it does not undulate.

The stanza form is among all poetic forms the one that lends itself best to the collaboration of music. And furthermore, allusions to music are innumerable in the *Odes*. Should we take this merely as a manner of speaking? And what of the perpetual repetitions of phrases, devoid of sense since the ancient bards and rhapsodies had disappeared? "Poet, take your lute." I wonder if it is not at least as serious an anachronism to look upon Horace as a sort of Valéry or Mallarmé. Even during the Renaissance, light poetry still had a part that was linked to music. In Rome in Horace's time, musical entertainments had a place in the life of society. Why should our poet not have liked music? Why, reciting his poems during banquets with friends—we must never forget that the relations of friendship were the setting of all Horace's life—should he not have supported his voice with a musical accompaniment? As for pieces of a more serious inspiration, the example of the *Carmen saeculare* assures us that their musical accompaniment did not risk shocking either the habits or the aesthetic tastes of the ancients. Besides, there are so many ways of musically accompanying a recitation!

A systematic skepticism, therefore, seems to me to be unjustified in the face of the texts in which we see Horace defining in the most explicit fashion what seems to him to be the essential part of his art: to compose a text that will support music, *verba loquor socianda chordis* (IV 9, 4 cf. II 12, 1–4). Besides, there is no reason to doubt that Horace, as he claimed, directed the rehearsals of his choristers (IV 6, 35–36) before the performance of the *Carmen saeculare*. Certainly more than one

reader in antiquity must have read Horace as we read him ourselves: but is it not also possible to read in one's chair the
comedies of Molière and find much pleasure in them? Who
would wish to conclude from this that performance adds nothing to them, and that apparently Molière must have taken no
interest in that question? So music for Horace. We learn from
the correspondence of Pliny the Younger (*Ep.* IV 19, 4; VII 4,
9) how a simple amateur could improvise a cythera accompaniment or a sung melody on a lyrical text. It was, apparently, the
normal practice when one wanted to give a poem all its luster.
There is no reason whatever to confine the *Odes* of Horace to
speech and literature.

THE COMPOSITION OF THE BOOKS

As is often the case in lyrical collections, reading the eighty-
eight *Odes* of Books I–III leaves us an impression of glitter, but
also of disorder, and the mind has trouble taking hold of them.
Perhaps it is not a very good method to begin by grouping the
pieces according to their genres or their subjects: the undertaking, besides being difficult, would have the effect of erasing
and undoing precisely that order (if there is one) or that disorder (if there is disorder, in which case it can only be inten-
tional) that comes from the poet. It is better to take up one's
reading again and go forward into discovery.

One sees at once that at a certain time the three books were
conceived by Horace as being elements of a whole. *Ode* III 30
(*Exegi monumentum*) takes up the Asclepiadean line of *Ode* I
1 (*Maecenas atavis*). In the three books, these are the only pieces
in this meter; the conclusion corresponds to the preface. We
see too that each of the three books begins by a poem or a group
of poems of a particular solemnity: in Book III, it is the group
of six *Roman Odes* (to which we shall have occasion to return);
in Book II, it is a dedicatory poem that celebrates Pollio; in
Book I, after the general introduction to the collection, it is an
ode to Augustus.

Apart from the preface *Maecenas atavis* and the charming
vignette (I 38) of the end, Book I is enclosed within two poems
directly celebrating Augustus and placing the reader back in
the atmosphere of the battle of Actium. One poem has to do

with the death of Cleopatra (I 37), the other (I 2), inseparable from the prayer that concludes the first book of the *Georgics*, evokes the expectancy of the return of the emperor in the spring of 29. While the second book of the *Odes* contains twenty poems and the third, thirty, the first brings together thirty-eight, an unusual and irregular number. Perhaps this anomaly should be ascribed to the extra weight, at the beginning of the book, of that group of eight odes (2 to 9) where Horace successively presents to the reader nearly all the stanza forms that he will use later. In fact, after this group, *Ode* 10, a hymn to Mercury, patron of the arts, rather recalls the religious invocations that often open the poems or the collections of poems of the ancients. It has been wondered whether that metric parade was not, in part, an answer to practical necessity. Let us not forget to what an extent Horace was an innovator in versification. Somewhat as a technician at the beginning of his work defines the conventions that he will use, so our poet may have felt the need to present once and for all to his reader (and perhaps with a minimum of metric or musical annotations) the rhythmic instruments to which he would then have recourse.

Although certain indications can be glimpsed here and there, one cannot be certain of having rediscovered an order in the body of this book. On the other hand, there is no doubt that starting with *Ode* 31 Horace intended to create an ensemble of serious pieces that correspond to the solemnity of the beginning.

One ventures into the second book with an entirely different confidence. The book is divided into two parts, each of which is introduced by an ode dedicated to a great personage: Pollio (II 1) and Maecenas (II 12), whom the poet invites to write, or thanks for writing, a history of the present times; the two parts (1–11 and 12–20) contain practically the same number of lines (288 and 284). The architecture of the first part is very visible: The even pieces are in Sapphic stanzas, the uneven in Alcaic. Each subject is treated in two successive odes, and the couples thus formed correspond to each other in accordance with a plan that may be plotted as follows:

2–3   Moral counsel: liberality; taking advantage of the passing moment.

4-5   Love: servant girls and young girls.
6-7   Friendship: dying in the arms of a friend; the return
      of a comrade.
8-9   Love: infidelity and fidelity.
10-11 Moral counsel: the *aurea mediocritas*.

To draw a plan of the second part of the book, we do not
have such objective verifications as metrical analysis has given
us for the first. Still, it seems to me that the pieces would be
disposed in a probable manner, and would take on both relief
and weight, if they were read thus:

13-14 Death of the poet.
15   Against the luxury of gardens.
16   *Otium.*
17   Friendship.
18   Against avidity and luxury.
19-20 The poet feels himself to be immortal.

Each time friendship is in the center. But the first part of the
book has a more sententious character, while the second has a
more personal accent or a more incisive tone. We are, therefore,
not surprised to find that the Alcaic-Sapphic balance of the
first part is later countered by a distinct predominance of the
Alcaic stanza (six odes). Only *Ode* 16, in praise of leisure, the
true happiness of the wise man, is composed in Sapphic stanzas.

These embracing arrangements, these carefully studied nu-
merical balances correspond, as we know, to the taste of the
times. Analogies have been found in Tibullus and Vergil.
Whatever the current traditions as to the beauty of lyric disorder
may have been, it would have been surprising if Horace, so
meticulous and rigorous in all that concerned the exactitude of
art, had not, he too, sought to erect in at least one of his books—
and he chose the central book—one of those monuments of
interrelationships in which poetry seems to become architecture.

It has been long recognized that the first six odes of Book III
form a unit: six poems on connected subjects, all six composed
in Alcaic stanzas. The whole book seems to have been constructed in relation to this magnificent group; is it by chance
that the 336 lines of *Odes* 1-6 are followed by the 336 lines of
Odes 7-19 and the 336 lines of *Odes* 20-30? Horace was much
concerned that this monumental portal should not throw his

book out of balance, and that is what explains its exceptional length, with 1008 lines, whereas Book I has only 876 and Book II, 572. After the grandeur of the beginning, he continues the book with a number of light, erotic, and bacchic pieces. The Alcaic stanza does not reappear until *Ode* 17 and after. No doubt it is not by chance that at the end of the book we find three odes (24, 27, 29) of exceptional length. F. Altheim has, it appears to me, accurately seen in *Odes* 26, 27, 28 a sort of feminine cycle (three ages of the woman) intended to be understood as a unit; an epilogue that, to a certain extent, corresponds to the ample compositions of the beginning of the book.

The organization of the six *Roman Odes* is a very carefully studied one. Mr. Paul Maury, to whom we owe such admirable discoveries on the "architecture of the Bucolics," has made very happy contributions toward bringing it to light, and I shall take my inspiration here from his notes on the subject. If one examines only the content of the poems, it is already apparent that *Ode* 4 is the peak of the whole, with the solemnity of the invocation of the muse: "Come down from heaven, O Calliope . . .", and the indication from the very first stanza of the amplitude of this song *longum melos*; with its eighty lines, it is in fact the longest of all the *Odes* of Horace. The composition is absolutely majestic: between the poet beloved of the Muses (ll. 1–36) and the all-powerful gods (ll. 45–80), "Caesar," that is, Augustus, appears for an instant in the heart of the ode (ll. 37–44), conversing familiarly with the goddesses and receiving their counsel of goodness. We then become aware that this exceptional poem is buttressed, as if by two equal masses, by the two that precede it and the two that follow (104 lines in each case). But while *Ode* 1, as prologue, is external to this grouping, we will find again in *Odes* 2–6 those embracing correspondences of the type familiar to us: *Odes* 2 and 6 are exhortations of a moral character; 3 and 5 correspond also, illuminating the present times by the perspectives of history, in *Ode* 3 the ruins of Troy, in *Ode* 5 the Punic Wars. In each the ode is animated by a veritable speech, by Juno in 3, by Regulus in 5. The sovereign is regularly designated there by the name of Augustus, which on the other hand does not appear in the other poems of the same cycle. To adopt the always happy

phrases of Mr. Maury, there are ethical odes (2 and 6), mythical
odes (3 and 5), and a mystical ode (4).

Thus one cannot say that there is no order in the collection
of *Odes*, or that there is merely a simple desire for variety, which
would amount to the same thing. Comparing book to book,
we see, too, that Book II, the composition of which is
more rigorous, contrasts with both Book I and Book III, which
are more uncertain in that respect. But there is also more
diversity of meter and inspiration in Books I and III; Book II,
more austere, more occupied with moral thoughts, is without
doubt the heart of the work. Without being ignorant of the
fact that each piece would usually be savored apart from the
rest and in itself, the poet did not give up the idea of setting
before us a work, a monument—*monumentum aere perennius*—
whose parts would set each other off, and which a careful reader
could receive into his memory as a coherent and balanced whole.

The group of three books must have been published in 23
(after the spring of 24, when Augustus returned to Rome after
the Spanish War, *Ode* III 14; before the death of Marcellus
in the winter of 23–22, a cruel cancellation by destiny of the
hopes of *Ode* I 12, 46). It is obviously much more difficult to
recognize and date the ode that may perhaps be the oldest, *Ode*
II 18; it recalls the tone of the *Satires*; it is a veritable "diatribe"
addressed to a fictitious interlocutor; the iambotrochaic meter,
which does not reappear in any other ode, recalls the rhythm
of the *Epodes*; the lines are difficult to group into stanzas. All
these are indications of a relatively early date. It is generally
allowed, and with much probability, that the composition of
the greater number of the *Odes* cannot have been anterior to
the publication of the *Epodes* and the *Satires* in 30. But in that
eight-year interval chronological signposts are rather rare, except
for the poems more directly linked to political current events.
It is clear that I 37 is inseparable from the death of Cleopatra in
the autumn of 30; that I 2 dates from the spring of 29, I 12 from
summer of the same year; I 31 celebrates the dedication of the
temple of Palatine Apollo on October 9, 28; the *Roman Odes*
date from 29–27. We can suppose that the *Ode* to the ship of
the Republic (I 14) was composed in 30: hope is beginning to
rise out of anguish, and the poet, in lines 17–18, seems to wish

to recall to us the sentiments that he had expressed in *Epodes* 7 and 16. To these fairly certain dates we can add those resulting from a reference to personal events: on March 1, 29, Horace was nearly crushed by a falling tree; this allows us to place II 13 and III 8. Similarly, he was forty years old when he wrote II 4; it is therefore 25–24.

Certain characteristics of inspiration, technique, or meter can have value as chronological indications. It is tempting to consider those *Odes* that most nearly recall the *Epodes* as being older: for example, I 7, in which Teucer's speech is introduced as Chiron's was in *Epode* 13; and I 28, whose *ex abrupto* beginning, like that of *Epode* 5, is intelligible only in retrospect, when we understand that it is not the poet but an imaginary personage who is speaking. When apparent indications converge, we can be more affirmative; in I 15 Nereus' speech somewhat recalls those of Teucer and of Chiron; the story of Paris and Helen could well be a transposition of that of Antony and Cleopatra; the allegory here might recall that of the *Ode* to the ship of the Republic (I 14); a metric irregularity in line 36, a technique of word order that recalls that of *Ode* I 37, a sea setting (as in *Epodes* 13 and 16, and in *Odes* I 7, 14, 28), which is particularly appropriate to the events of the years 31–29; one sees that there are reasons to date this *Ode* among the first ones. But are we not in danger of going too far if we date III 11 and III 27 in the same period, because there too we find mythology, speeches, very complicated composition, and, in III 27, a sea setting?

We must not attach too much importance to metric irregularities. In I 23 there are highly abnormal interlinear hiatuses at lines 3 and 7. But are they not intended to make us feel the distress of Chloe? Similarly, I 26 teems with metrical accidents; but the piece was conceived with the intent of appearing impromptu. It would therefore be dangerous to deduce indications of chronology from these observations.

The very conditions under which chronological investigations are made expose us to illusions of perspective. The greater number of the pieces that we can manage to date belong to the years 30–27; one would be tempted to believe that afterwards Horace did not work at the same rhythm. But that is partly because we easily date pieces that have connections with political current events, and that those current events, naturally enough, stirred the poet's imagination more in 30–27 than in 26–23. Let us content ourselves with saying that from 27 on, and after the consolidation of the Augustan regime, national events ceased to feed the flame of Horace's lyricism. This is perhaps of great consequence if we are to believe, as I have proposed, that at the very origins of this lyricism the shock of great historical events, the awareness of living through a drama of vital importance, had played an important role. The *Roman Odes* are perhaps a culmination, marking the end of a period after which Horace ceased to Pindarize and allowed himself to follow the natural path that led from Eolian song toward a short poem that would be light, intimate, or gnomic.

Two more points are important to make clear. It does seem that most of the longest odes (those of more than 40 lines) belong to the first period: political odes I 2, 12; III 1, 3, 4, 5, 6, 24; mythological odes, III 11, 27. The dates of III 16, 29 cannot be determined. Besides, Book II, in which we find the shortest poems (none has more than forty lines), where political inspiration has a minimal place, is also the one in which there is the least metric invention. Should we not put all this together? Thus we would see that after beginnings in which daring and lyric expansion knew no limits, Horace, beginning with the period of the *Odes*, started to turn toward the type of inspiration, indeed toward the wiser writing, of the *Epistles*. Later the *Carmen saeculare* and the epinicia of Book IV of the *Odes* would show clearly what could still be expected of the Pindar whom he carried within him. But our poet probably never wished to exhaust a form of art. We have already noted an analogy in his career, in the case of the *Satires*: a great deploying of efforts, struggles, and imagination to invent and impose a new form and a few masterpieces, after which the poet abandoned the career to which he had only seemed to commit himself—free to return to it later.

THEMES OF INSPIRATION

Faced by the lyricism of Horace, each age has made a choice and defined its preferences. The Middle Ages saw him as a moralist: *Ethicus*. The Renaissance thought most highly of his light pieces. Later Horace was appreciated as the master of a life that was thought to be easy and undemanding, and which we now judge to have been a little selfish. Finally, there are the civic *Odes* to which our own time has applied itself by preference, because we are serious people, haunted by a concern for the public good. It is not easy to like everything at once, or even to understand everything. Perhaps no author demands a greater subtlety, a greater opening of mind and heart, of his students.

In the light of what I believe to be the composition of the *Odes*, it is probably suitable to study the national *Odes* first, and then the others as a group, since, diverse as they are, they are connected, as we shall see, by the same manner of understanding life.

Obviously the study of the political poems cannot be conceived of except from within a chronological framework; it was a succession of public events that brought the disgracefulness of the civil wars before the poet's eyes, making him ponder both on ways to achieve the moral restoration of the city and on the role and person of the prince. In *Ode* I 14, he recalls a period in the past (ll. 17–18) during which public affairs had caused him nothing but disgust. No doubt it was the sort of despair that is so pathetically expressed in *Epodes* 7 and 16. But beyond that, and to give the word its bitterest connotation, we must probably go back to *Epode* 4. The war between the triumviri and Sextus Pompey is still going on. Horace is not tender toward Pompey. When he accuses him of placing slaves and pirates under arms, he has a definite appearance of adopting the rancors of the Roman populace against the organizer of a sea blockade. But the adversaries of Pompey are no better (that is why the date of 38 seems more likely than that of 37–36), because they allow a former slave to usurp the insignia of knighthood in the streets of Rome. On the scandal of the civil wars, not a word. Our poet will never again be moved to write on this rather paltry subject.

Epode 7 has quite another tone. Horace now wishes to see the two adversaries, who are about to come face to face, only as Romans and fellow-citizens. It had been thought that peace had been restored, and suddenly it was war again: like Ferrero, I lean toward dating this little poem at the beginning of 32, when Octavius' coup d'état aroused a real panic in Rome. "Is it a blind fury, an irresistible force that drags you along? Is it a sin? Answer! They are silent, a deadly pallor blanches their faces, their stricken minds are in a stupor." A stupor before the abyss, and the lure of the abyss. It is easy to believe that here Horace, always pliable and sensitive to external influences, gave voice to sentiments that must have been very widespread. Yet, as a close friend of Maecenas and thus linked to the fortunes of Octavius, he has perhaps more merit than another in not making a distinction between the two adversaries, ignoring possibly legitimate grievances, and seeing Octavius and Antony only as brothers who are, inexcusably, enemies.

Epode 16 is apparently contemporaneous. It has often been assigned a very early date because it seemed to be one of the sources of the fourth *Bucolic* (composed in 40). After the work of Snell, and especially that of Becker, I am now convinced that the influence was in the other direction. Besides, the *Epode* bears the marks of the entire collection of *Bucolics* (published in 37). If it particularly recalls the fourth *Bucolic*, it is because despair has risen up against hope and because war, now imminent, is destroying the agreement of Brundisium: Octavia, sister of Octavius, who had in accordance with that agreement become Antony's wife, has now been repudiated by him. It should be added as well that in more than one way this *Epode* announces the *Odes*—by its extent, its setting, its insertion of a speech, and a structure in which two distinct themes are juxtaposed, as in some of the earliest *Odes*. The proposals of Horace, who is already speaking as a *vates* (l. 66), as he will do in the *Odes*, are extremely strange: to abandon Rome, an accursed city condemned by the gods, and to allow anyone to establish himself there who wishes to do so. The whole city, or at least its elite (l. 37), will leave without thought of return and will go to install themselves in the Isles of the Blest. It is certain that Horace never envisaged the eventuality of a real emigration. Is this a cry of despair, a call for an impossible escape? The tone of the poem does not recommend this interpretation. Besides, it would be difficult to understand Horace's claim that he was chiefly addressing the valiant. But here, too, a comparison with the *Odes* (where mythical themes are used in allegories) can put us on the right track: these *arva beata* are very probably identical with the *beatos portus* that a contemporary poet (*Catalepton* 5, 8) sees opening up before him if he devotes himself solely to the study of wisdom and "regains his life, which has been devoured by cares." These apparently far-off lands, situated at the end of the world, are in reality the kingdom within, not the kingdom of dreams but instead that of a virile courage—"leave groaning to women"—and the only recourse for the individual in time of collective disaster. We will often note again this propensity in Horace to withdraw into himself. But here there is nothing else to do (l. 23); when all efforts have been vain, and when all outside us has, in one mass, slipped into the abyss, ah! let us remember at least that we still have our soul. Again in these two *Epodes* we see a strange idea obsessively returning: a curse hanging over Rome. Vergil, it is true, also saw the civil wars as the punishment or the consequences of very old offenses (*Buc.* 4, 13, 31; *Georg.* I 501). It is more surprising to see Horace, who is so unmystical, sharing such views. Perhaps nothing can give us a more accurate idea of the horror and anxiety of those last months of waiting, when no one in Rome can have doubted that it was on the point of undergoing another Pharsalus or another Philippi.

As a matter of fact, we know that the war of Actium—one of the masterpieces of Octavius' genius—was as nearly as possible a war without battles, and at the same time a war with decisive effects. *Epode* 9, written in Rome at the announcement of the first news of the battle, is unique in the whole body of Horace's work: a true "war poem," in the somewhat pejorative sense that the expression has taken on today—a liberation of elemental sentiments, denigrating the vanquished and exalting all those who had been on the right side, even the most dubious auxiliaries, like the Galatians whose opportune treason paved the way for Antony's defeat. Horace's excuse is that the frightful cloud that had been darkening the whole horizon for two years had collapsed before his eyes without a storm. The true Horace would reappear in *Ode* I 37, written a year later, after the death of Cleopatra; there all is, to be sure, triumph and joy; but the poet does not forget that a dangerous enemy has had the strength to die nobly.

During the following years, reflections on the civil wars had a considerable place in his thought. It would hardly be forcing the meaning of the *Roman Odes* (*Od.* III 1-6) to give them the collective title, "What must be done so that there may never again be civil wars?" Our poet recognized, he believed, that these historical disorders had their origin in the soul, particularly in greed and in the inability to enjoy a simple life. In this greed, in this desire for novelty, he did not see an admirable dynamism that merely needed to be better oriented; he saw the fruits of mental inconsistency and instability. It seemed to him that the health of the State could repose only on an upbringing that would stiffen men's souls. It is rather strange to us that so much place was given in this educational program to apprenticeship in military virtues, indeed in the practice of war. In Horace's eyes, frontier combat was one of the conditions contributing to those values of virile simplicity on which the peace of the Romans would be founded. The true subject of *Odes* III 2 and 6 is the educational value of war. Here Horace uncritically shared a traditional and narrowly national ideology. The Romans' excuse is that at that time they did not have around their empire other nations comparable to their own, organized, civilized, worthy of life and able to inspire them with respect. It is difficult not to be somewhat selfish when one is all alone in the world. Yet, in Rome itself, we know that some persons were already beginning to question the right of the conquerors. For our poet, the problem was completely eclipsed by the educational value that he lent to camp life.

This, I believe, explains the enthusiasm with which he celebrates the expeditions, in reality very modest, thanks to which the Empire then maintained peace during its long marches. When he speaks of humiliating the Parthians, or of cleaving the Arabs asunder, or of conquering Britain, certain critics have imagined that he was prostituting his art to the imperialistic and colonial demands of the rulers. Surely not, since, as everyone knows, Augustus always carefully avoided involving himself in war anywhere, and above all in the Orient. Others have thought that it was business factions that, faced by the cunning inertia of the emperor, were applying pressure on Horace, as the mouth-piece of the war party; but at that date did any war party exist in Rome? And how can we imagine a favorite companion of Maecenas opposing the Emperor's policies? In a very subtle study, A. Oltramare has conjectured that Augustus, at the same time that he did not wish to make war, did wish to be believed to be disposed toward it, so as to intimidate the Parthians and to prepare a climate of opinion in Rome that would sustain him if war should, in spite of him, become inevitable; and that Horace, more or less of an accomplice, had entered into this subtle game. Perhaps; although in my opinion one is always wrong in postulating Machiavellism in anybody. It would seem much more believable to me, as it does to J. Gagé, that Horace, together with a whole body of prevailing opinion, allowed him-self to be influenced by an insistent prophecy: that the estab-lishment of a definitive peace depended upon subjugating the last still independent nations or peoples within the inhabited world. Augustus would have known better than to let himself be deceived by the mirage that had successively finished Crassus, then Caesar, then Antony. With less responsibility, a poet could be less prudent. This explains *Ode III 5*, which recommends a policy of purely military revenge to liberate the standards and captive prisoners still in the power of the Parthians; while it was by diplomacy that Augustus was no doubt already planning to accomplish his goals, and seven years later would indeed ac-complish them.

From 29 on, the person of Octavius Augustus has an impor-tant place in Horace's national poems. Our poet had become convinced—and it does credit to his good sense—that the Roman State and civil peace depended entirely upon the person of the prince; he thought too that that success, continued year after year, required, but also demonstrated, a nearly superhuman genius. To speak in praise of the prince was to expose oneself to the accusation of servility; but not to speak of him when the subject required it, or to speak only with indifference, was this not to confess that one had a base, timid, ungrateful soul? Better to appear to be a courtier. It is notable that in Horace's poetry the emperor is exalted only as the representative of an ideal of morality that becomes, through the poet's praise, a kind of obligation: Augustus will be lodged in the empyrean between Hercules and Pollux (*Od.* III 3, 11), but only because he is, like them, "the just and firm man who is frightened neither by the threats of a tyrant, nor by the ferment of a delirious crowd, nor by the caprices of the Ocean" (*ibid.*); because he listens to the counsel of moderation that the Muses give him (*Od.* III 4, 41–42); and because he is the embodiment of prudence and tempered strength (*ibid.* 65–66).

The significance, the very content of texts of this sort, is obviously very complex. They teach us, certainly, how and for what merits Augustus liked to be praised. Yet we should not give the poet's share too little importance, for he certainly had his own opinions on justice, liberty, and strength. And certainly too if there had been too wide a gap between that political ideal and Augustus' idea of his role, the poet, unless he had gone over to the opposing camp, would have said nothing at all. But he did speak, and rather than seeing what he wrote as a mere reflection of an official ideology, we should at least ask ourselves whether he himself, by his personal effort of moral thought, did not contribute toward the creation and orientation of that very ideology.

An analogous problem is posed by the work of Vergil. It is striking to see our two poets announcing in advance some of the great things that Augustus brought to pass: the restoration of the temples, moral reform, the opening of a new age. It has often been suggested that the prince let them know his plans so that they could prepare public opinion for them. Is it not more probable that on several occasions Augustus allowed himself to be guided by his poets? It is the role of high consciences and of men of imagination to open up the exalted perspectives into which men of action can fling themselves. When he gave himself the title of *vates*—the word had not yet been worn down to the point of becoming the equivalent of *poeta*—Horace was without any doubt thinking of such a mission. In the midst of modern Rome, he aspired to the role of those bards and prophets who in ancient times assisted the chief, being capable of indicating to him by their very praises—for praises create bonds and obligations—the way to his highest duties.

We are not surprised to find that in this poetry the person of

Augustus seems to belong more to the empyrean than to earth. Nothing could be more natural in a civilization where no one thought of placing the impassable barrier between the great man and the hero or god which the Judeo-Christian tradition acknowledges between the creature and the Creator. For the philosopher there is, within the most rigid definition of terms, no difference of nature between the gods—that is, the supreme God—and man: Seneca treated this subject to the satiation point. The differences are only of degree, and are finally more accidental than real. *Ode* I 12 naïvely expresses that insurmountable problem: "man, hero or god" (l. 1); but the categories are even more mingled than we are likely to imagine, since the structure of the ode, divided into triads of stanzas, makes it appear that in Horace's eyes Romulus, Numa, and Cato of Utica were heroes, like Hercules, while Regulus and Camillus were men. What will the prince be? Everything together: man, hero, and god; the poet cannot distinguish any more than the sage. There is perhaps a little more in *Ode* I 2, where Octavius is presented as an epiphany of Mercury; Horace would not go so far again. It is possible, as D. Norberg has proposed, that one should recognize in this poem, written at the beginning of 29 before the return of Octavius, something of the incertitude and disarray of those still anxious years. In what guise would the new master of the world return to Rome? Having vanquished Egypt, would he not wish to retain something of the ideology of the Pharaohs in which Antony had cloaked himself? The beginning and the end of the first book of *Georgics* hang upon a question of the same kind: *quis deus esse velis*, "what god will you wish to be?" But while Vergil invoked the protection of the national gods, Vesta and Romulus, upon the prince, Horace ends his ode on the words *princeps, pater, dux*, words of the Roman tradition to which Octavius, of course, had the sense to hold fast.

It has seemed to many readers that a disharmony exists between the wisdom commended by the *Roman Odes* and that which is exuded by the ensemble of the other pieces in the collection: on the one hand, a summons to heroism and to the virile virtues; on the other, tolerance toward facile and selfish pleasures. This contradiction may come from a misunder-

standing of the poet in both places. In our civilization, heroism
is required as the inner climate in which one must live to know
his duty, and his duty consists essentially in devoting himself
to working for an objective goal: the greatness of a nation, the
liberation of an oppressed people, a fight against want. It is
obvious that a man dedicated to tasks of that sort can never
know any relaxation, or will know it only as a kind of contra-
band, his mind tormented by remorse. It is not thus in Horace,
who wants heroism to be practiced so that one is always ready
for it and thus certain of being able to save one's inner dignity:
but unlike modern man, Horace's man can sometimes, even
often, like Apollo himself (Od. II 10, 19), relax his bow. Besides,
Christian puritanism, abetted by "social" puritanism, finds
every entertainment, every somewhat refined pleasure, scandal-
ous: one might perhaps excuse the drunkard who was ashamed
of himself, but drinking with friends, crowning oneself with
roses, playing the lyre, asking nobody's pardon, seeming happy
—fie, go hide!

As a matter of fact, the manly education, the somewhat military roughness and resolute courage that Horace praised, make
the soul capable of those simple joys from which he knew how
to derive pleasure. Unstable imaginations and minds softened
by luxury would find only boredom and immediate satiety in
them; inner emptiness constantly requires exaggerated projects.
The poet of the light odes and the poet of the Roman Odes
have a common enemy: the ambitious man with the empty
soul, incapable of recognizing the price and the weight of the
day that is passing. It is understandable that under these conditions Horace sometimes seemed to contradict himself: praise
of military life in Ode III 2, dispraise of the same thing in Ode
I 29. But that is because the addressee of the latter ode is leaving
for the armies to make his fortune, while the young man of
Ode III 2 is learning under arms "to bear poverty and restric-
tions as friends"; this young man, after years of hard life, will
one day be one of Horace's companions "under the rose"; the
other will swell the number of those whose mad dreams constantly threaten the happiness of everyone.

The famous phrase Carpe diem, "Pluck the passing day,"
makes us grasp, I believe, one of the most essential aspects of

Horace's moral personality. It is, naturally, in rapport with his temperament: this man of Mercury had the mobility of quicksilver; he was impulsive and volatile. Nevertheless, it is doubtful that he would have adopted this point of view if he had not attributed a true moral value to it. In fact, he places it in opposition to those vices that always most horrified him and that he battled all his life. One of the greatest reproaches that he makes against ambition and the love of riches is that these passions mortgage and annul the present—which one neglects to experience for what it is—in favor of a future that is surely chimerical, since, even if it were to be realized, and nothing is less certain, one would turn away from it at once: for one would not know how to live in it, forever driven on by the same incapacity that makes us strangers to the time in which we are living now. In future projects Horace always feared a treason to the present, the surest mark of moral instability and weakness.

We are speaking, then, we can be sure, of quite another matter than picking "the roses of life." Or rather, as that pleasant phrase would probably not have displeased Horace, life has no roses, or at least does not keep them flowering for any spirits but those that are singularly heedful, self-controlled, open to the real, loving what is, capable of living in the present. On this point Horace may have been feeling the influence of Epicureanism. The doctrine of the school, as it is seen in Lucretius (I 459 ff.) and in Epicurus himself, does in fact in many ways bring about a devaluation of time: the only happenings that exist are those which have an existence only at the moment when they occur; they disintegrate afterwards, leaving nothing of themselves to subsist after them except other events, taking place in a new present. This, among other things, is what permits the orthodox Epicurean to be sure that death for the living is nothing. We shall see, however, that on that vital point our poet did not think as an Epicurean. In fact, he had a much broader connection with that whole family of minds for whom the authentic place of man is not duration, with its illusions that inhere in memory and plans, but the single moments in which our liberty braves the world.

This allows us to come to grips with the problem of Horace's selfishness. Certainly, the word cannot be applied unreservedly to a man who according to all evidence was so thoughtful and tactful a friend. Also one cannot accuse a man of being a mere "enjoyer" when he was a good workman who worked so much and so well that, two thousand years after, his works still nourish our moral life and our joy in living. But selfish, if we will, in that he did not feel obliged to devote himself to some immense enterprise that would in any case have been beyond him and to which he would have had to allot time. In the same period, Vergil saw Rome as a palpitating and grandiose story, a work to be constructed: the whole *Aeneid* is animated by the dynamism of a great divine and human plan that is being realized; Augustus is a man of destiny. What Horace saw in Roman history was chiefly a series of images of a high morality. Rome is not a work to be created; it exists, and it would suffice if its morals were purer; Augustus sets the example. If politics is the art of foreseeing and consequently anticipating the future, Horace's is the least political brain possible. One need only reread the counsel dedicated to Maecenas (*Od.* III 8 and 29): its affectionate naïveté—"Think of correcting today's affairs, but do not bother with the future which is unforeseeable"—will give us a clearer understanding of other poems where we would otherwise be tempted to believe that it is a selfish or lazy man who is speaking and revealing himself. He was neither one nor the other; but a whole section of the human horizon was always more or less closed to him.

Horace, then, did not like to think of the future. For him, tomorrow was the place not of hope but of uncertainties, and it was better not to try to dissipate these, for the only certitude that one risked finding instead was death. Yet death has a considerable place in the *Odes*, and it is clear that Horace did not like it. He did not seek to dress it up, or to volatilize it, or to persuade himself that it is a natural phenomenon that we should accept with indifference or at least without sadness. On that head, how little of an Epicurean he is! He did not succeed—but very rare, I think, are those who do—in living really entirely in the succession of present instants. Instead of feeling moment grains under his fingers like so many infrangible diamonds, he had a feeling of evanescence, and in the presence of that feeling he was without recourse. Most of us escape that anguish only by placing all our interest, all our love, in some great continuity external to ourselves, the fortunes of which will not be compromised by our own death. Horace's morality does not offer him this remedy. Should we pity him? Pity and condemn him both? If we could undertake a dialogue with him, would he not have much to say to us on the inhumanity, oversimplifications, and rejections that our behavior often dissimulates?

This sadness in the face of fleeing time and approaching death shows well enough how far Horace is from Epicurus. We would see it equally well if we were to analyze the very point where the spiritual attitudes of the two seem closest, the concept of *otium*. For Horace as well as for Epicurus, repose is an answer to the deepest wish of nature, and certainly both would willingly battle against a doctrine, if there were one, that conceived of happiness as indefinite activity. But if to be an Epicurean it were enough to aspire to repose, if it were enough to wish to banish desire and fear from one's heart, if it were enough to have convinced oneself that power and riches are powerless to bring peace, then Saint Augustine, all mystics, and many others would also be Epicureans. What characterizes *otium* in the *Odes* is that it is acquired at little cost; it is more or less the same thing as that material tranquillity that, in a balanced civilization, is the ordinary lot of those who are not troubled by the desire for either honors or fortune. Epicurus would certainly not have contented himself with it. He would have reminded us vigorously that superstition, fear of death, the curiosity of the mind, and the passions of love haunt the common man too, and thus there would have been no more repose for him. But he would perhaps have rebelled even more to see Horace apparently convinced that ideal tranquillity escapes the sailor in a tempest and the soldier flung into war; he would have reminded him that the principles of wisdom, without which the most peaceful citizen will never know any real peace, have the same efficacity whatever the external circumstances may be. It appears, then, that for Epicurus—who is very near, in this, to the Stoics—the enemy is within: it is disorder and illusion, and inner therapeutics can procure an absolute liberation. For Horace, less worried over the health of his soul, the external world exists and its blows reach one's being at its inmost depths; one must try

to protect oneself from Fortune, but no one can believe that he
can escape it. Of Horace and Epicurus, which is nearer to
reality?

It is difficult to define Horace's religion. He tells us himself
(*Od.* I 34) that the thought of the gods hardly occupied him,
and I think that this was so during his whole life. Yet he tells
us in the same poem that, after long professing an unthinking
virtue, he had one day been finally shaken in his skepticism
by a burst of thunder from a cloudless sky. The context seems
to suggest that that thunderclap is to be understood meta-
phorically: what was this thunder that shook the whole universe
from Taenarus to the Pillars of Hercules? What was this prodigy
that brought about strange mutations in the political order,
casting down the great and exalting their weakest adversaries?
Since there is reference in the piece to an oriental tiara, it has
been wondered whether it was not the substitution of Phraates
for Tiridates on the throne of the Parthians, or the downfall of
Cornelius Gallus. But would it not be a more natural inference
that Horace was thinking of the event, the great event, that
dominated that whole period, the battle of Actium? For there
Antony had fallen and Octavius become absolute master in an
unforeseeable, almost supernatural, fashion, since in the supreme
engagement the enemies had fled almost without fighting and
had later killed themselves.

But what power is it that is manifesting itself in these superhuman occurrences? Jupiter, says line 5; a god, says line 13;
rapacious Fortune with her strident wings, says line 15, and
that interpretation must be the real one, for the poem leads almost without a break into a meditation on the powers of Fortune (*Od.* I 35). We perceive that this is by no means a
conversion to a providentialism of the Vergilian type. Rather,
the ode would seem to mark the discovery of something beyond
a too easily contented and self-assured pedestrian virtue—let us
say, the rather limited moralism that is perceptible in the
Satires; the discovery of all that is unknown and inhuman in
the universe. Far from being a farewell to Epicurus, it may be,
this time in an orthodox Epicurean spirit, a taking of the measure of man, minute in the immense natural chaos. The pessi-
mism to which such a feeling ordinarily gives birth in the mind

duly appears in the following poem: all are praying to Fortune, all fear her, but she listens to no one, happy in her senseless works. She enters and goes out, preceded by the Irremediable, drawing after her Hope and Fidelity, those great names among men.

Yet religious, or at least irrational, themes are not lacking in the work of Horace: the theme of the sin, or inherited crime, that was causing Romans to massacre each other; the theme of civil wars to be expiated in foreign wars; that very disconcerting theme of the curses that would fall upon the Empire if the Romans were to raise up the ruins of Troy. Is all this merely literature? Or, as has been suggested, did Horace at one time in his life, for the sake of friendship, or mimicry, or a game, give way to the influence of Vergil, in whom some of these themes are in fact to be found, but rooted in a general philosophy where they seem to us to be more natural and more true? These explanations, each of which may contain some of the truth, seem to me to be false in their principle, or rather in their intent. Yes, Horace was irreligious. But it is precisely irreligious minds—not religious minds—that stumble into superstition. With them religion itself disintegrates and deteriorates into superstition. These small matters do not hold a large place in their life: from time to time, they pause over them. Horace was probably such a man. At the end of the *Epistle* to Florus (*Ep.* II 2, 205–16), I believe that he made his personal examination of conscience before us:

You are not avaricious; fine, let us go on. But what then? Have all other vices gone with this one? Is your heart exempt from fear of death, from anger? Do you count your birthdays without sorrow? Can you forgive your friends? Do you become gentler and better as old age approaches?

The reader of Horace recognizes his poet well in each of these words. But in the same passage the question arises of being able to be unaffected by dreams, prodigies, phantoms, or spells. Our Horace may have felt himself menaced in that quarter too.

Let us not darken the picture unduly: the *Odes* as a group profess that happiness has been realized. It has finally been on that point that posterity has judged them—nearly always severely. One is tempted to think that a happy man is one who is willfully blind or who does not do his entire duty. If he is happy, it is because he has a little too much: too much money, time, or strength. Why does he hesitate to dispense this super- fluity to those who are suffering, relieving their burden a little— however little—and returning to the common level instead of saddening the poor by the contrast of his comfort? Horace would answer that, on the contrary, it is good that there should be witnesses on earth to the possibility of happiness, a happiness such as his, acquired at little cost and, in short, coming from within. This happy sage may be the means of helping those who envy him to avoid temptations and the disappointments that give rise to disorder. If he reconciles his fellows to a simple, cordial, measured life, who knows if he will not save them from the horrors of civil war? But let us be more basic: in a world like the one that was beginning, in which, to the ruin of the Empire, sumptuous edifices, baths, theaters, amphitheaters, and forums would absorb the best of the fruits of economic activity, as if they had been necessities superior to all the real needs, in this world there was perhaps no sermon of more social value than the example of that man, living in his house in the fields, careless of luxury and its splendors, contented and happy.

4 . The Book of Epistles

THE POEM that concludes the third book of *Odes* not only expresses the pride of having completed an imperishable work; it
expresses also the conviction that that work is finished. To a
certain degree it excludes the possibility of something to follow;
it is almost a farewell to poetry.

If I am not mistaken, it is during the years following the
battle of Actium, between 30 and 27 B.C., that Horace seems to
have taken the most pleasure in expressing himself in the lyric
form. With the years, in the ungrateful effort of final retouching, perhaps some lassitude came over the poet's spirit. He had
passed the age of forty; he had renounced the love of the fair.
He imagined that old age had come. Like all mobile minds,
he worked in spurts, with interludes of laziness, but accomplish-
ing in a few months what would have required years of others.
It was in the conviction that his work was already behind him
that Horace wrote his *Epistles,* not only as a farewell to poetry—
this point is already covered—but as a final pledge to the love
of literature. Certainly the prodigious virtuoso that he had
become would have resigned himself with difficulty to ceasing
suddenly to write; but he now conceived that nothing further
was possible for him than a terminal book that would bring him,
before his death, to that great calm of *otium* in which he still
had, he felt, so many discoveries to make for his happiness and
the health of his soul.

HORACE'S RETREAT

It has sometimes been suggested that this desire for retreat came to Horace as the result of an indifferent reception to his lyric works. But it appears to me that the very text most often advanced to support this hypothesis refutes it:

You would like to know [the epistle is addressed to Maecenas] why, in his ingratitude, the reader praises and likes my little works (the *Odes*) when he is at home and maliciously denigrates them beyond his threshold: I do not purchase the commendation of a common people as changeable as the wind, putting myself to the expense of dinners for them or paying them with used garments; I am not to be seen alternately listening to illustrious writers and taking my revenge on them, finding it good to dance attendance on troops of grammarians. Hence these tears. If I say: I blush to read my unworthy writings before the serried ranks of an audience, and to give importance to trifles, they answer: You are joking, you are saving your poetry for the ears of Jupiter . . . [*Ep.* I 19, 35–44]

This text shows that Horace felt confident of the esteem of private readers, that is to say of the public, and also of that of Maecenas and Augustus (Jupiter). Those who turned him a cold face were the professionals whom he would have had to win by political means—meals and bribery; here we recognize those persevering enemies who, ever since the time of the *Satires*, had not stopped plaguing him. But Horace had never paid much attention to them, being too sure of the understanding that he found elsewhere. Perhaps we are even permitted to wonder if he did not exaggerate that hostility to make his success stand out the more. Thus Molière, sure of the king and the theater pit, liked to describe himself as the butt of the hostility of marquises. In the same *Epistle*, we see Horace complaining of the "stupid imitators" who turn his lightest sallies into oracles and regulate their pace on his: *O imitatores servum pecus.* . . . Now one does not think of imitating a man unless he is successful. Elsewhere, in the more or less contemporary second *Epistle* to Florus, we see that among his colleagues Horace had the place of an important man (*Ep.* II 2, 87–105). A Horace whose *Odes* had not had a very handsome and widespread success would not have been chosen by Augustus five years later to compose the *Carmen saeculare*. So let us refrain from confusing the issue of the poet's change of style by advancing the hypothesis of rancors or discouragements; the change was more deeply linked with the inner history of the poet.

So far as the form that he adopted is concerned, it can be readily believed that Horace, convinced that he was finished with great poetry, found a certain pleasure in recalling the memory of his first work. These *Epistles*, which were being sketched on his tablets and would be his final work, would be a counterpart of the *Satires*. The lyric work would rise like a peak between these minor books. This explanation is indicated by many details that show a desire to establish such a relationship. "You who were named in the first accents of my Muse, and will be named in the last, Maecenas, . . ."—so begins the first *Epistle*, in an explicit reminder of the beginning of the first *Satire*, "Whence comes Maecenas. . . ." In the fourth line of this *Epistle*, we see again the style of the *Satires*: the gratuitous introduction of a minor personage who is the hero of the most commonplace occurrences, in this case an old gladiator by the name of Veianius; a little later (l. 56) a line of *Satire* I 6, 74 will be repeated word for word; then there will be fragments of dialogue, the appearance of a more or less fictitious interlocutor, an Aesop-like fable; Horace purposely plunges us back into the atmosphere of his first collection. These "Satiric" *Epistles* are spaced out through the whole length of the book; the sixth, for example, is addressed to one Numicius, who is completely unknown and has even been suspected of being an imaginary personage, since he seems equally tempted by money, ambition, good dinners, love, and games—tastes that are not ordinarily all found in the same man. And in such a context it is quite natural to find again Lucullus' chlamys, Mutus' properties, the manner in which Gargilius did his marketing, and so on. As in the *Satires*, the sixteenth *Epistle*, to Quinctius, also swarms with those little quarrels with personages who disappear as fast as they appear, a praiser of Augustus, a slanderous accuser, a timid slave, Horace himself, a man of quality who is in fact a thief; as in *Satire* II 3, 303, a passage from the *Bacchantes* serves as the theme for a moral sermon.

Naturally, Horace always recalls with amusement the excesses of the Stoic puppets of whom he had made fun or who had

formerly aroused him: the Stertinius of *Satire* II 3 comes back
to rave a moment in *Epistle* I 12, 20. He will mention again the
universal kingdom of the wise man, compromised by a simple
cold in the head (*Ep.* I 1, 106–108). We must see *Epistle* I 17
as a true satire, from the first line to the last: there Horace as-
sumes in his own name a role analogous to the one he gave
the virtuous Tiresias in *Satire* II 5; but now it is not the art
of snaring wills but rather the art of success, or, better, the art of
parasitism: it is this art that constitutes virtue itself (37–42).
Reserve, a spirit of independence—that is, everything that the
true Horace made the law of his life—are derided as the ridiculous appurtenances of cowards, the pusillanimous, and weak-
lings; the essential (*rerum caput*) is "to carry off as much as possible" (*plus ferre*); it is amazing that such outrageous remarks—
the bore in *Satire* I 9 did not go so far—have not alerted certain
critics who have believed that this caricature represents the true
thought of Horace.

It sometimes happens that the *Epistles* are intended to recall
the *Odes*. Bullatius, who is supposedly the addressee of *Epistle*
I 11, is an elusive shadow; but the letter addressed to him, with
its abundance of picturesque evocations, its metaphorical vocabulary, the warmth and emotion with which the poet urges
him to live from day to day, somewhat recall the tone and the
structure of an ode; it too has the tripartite construction and
the elliptical expressions. It is probably not by chance that this
exquisite "poem in prose" is the first in the second half of the
collection; like the satirical *Epistles*, but in another way, it links
the new book of Horace to those that preceded it.

The prehistory of the *Epistles*, if I may so express myself, is
perhaps not to be sought only on the literary plane. Cautious
as one should be in reconstructing biographical events, we cannot escape the conviction that at that moment, in 22 or 21,
"something" happened in Horace's life, an experience that convinced him more firmly of the urgency of thinking of perfecting
his morals and renouncing all ambition. Furthermore, what
happened was nothing mysterious: He recounted the whole matter in *Epistle* I 7, addressed to Maecenas. No doubt that letter
was limpidly clear to his contemporaries, and it is not the poet's
fault if it no longer is to us. These uncertainties are vexatious.

Yet it is impossible for criticism not to take a position with regard to this vital text, since the events of those years, the very character of the poet, and the perspective in which we will read the *Epistles* will all appear in a very different light according to the interpretation we give to it.

Before any exegesis, let us see first what is yielded by the text. Horace had promised not to be away for more than a few days. But it is now August. Rome is unhealthful. The poet fears to fall ill and stays in the country. May Maecenas excuse him as if he were ill indeed! Similarly, in winter, Horace will go seek the sun near Tarentum; he will take care of himself and will not return until spring.

I know that the fortunes that you have bestowed upon me were an expression of esteem; you know men, and you attach value to what you give; this double merit on your part gives me the more reason to show myself worthy of you. But if you wish me to be always in Rome, give me back my former health and my youth. Through a narrow slit, a lean fox once entered a box of grain; big and fat, he could not get out; he would have to become thin again to pass through the hole that, once thin, he had entered. If this fable is to be applied to me, I renounce everything (*cuncta resigno*): against all the riches of Araby I would not exchange the liberty of my leisure. You have often praised me for my reserve, you know the sincerity of my affection, I make you the judge: see if I am able—if I desire—to renounce what you have given me (*inspice si possum donata reponere laetus*). Telemachus did well to leave Menelaus the equipage that the latter had given him: what would he have done with it in Ithaca? Small things suit the small: it is not the Rome of kings that pleases me, it is the solitary Tibur, the peaceful Tarentum. Mena, poor devil, lost sleep because he had received a rural property that he was not made to run; he found happiness again only by returning to his life as a small wage-earner. As soon as a man realizes how much things he has abandoned exceed in value the things sought out instead, he must hasten to come back to them, to return to what he has left. To know one's true measure, that is what is fitting.

We can be sure that in this letter to Maecenas Horace was proposing to return something that he had received, a gift that was no doubt flattering but in the use had proved to be incompatible with the tastes of the poet, with the liberty that he clung to beyond all else. Obviously, the letter was a matter of some delicacy: the multiplicity of apologues and a thousand details of style show that Horace was conscious of dealing with one of those subjects where the slightest clumsiness of expression becomes extremely disagreeable.

Exactly what is being discussed in the *Epistle?* And what was this present, this liberality, this favor of Maecenas, this "benefaction," to use the Latin term, that Horace wished to renounce? For us moderns, who, unlike his contemporaries, know Horace's life only from those traces he left in his works, it is natural that we should think immediately of that gesture of friendship whereby Maecenas, many years ago by this time, had given the poet a charming property in the Sabine hills: Horace spoke of it so often, *Hoc erat in votis.* . . . This, they tell us, is the "benefaction" that he now proposed to Maecenas to return.

Such is, I agree, the first idea that presents itself to us. But is it probable? Let us put ourselves in the position of those Roman readers for whom Horace intended his *Epistles,* and who had first been the entertained or enthusiastic readers of the *Satires* or the *Odes.* Each still remembered the fountain Bandusia, the races of Fauns on the Lucretilis, the city rat and the country rat; they all know the happiness, the pleasant and moderate life that Horace knew in that solitude. And now their poet was claiming that this was not the gift for him (l. 43)! That that property, so simple, so small, where he had found his true self, was now as confining to him as the riches of Araby could be. He wished to return quickly (*mature* l. 97) to what he had been before. He spoke of giving the gift back with a joyous heart (*laetus* l. 39), thus, joyously, canceling nearly ten years of life. But why did he want to give back his Sabine farm? Maecenas was not asking for it. What had happened? There must then have been a falling-out: one of those in which one returns gifts once received in confidence and joy, in order, by that shabby gesture, to gain back the appearance of a moral right to one's liberty. . . . Who can fail to see that the mere envisaging of such a prospect would have been as dismaying to the reader as a disaster—the quarrel of two freinds? And what ugly things was he forced to imagine? A Maecenas who was tyrannical, tactless, and demanding, incapable of getting along without Horace for a moment? A Horace who was balking, who probably could find no other way to regain a little breathing space, who was making a point of saying that he did not judge himself bound by any gift, and who would give everything back if the self-styled benefactor were not pleased?

Really, if such were the case, how can we imagine that Horace could be moved to give a literary form to this painful episode in his relations with Maecenas, and then to wish to make it known in this form to the public? And how can we imagine that this publication could have been equally agreeable to Maecenas, or that he could be happy to see such a letter in a collection dedicated to him?

Let us consider, too, what followed these events: No one questions the fact that Horace kept his Sabine farm. *Ode* IV 11 describes it to us on an April 13, all full of joyous preparations for a party: Maecenas' birthday is to be celebrated. Is it possible that Maecenas had, as they say in the regiment, "understood" —that is, had taken it that he had received his orders, had re-coiled before the ugliness of a quarrel, had lowered his flag, and had begged Horace to keep that gift which had been so readily offered back to him in case he should not be willing to give in? Very well. There are those who feel that in doing so Maecenas would only have been doing his duty, and that his capitulation does him honor. Very well again. But then it was his former demands that dishonored him or made him ridiculous. Besides, is it every very honorable to give in to blackmail, even when one has been partly in the wrong? In any case, it is difficult to see how anyone who had given in could be pleased to see the publication of the double evidence of his mad demands and his humiliation. And what are we to think of the poet who insisted upon triumphing publicly over his benefactor?—in order, they tell us, to do honor to his liberalism. . . .

Fortunately, nothing obliges us to read the *Epistle* in this sense. Horace may have been thinking of something entirely different, which his contemporaries, knowing the concrete situation, must have understood without hesitation. In fact, we know that Maecenas' friendship did not content itself with having installed his poet in a country villa. Often in the *Odes* we find Horace affectionately defending himself against other offers, affirming that he is contented, and that anything more would add nothing to his happiness. We can readily imagine that Maecenas, as he became more and more cognizant of all his friend's qualities, resigned himself with difficulty to seeing him permanently ensconced in a Sabine retreat. He constantly constructed plans and invented arrangements that would permit the poet to live in Rome, to hold a position of prominence there, to be happier there. *Ode* III 16 concerns projects of that sort: Horace might be capable of being lured by the prospect of gold toward a more brilliant position, but the prospect of inevitable cares, the fear of laying his soul open to cupidity, the horror he has of inspiring envy keep him permanently in his little domain. The same expressions recur in the *Ode* and in the *Epistle* that we are discussing. In both cases the contrast is the same between a brilliant placement that Horace repulses and the humble country life in which he is so happy to see his days slipping by. But between the *Ode* and the *Epistle* a change in facts took place: after having refused and fled for a long time, Horace had finally allowed himself to be won over to Maecenas' plans. But, since his heart had not changed, a short experience had sufficed to convince him that he had been wrong to accept, and that it was decidedly in the liberty of his retreat that he wished to live. He must then give up, with Maecenas' consent, what he had a little imprudently accepted, which, he says, certainly honors him (l. 22), but which he now doubts that he can keep and remain worthy of himself and of his friend (l. 24). Has he really lost his freedom to do what he wills with himself? He much fears that he has, and that the fable of the fox who was the prisoner of his own opulence applies to his own case: Maecenas must be the judge. Then, if it is truly so, he prefers to renounce (*cuncta resigno*) and to return to his hole, that is to his dear Sabine farm.

To the same degree that it was difficult just now to understand the publication of an *Epistle* describing afflicting, indeed dishonorable, situations, so publication under the present hypothesis seems natural, opportune, and perhaps even necessary. Horace did not stay in Rome, he returned to his countryside, he was traveling in southern Italy. It was necessary to explain that this absence did not result from any fall from grace; it was necessary that the poet himself request, as a favor, permission to release himself from obligations that were certainly flattering but had been imprudently contracted. Maecenas would share his views, and no one would be able to believe— quite the contrary—that he had withdrawn his confidence from the poet. We then understand that the two friends, together, desired that publication. We understand that it was with a joyous heart, without reservations, that a little later Horace celebrated Maecenas' birthday in that countryside now twice beloved, in that it had been first received and then regained through the obliging comprehension of his friend. Although this was a touchy moment in the story of their relationship— it is always dangerous to have erred in one's kindnesses, how- ever affectionately—we understand how it can have left no cold- ness between them. "Remember Horace as you would me." This was, as we know, the last recommendation of the dying Maecenas to Augustus. And perhaps there is some point in remembering that Horace survived his friend, as he had promised in *Ode* II 17 fifteen or twenty years earlier, by only a few months, and was buried very near to Maecenas' grave.

It is rather striking that, outside of *Epistle* I 13, the verse dedication of the collection of *Odes*, almost all the *Epistles* that can be dated (*Ep.* I 3, 9, 12, 18) fall together in a rather short period, between autumn 21 and summer 20. Perhaps the very genesis of the book has a relation to that moral crisis, which we should place in 22 or 21, the friendly outcome of which is shown to us in *Epistle* I 7. Horace, a little intoxicated by the success of the *Odes* (*Exegi monumentum* . . . and we shall soon see that after the *Carmen saeculare* he experienced a similar intoxication) was for a moment unfaithful to his re- treat. It is the period described in *Epistle* I 1: "Sometimes I become a man of action, I plunge into the agitated waves of politics" (l. 16); but he was a man of action forever haunted by the feeling that he ought to be elsewhere: "Night seems long to those whose mistresses deceive them; long, the day to those who have a task to fulfill; so there pass for me with a painful slowness those moments that delay the hope and plan" of devoting himself entirely to a life of wisdom (l. 20–26). One day, he realized that he had to return to his solitude. But when one "returns" in that way, it is never the same man who returns: there is more gravity, a little sadness, and a keener feeling that one has truly only one life, that it is already fixed and irremediable in many ways, and that the only thing is to see to it that it is inwardly as little empty as possible. It is just this that essentially constitutes the true note of the *Epistles*.

WHAT IS AN EPISTLE?

The verse letter for which Horace, so far as we know, invented the model and the tradition seems to me to be the end result of many converging quests. As soon as there was a philosophy or a political thought, it was natural that philosophers or men of action, prompted by an important occasion, should write a letter to a friend, partisan, disciple, or adversary which was connected with current events, but which at the same time, from the very fact of the importance of the circumstances, had an import extending beyond its immediate object. Plato's are certainly real letters; yet it matters nothing that the circumstances which caused them to be written no longer exist, for we still find them fruitful reading. No doubt many of his contemporaries could have profited from reading them even without having either reason or opportunity to concern themselves with Sicilian affairs. In the same way certain of Cicero's letters still have all their value as political programs.

The ancients also practiced a paraepistolatory genre, wherein the "letter" was less addressed than dedicated to its apparent addressee. The writer thinks of a public, and he dedicates his work to a particularly eminent representative of that public. Is not every dedicated work considered in principle to have been especially, if not exclusively, composed for the person to whom it is dedicated, so that the whole thing may be considered as an extended letter addressed to him? Nothing prevents us from seeing the *Dialogue of the Orators* as a letter to Fabius Justus; the body of the work is presented as an answer to questions raised by the addressee, a follow-up of conversations carried on with him. If we are apt to consider it more as a treatise preceded by a dedication, it is because after the first chapter of a work that has forty chapters it is no longer concerned with the person to whom it is dedicated, and because it seems to us that nothing in this *Dialogue* would have been written or presented differently if Fabius Justus had not existed.

As much could be said of most of Cicero's treatises. The *Letters* of Epicurus to Herodotus and to Pythocles also belong to this genre; in the tradition of the school they continued to pass for letters, probably because they had been placed in the same collection with other analogous pieces, many of which had a more clearly perceptible epistolary character.

Besides, it is clear that between literate persons, between poets, the simple circumstances of daily life or of friendship sufficed to give rise to an interchange of epigrams and notes in verse: the *Anthology* and Catullus give us charming examples. Many of the *Odes* of Horace are very near to being letters. It has been said that Horace always respected a fiction according to which the ode requires the presence of a friend or witness. It seems difficult to be sure of this, and I would not even wish to claim that there is any truth in this alleged principle. The connection between the epigram or note in verse, on the one hand, and the doctrinal letter with moralizing or philosophical intent on the other, took place before Horace's time. There is good reason to think that some of Lucilius' satires took the form of letters. Lucilius even cites an *epistula non magna* (l. 341) as the very type of the *poema*, the genre of composition in which he hopes to distinguish himself.

What brings Horace's originality into view beyond any doubt is the fact that he found that form sufficiently interesting and rich for him to remain faithful to it exclusively throughout a collection of twenty pieces addressed (or dedicated) to nearly twenty different persons. As is almost always the case, the apparent generalization of a form that until then has been fairly narrowly restricted is evidence that the form is no longer exactly the same: under an exterior that is unchanged or barely changed, something new has been born. The object of the Horatian *Epistles* was in fact new. What they tell us is not the thought of Horace on one subject or another, or even the conduct or the principles of his correspondent; they yield up to us, in an often entirely disinterested fashion, without the prospect of imminent or later action, the very person of the poet. This intention, this new reality, is felt particularly if one compares a pseudoepistolary satire, like the *Epistle* to Numicius (I 6), with the very short note to Celsus (I 8), which is, in the sense of our definition, a true letter. The *Epistle* to Numicius exposes a program of life: positively, the *nil admirari*; negatively, a triple condemnation of cupidity, ambition, and pleasures. Suppose that Numicius really existed, and even that in writing him this letter Horace hoped to work toward his improvement: the letter is nonetheless a little treatise of practical philosophy, without any true connection with the person of the author. Doubtless it expresses ideas held by Horace as well as by many others; but it is not Horace himself. In contrast, read the letter to Celsus. There is nothing here that would interest anyone who was not interested in Horace. It is no longer a parade of principles, but the position of a man, the poet himself, with regard to these principles. It is still a letter on morals, I admit, but its center of gravity is a person, not ideas.

It is obvious that this new, personal note, which one can isolate sometimes by taking one's point of departure from extreme cases such as those we just considered, is most often internal to developments of a theoretical aspect. Let us take, for example, those *Epistles* where the countryside is presented as the ideal framework for a life devoted to wisdom. General ideas can be drawn from them and abstractly formulated in a universal way. No doubt Horace himself read more than one treatise on this subject. But what is new in the *Epistle* is that in the foreground of the abstract theme, "wisdom and life in the country," there appears a man engaged in this adventure. We can no longer feel or grasp the generalities except through him, for they have become interior to the fellow-feeling and interest that he arouses in us, and are intermingled with his own particular adventure. It is no longer life in the country that we see, but Horace in the country, trying to become better. Conversely, if our fellow-feeling fails all disappears. There remains only a shell of commonplace. Will we even be able still to appreciate their general truth?

Horace, then, wrote a whole book of *Epistles*, taking magnificent advantage of a hardly recognized literary form and revealing its possibilities for specific expression. He would not, as his predecessors had done, use the epistle for matters that other literary forms could transmit just as well. He has something else to say, something else that only the letter can render, in that it springs from one person to another, being really a substitute for the meeting of two persons. It was inevitable that one day humanity would come to use writing, that fresh discovery, to such an end. Horace was the first to do it, doubtless because he had an acute sense of himself as an individual: he had that ability to be an object of interest to himself and to others that is the foundation of true friendship, a rare virtue that so many fine geniuses have lacked, sometimes looking upon the lack as a virtue.

We can see that the question of knowing whether the letter was sent, or whether it called for an answer, or whether it was itself an answer to another letter, is probably of little importance. The essential difference between the letter and the treatise has to do with the original intent, not with their final fate. Anything is a treatise that arises from our having ideas and principles; a treatise is anything written in which we efface ourselves behind what we propose, in which we use what we are to create something which will have a value apart from what we are. A letter is whatever is written in the opposite way, when the communication of ideas is only a means, an instrument, of the communication of persons.

This does not cancel out the addressee. Quite the contrary, for it is only in relation to another person that one manages to grasp oneself, to know oneself as a subject. Horace is Horace only because he is face to face with Florus, Tibullus, Maecenas, Aristius Fuscus, and even the unprepossessing Lollius Maximus. It is neither because of a studied condescension nor because of a mechanical imitativeness that we change our countenance according to our interlocutors; according to what each of them is, different aspects of ourselves become accessible to us; man alone very often goes around in circles in his ideas or degenerates into idea systems. I do not believe that there are serious reasons to suppose that *Epistle* I 14 "to his gardener" never reached the hands of that gardener (or rather agent). We always have a tendency to suppose that the ancients were more stupid or less literate than ourselves. Why should that slave or freedman, who knew his master well, whom Horace could associate with mourning for a lost friend or with the affectionate memory of a former mistress, have been surprised

one day to receive a letter in verse? But even if we suppose that
the letter was not sent, what is important is that without the
existence of the "gardener," without the spiritual—and thus,
vividly evoked—presence of that man near to him, Horace would
not have gained access to that part of himself which he disclosed in the *Epistle*. Of course he would not have been ignorant
of the fact that everyone is discontent with his lot; how many
times had he already said and resaid it! But he would probably
not have seen himself with eyes so full of perspicacious slyness.
Our ideas we can maneuver very well by ourselves, but to grasp
our own essence we have need of others.

The *Epistles* of Horace, then, represent an important moment
in the history of our mental development. If we search the
world's literature for minds that can be compared here to
Horace's, we think at once of Montaigne, the butt of the same
condemnations of selfishness and futility that were hurled at
poor Horace. "That idiotic project of his of depicting himself.
. . . The 'I' is detestable." If such judgments could still have
currency after 1600 years of Christianity, that is, after 1600
years of inner experience, what intellectual freshness, what an
upspringing of life must have been necessary to undertake that
"idiotic project" in an age when the individual was ineffable and
came down to absolute materiality and opacity! In his enterprise, perhaps Horace succeeded better than Montaigne. It
seems to us sometimes that our Montaigne became entangled
and drowned in his papers, that he was too much alone with
his books; while in Horace all is dialogue with the living. La
Boétie died too soon. As much could be said, I think, of Seneca,
clinging to poor Lucilius, all enclosed in himself—and too dogmatic, besides, which hardly permits one to be interested in
people. In the last analysis, one has the friends one deserves,
and as one grows older it is not a minor success to keep a
few of them or even one. Let us ask ourselves: Would each
of us find the fifty or so friends to whom he could write, in
the same confiding tone, the equivalent of Horace's *Epistles*?
We had them once, perhaps, but when we were twenty years
old. The Horace of the *Epistles* was forty-five which by our

reckoning would make, I believe, more than fifty. This one calculable fact perhaps tells us more of the quality of the man than the longest reflection.

COMPLETION OF A MORAL DOCTRINE

We saw a little while ago that in the *Epistles* Horace more than once wished us to remember his earlier works, the *Odes* and *Satires*. Certain processes of development are to be found in all of them, and of course in its broad outlines his moral doctrine remained the same. Our poet was always very determined to keep himself from ambition and cupidity, very much convinced that there is much naïveté in wishing any other life than the one one has. The list of these principles could easily be extended. But in comparison to the earlier works, new elements that are less immediately visible may come closer to the essential. The *Satires* have to do very much with others, usually for the poet's amusement. Horace had now passed that picturesque stage, which is probably, at least for certain minds, inevitable: the sense of the concrete, which will later, if all goes well, make them grasp the presence of the spiritual, begins by practicing on externals, and naturally amuses itself in doing so. Damasippus himself, desirous as he is to help his listeners, moves continually toward caricature. In time, Horace left these futile games behind. Henceforth he would think about himself above all, and when he thought of others he would be friendly. Also, in comparison with the *Odes*, we see him much less preoccupied with living in the instant, less desirous of seizing a fugitive present that will perhaps be the last flash of his life. These themes return again in the *Epistle* to Tibullus (I 4) as instruments of a therapy proposed for the uneasiness of an anxious man; for where he himself was concerned, our poet, in opposition to what he had formerly preached, now made plans for the future:

What is the true, what is moral good? That is what concerns me, what I inform myself about, what involves me entirely. I am putting aside and arranging provisions where I can later draw on them. . . . I see passing with painful slowness for me the moments which defer the hope and plan of ardently undertaking that task which is equally useful to rich and poor, which children and old men will suffer equally for having neglected. [*Ep.* I 1, 11–26]

He was going to devote himself to study, and to reading the words of the wise (*ibid.*, 34–37; cf. 3, 28; 8, 9). He felt that it is in this diligent work that one approaches happiness.

This is because, correlatively, his concept of happiness had also changed. More convinced of what he must do by himself, he gave less thought to the many unforeseeable occurrences that depend upon Fortune. "Let us content ourselves by asking Jupiter for what he puts at man's disposal or takes away from him: life, and resources; balance of soul I must provide myself" (*Ep.* I 18, 111–112). *Ipse parabo.* Decidedly the poet had not become more religious than in the *Odes.* His Jupiter, identical with Fortune, had influence only over things. But whereas earlier it had seemed so natural to him to be happy provided that Fortune was not cruel to him, he now understood better that in all circumstances, happy or unhappy, the essential remains in our hands, because it remains to us to make our own lives.

If the *Epistles,* as has been said, bear evidence of a moral conversion, it is here that we must recognize it. In the *Odes,* all was organized around a morality of the moment. The one way of living in safety was to seize Fortune's gifts as they came, without ever trying to anticipate. Horace later recognized that we must establish ourselves on a plane other than one in which the external world pays out our life, hour by hour. He recognized that our life has a continuity, and that we have the responsibility for it: it was a discovery of dimensions, of temporal responsibilities, of our liberty.

Such mutations somewhat change the very look that we turn on things, even on the dear countryside. Naturally Horace still appreciated its leisures, sleeping on the grass beside a brook. But the attachment he felt for the country had become more metaphysical. *Epistle* I 10, in particular, establishes a connection between *rus* and *natura* which hardly appears in other authors of antiquity, but which has become customary in our modern languages, where the word "nature," without losing its philosophical connotations, also brings up before our eyes fields, foliage, and landscapes. Horace's idea is that only in the country can man work out his true man's nature. Even when he believes that he is tired of the country it is what he seeks, and its image and reflections seek him out in the very refinements of urban luxury. In a general way, the country, with the regularity and evenness of its rhythms (*Ep.* I 10, 15–17), the simplicity of the relationships that it establishes between men (*Ep.* I 14, 37–39), its calm and its silence, is the ideal place for great spiritual undertakings, wisdom, and poetry, methodical contemplation and enthusiasm (*Ep.* II 2, 65–86). It gives man back to himself. We were just saying that in the presence of his fellows, Horace now attached himself to inner matters and was less curious about laughable or miserable details of appearance. It is also possible that, even when he gazed upon natural charms or splendors, this gaze, which was really looking at something else, no longer had all the precision of the past. To be sure, the description of the little domain at the beginning of *Epistle* I 16 is full of life. But in these *Epistles* we no longer find those vivid strokes that make certain *Odes* unforgettable and assure us that the most fleeting of the least ordinary sights can be fixed forever. Even in nature, Horace's gaze was now turned first upon himself. Even in that welcoming universe, the poet eminently felt the transcendence of his own inner reality. Nor did he any longer know that abandon, that vivifying communication experienced and rendered by Vergil in his *Georgics*, by which man receives the best of his soul from nature. It is true that he did not have the religious aptitudes that make such a discovery possible. He remained bound by his embattled temperament, he remained the man who took his position against everything external, "opposing it," as R. Heinze so rightly expresses it. The essential, he felt, he must accomplish all alone: nature, in the last analysis, only gave him a framework.

Everyone knows that our poet always refused to belong to any school (*Ep.* I 1, 14), and in the beginning nothing seems more ordinary. Yes; but usually those who claim their right to this liberty are skeptical or indifferent. They do not wish to be Stoics rather than Epicureans, or men of the left rather than men of the right, quite simply because the moral problem or political problems do not interest them. With Horace, as we know, it is quite another matter, and it is in this, especially during antiquity, that his attitude was unusual. Everyone thought then within a family of thought. The schools, whatever they were, kept up a tradition by which the piety of their followers was nourished. One was the disciple of a master; one did not change one's mode of thought without the fear of being treacherous to someone. This is because for a long time philosophical teaching, essentially oral, had been a tradition from person to person. The book was to change all that, and Horace is perhaps one of the first witnesses of this liberation. It is clear that his first move when confronted by a preacher was to kick and joke. On the other hand, he has not allowed us to be ignorant of the fact that for the conduct of his moral life he was a man of books. He reread the *Iliad*, and was astonished to find more teaching there than in Chrysippus and Crantor (*Ep.* I 2, 1–4). He asked the gods to let him have a good supply each year of books and wheat (*Ep.* I 18, 109–10). When his laziness or his faults carried him away, he became angry with his books as a sick man does with his doctor (*Ep.* I 8, 9). The best advice that he had to give to young Lollius was: "In the midst of all these occupations you will read" (*Ep.* I 18, 96). Here again, we think inevitably of Montaigne: always suspended, always an apprentice, alone before the diversity of doctrines; obliged, in order to choose, always to refer to himself, his sole stable companion; with hesitations, or rather inner attempts, and application in lending himself to doctrines, not as a game but in the hope and will of becoming better himself; and feeling the necessary indecision of one who is never sure that he has found the place in which to fix himself, of one who wishes always to be capable of seeing the truth that lies in something that he has not yet assimilated, or which even is not, may perhaps never be, for him.

Wherever the wind takes me, I allow myself to be carried, a passing guest. Sometimes I become a man of action, I plunge into the agitated waves of politics, I, guardian and austere satellite of true virtue; sometimes I allow myself to slip unconsciously again into the principles of Aristippus, and I force myself to place my yoke on things instead of submitting to theirs. [*Ep.* I 1, 15–19]

Hospes. A passing guest. He is not speaking of assays, or initial tests. These are not the gropings that seek a sure passage and access to a port. There is no port: these gropings are wisdom itself. There is no end, for there is no valid formula, even for oneself alone, which one would only have to inculcate in one's soul. Wisdom is that extending of oneself that is always new even although in a continuous line, always unfinished although always in progress.

A wisdom so sought, through a constant attention to oneself, astonishes or scandalizes the dogmatic. How can one know what is proper to one's soul? On what will one guide one's choices? Will one not be simply the toy of conformities or, as Horace himself said, of the passing wind? Not necessarily, if in the soul there exists a sufficient, that is an indefatigable vitality, certainly capable of errors but also forever ready to take hold of itself again. So let us not be tricked by the aphorisms with which Horace was never miserly: we cannot encompass him in any one of them. The *nil admirari* (*Ep.* I 6, 1), for example, with its lapidary formation, is probably nothing but a landmark planted in the immense domain that, at that very moment, represents in the eyes of the poet only a part of the program of morality. We would also be wrong in reducing Horace's wisdom to a sort of middle way that would consist of the mere idea that virtue itself must be sought with moderation (*Ep.* I 6, 15–16). The only meaning of this aphorism is to affirm that the very qualities of virtue must, like all the rest, be submitted to judgment, that there, too, are found traps, that virtue can become a fallacious idol. Other texts, on the contrary, would show us Horace as a man ready to make any sacrifice to safeguard what appears to him at that moment to be his spiritual liberty and his dignity (*Ep.* I 16, 73–79). There is also the "pig of Epicurus" reference, which, joke as it is, surely has some reality in it, at least if we gloss it, as Horace did, as a "fat man, polished, with well cared-for skin, liking to laugh" (*Ep.* I 4, 15–16). All these expressions are to be taken together, and not as precluding one another or replacing one another as if at stages of an itinerary. Horace's life was such that they could all be affirmed together. All is true.

Finally, a life so led is judged not by its conformity to such and such an external model but by its density and its capacity of reacting to the unexpected and taking the curves like a well-driven automobile. That Horace was still Maecenas' friend after the events recalled in *Epistle* I 7, that he was open to correspondents of very different ages and makeup, that he maintained his contact with youth, and that he had the very ability to write the *Epistles* and later works that at the moment he could not even foresee—all these are the fully authorized guarantors to us of the legitimacy of that conduct.

All is true. Because in reality there exists more than is covered by the most universal of systems. Because the least individual life contains complexities that make the best worked-out ideal appear oversimplified and arbitrary. The concrete and the individual are of prime importance. With these principles, how can one direct the morality of another? Can one profess anything else but skepticism? Yes, because one is oneself the opposite of skeptical and indifferent. Only, outside of a few maxims of general hygiene like *nil admirari*, and some episodic bits of advice with reference to very visible faults (Quinctius is a bit of a comedian, Lollius is hard to get along with, Aristius Fuscus seems frivolous), Horace will act chiefly by the example and the success of his life. The trust, the self-communication that make the note to Celsus (*Ep.* I 8) or the end of the second letter to Florus (*Ep.* II 2) so moving is the privileged instrument of moral action. Everyone has his own life, but the example of one who lives well is an encouragement to everyone to live in the same manner. The moralist may still feel free to throw out a call to reflection and invite each person to take up his burden, that is, to look his own life in the face, but he can hardly go further: everyone does not have the same road to travel. Such is the principle of a liberalism that has surprised more than one reader. To comfort Tibullus (*Ep.* I 4), Horace reminds him of all the good things heaped upon him by life: wealth, the art of enjoying it, reputation, an elegant mode of life. Are these truly good things? Yet we know that Horace does not seek them out for himself; more, he now and then has to forbid himself to desire them. But for Tibullus perhaps they are good things, at least at the moment. Similarly, in *Ep.* I 17 and 18, along with the humor, the causticity, and the needling tone, along with the prudent expressions inspired in him by the thought of ungrateful figures, we must not exclude the possibility that Horace, at the moment he was writing, felt a certain sympathy and a kind of attraction toward values that were not proper to him, but which after all were perhaps proper to others. Even in the rather repugnant parasitism into which Scaeva was slipping, is everything thoroughly detestable? That suppleness of spine and ease in ignoring all public contumely, are they not at least the minor reflection of another elasticity, that of the wise man? Is one not always someone's fool? And here Horace doubtless thinks that he should reread Aristippus. It is also possible that the retreat in which he himself finds happiness would not bring Lollius what he needs; and so we should not see irony in the line where the poet asks his friend to examine himself on this point and to ask himself what could bring him honors and money. Each man has his own burden.

Horace did decide not to write any more, that is, not to write lyric poems, for epistles or conversations do not count. He wished to devote himself entirely to the liberation and progress of his soul. But it is not so easy to break with one's past, especially when one still has friends. Many *Epistles* show us that the poet remained very much interested in the literary projects of his correspondents. Among the young officers whom Tiberius took to the Orient among his cohorts in the autumn of 21, many had ambitions: Titius was hesitating between Pindaric lyricism and tragedy, Florus, between juridical eloquence and light poetry; others thought of epics (*Ep.* I 3, 6–25). Elsewhere, Lollius was in love with poetry to the point of becoming unsociable and shunning the most innocent amusements (*Ep.* I 18, 47–48). It is clear that all these young people, no less than Maecenas himself, kept plaguing Horace to start writing again.

He defended himself as best he could, praising the charms of wisdom and the intention that he, at least, had of devoting himself to it for the time that he still had to live. But, as we have seen, he never dogmatized. What he believed to be good for himself he would not dare to impose upon, nor indeed to propose directly, to any of his correspondents. He said to no one that poetry is futile. To no one did he give the advice of abandoning poetry. Quite the contrary, the *Epistles* often put him in the position of having to give guiding advice to those whom he himself had formerly involved, if only by his example,

in friendship of the Muses. We shall not be surprised to find
him informing Titius of the difficulties that await an imitator of
Pindar, and how one must adroitly transpose the inimitable;
the advice that he gives Celsus touches on the more general
problem of imitation, so important in the aesthetics of the
ancients.

Besides, Horace could not so soon forget "the imperishable
monument," raised only yesterday, which was to ensure that he
would not die entirely (*Od.* III 30). How could he lose interest
in the audience that he had found in the public? And also what
was becoming of those poetic ideas, those forms that he had
introduced and whose fecundity was being demonstrated or
their efficacity compromised by other poets who had been inspired by them? It is a problem of that kind that he approaches
under the form of a pleasantry in *Epistle* I 19. Will the poet be a
water drinker or a wine drinker? That is, will he be an artisan-
artist, a craftsman (twenty times on the loom . . .), or someone inspired? We are to understand that here he wished to
have his say. Literarily speaking, he was on the side of the
water drinkers, this is sure. In the first *Satires,* he had already
praised the work of the file and told of the enervating fatigues
of perfecting. His last work, the *Ars poetica,* would end with the
comical portrait of the inspired man, hirsute and barely dis-
tinguishable from a madman. The *Odes* themselves are masterpieces of construction and precision. But we also find there
the least equivocal portraits of inspiration of a dionysiac type:
"Where are you leading me, Bacchus, all filled with you? . . .
Evoe, evoe, spare me" (*Od.* II, 19, 507; III 25, 1-2); and it is
normal that these very striking texts should have caught readers'
attention more than others. Horace thus was irritated to find
that he himself had seemed to stand surety for a type of poetry
that he had always detested, one that under the guise of being
inspired resigns itself lazily to disorder. It is possible, too, that
the sharpness of his mockery was a response to the appearance
of a new style: the doctrine of the "sublime" appeared in
precisely the years we are discussing, and one of its essential
dogmas was that certain negligences are the inevitable price
to be paid for the highest beauty.

Thus the interest he felt in his young friends, the very

existence, whatever he might say, of his lyric works, kept bringing him back to thought on to aesthetic problems. The date of the second *Epistle* to Florus (*Ep.* II 2) can be set at 19, and thus very near to those of the first book and doubtless anterior to its publication or distribution (since Florus is still surprised not to have received either a letter or an ode from the poet). Horace here approaches in the most explicit fashion the problem of the poetic vocabulary: the repudiation of colorless and inefficient words, no matter how commonly used; the revival of old words, the adoption of neologisms; the necessity of pruning the vegetation of synonyms, of adroitly composing the sentence so that all roughness, all displeasing shocks, are avoided.

It is difficult to believe that a writer who had a taste for giving his opinion on such specific details did not somewhat frequent the books of the theoreticians. The *Ars poetica*, in fact, does repose upon very extended and deeply assimilated reading of these special works. In the solitude of his country retreat, Horace did not confine his reading to philosophers. Doubtless firmly determined not to write any more real poems himself, he read with pleasure those that were sent to him, he thought about those that were being prepared, he pondered, perhaps more diligently than ever before, the theoretical problems posed by poetry. All this would happen again; but until then it was this still lively curiosity of his on these matters that would make others turn again to him, this time leaving him no way to escape, for the composition of a new poem.

5 · Glorious Epilogues

IT IS REALLY very difficult to sustain glory. In spite of oneself, the passing years consolidate one's burden of obligations. One could not have written the *Epodes*, the *Satires*, the *Odes*, and recently the *Epistles*, and protest that from now on one wished to live like a hermit and concentrate on saving one's soul. Society accommodates itself ill to these sudden reversals, which it is always tempted to see as some kind of caprice, and a waste, if not trechery: the old literary man was required to remain true to his type. He must play his role to the very end. He must lend his talent to add luster to an official ceremony, and the result would be the *Carmen saeculare*. His opinions would be sought, and he would be consulted on a grave matter that preoccupied Augustus himself: the conditions under which the theater could take on a new impetus, in such a way as to satisfy the exigencies of art but also please the people, and thus bring something to the building of the national community by bringing together and exalting the souls of all the Romans. Horace would therefore write an *Epistle* to Augustus. Then, a little later, desirous of developing his arguments, perhaps to modify his conclusions, he would write that *Epistle* to the Pisos which would soon be called the *Ars poetica*. Between times, some odes gathered in a new book bring to us, together with some state pieces that recall the *Carmen saeculare*, the last meditations of our poet. Glorious epilogues of a life that would continue for twelve more years, from 20 to 8, that we can be sure remained beautiful, active, and personal, but that we can no longer follow step by step.

THE CARMEN SAECULARE

During the years following the battle of Actium, the peaks of
Roman life were the moments when the prince, too often
called to the farthest provinces, re-entered his mother city with
his followers. In August 29, Octavius returned from the Orient.
He celebrated three triumphs in connection with his operations
in Dalmatia, the victory of Actium, and the subjection of
Egypt; Vergil published his *Georgics* and Horace, probably, his
Satires. In spring of 24 Augustus returned from Spain, conqueror
of the Cantabri. In 23, he regularized his own political position
by deposing the consulate and assuming the tribunal power
again; the edileship of Marcellus was an opportunity for him
to recommend and introduce the young man to the Romans as
the one who might some day be his successor; Horace published
his *Odes*. In the autumn of 19, Augustus returned from the
Orient. Through diplomatic means he had put in order a
problem that had been arousing passionate Roman opinion for
more than thirty years: the Parthians had consented to restore
the standards that they had taken from Crassus in 53 and had
accepted a sort of sovereignty of the Romans. With Tiberius,
Drusus, and Agrippa (who had become Augustus' son-in-law in
21), a group of solid personalities, a family, had grown up again
around the prince. In 18, Augustus, invested with a *regimen
morum legumque*, was striving to purify the Senate and promul-
gating laws against bribery, on the family and the celibate, and
against adultery; it is probably at this moment that the *Aeneid*
was published. He departed again in 16 for Gaul, for Spain, and
it is at the end of this new trip that on the occasion of his
return to Rome the *Ara Pacis* would be dedicated (July 13);
Horace then published his new book of *Odes*.

The secular games of 17 were the public celebration, the great
ceremony, that was to solemnize the historic moment of the
peaceful victory over the Orient. The emperor asked Horace
to compose a hymn that would be a part of the official liturgy,
and which we read in our manuscripts under the title *Carmen
saeculare*.

We have a particularly circumstantial knowledge of the
program of the celebration: Phlegon of Tralles and Zosimus
have preserved for us the text of the oracle, an extract from

the Sibylline books, which was a sort of rough draft for the organizers. Since 1890 we have also possessed an epigraphic memorial which gives us the *commentarium ludorum saecularium,* that is, the text of the official documents which instituted the ceremony, and then the transcript of the ceremonies themselves. A visitor at the Musée des Thermes can easily decipher the information that the third day, after the sacrifice offered to the Palatine, "twenty-seven young boys and twenty-seven young girls still having their mothers and fathers sang a hymn. And in the same way at the Capitol. *Carmen composuit Q. Horatius Flaccus*" (lines 145 *et seq.*). It is a very moving meeting for a man of today, since our own eyes can see lines on the stone which were without any doubt read by the happy eyes of Horace: official testimony by his contemporaries to a poem that we still admire.

This long inscription from which Horace's name emerges for a moment makes us very much aware that the *Carmen saeculare* is not a work of pure literature like, for example, the other odes of the same poet. To understand it, it is not enough to have taste and some knowledge of the poetry of antiquity; we must restore in our minds the liturgical ensemble, the intentions that governed the ordering of the ceremonies. Only then will we be in a position to appreciate the ingenuity, the emotion, the talent, all that part of himself that the poet put into this work and that his friends could immediately recognize in it, though others no doubt received only a more distant effect from a work that was a penetrating one, but difficult to disentangle from all the other contributions of the festival. It is thus that a man in lending his voice to a people gives it a part of his soul.

Originally, secular ceremonies seem to have consisted of rites of purification and propitiation. Their principal object was to conjure away or avert epidemics and, generally speaking, anything that threatened the development and health of a rising generation (*saeculum*). Theoretically they took place occasionally, when the need for one was felt, without a fixed schedule or perhaps every thirty years, the normal duration of a generation. But the influences that modified the sense of the word *saeculum* by giving it a definite chronological value —100 or 110 years (that is, the longest span of the life of a man)

—were to separate the secular festival from its concrete connections: it was now to seem intended to effect on the scale of the century the periodical purification and rejuvenation that the annual games had already long sought on a yearly basis.

It does not seem that the festival under its new guise immediately acquired very great prestige; neither in 249 (when it became receptive to Hellenistic innovation) nor in 146 does it seem to have marked an important date in the history of the Roman people. But during the second century some new religious conceptions and new preoccupations were introduced in Rome that would permit the secular ceremonies to exercise a powerful influence on the imagination. There are ages when, in the order of time, the real horizon—the one on which thoughts have their movement—is very near; chronology, when anyone thinks of it—and it is chiefly a matter for specialists— has only an abstract reality: it is merely a convenience for arranging the years, whose only importance is their concrete content. In other circumstances, on the other hand, it seems that periods of time themselves have specific qualities from which each year, each event arising from day to day, receives its beneficient or maleficient character. Then people wonder about the future and speculate about the ages of the world; gods and planets cross and join their influences to give each its well-defined character. Human impatience finds it difficult to entertain the thought that the next age may noticeably resemble the one in which one is living; every age must be decisive and mark a turning point; hope, after all, is one of the biological and perhaps divine ingredients of humanity. These general tendencies were reinforced in Rome by a certain catastrophism (which seems to have been of Etruscan origin) and by all the lassitude of a society that was exhausted by civil wars but sure that one day they would end. All through the first century and from the age of Sylla on, it appears, they had been waiting for something. Vergil's work, from the fourth *Bucolic* to the *Aeneid*, shows us the breadth and reverberations of these hopes: Augustus not only had to reconstruct Rome day by day but he also had to mark a conclusion of the past and open a new era: the golden age. It is probable that he had been thinking about it for a long time, perhaps since 23.

In fact, calculations were not enough to indicate a firm date: what was the exact length of a century, and starting from when should one count periods? It was necessary, at the same time, to recognize the signs of stars or events, which marked off periods of time. The comet that appeared at the time of Caesar's funeral ceremonies had been, at its time, such a sign. But the subjection of the Orient by the Occident (or vice versa) must also have been a very great sign; since the Romans had set foot in Asia, then in Egypt, a whole oracular literature had developed on that theme, and we have seen that certain of Horace's odes were influenced by it. No doubt Augustus thought that the surrender of the Parthians made it opportune for him to accomplish the solemn act that would fix and crown, to the benefit of his work, all the anxious and hopeful waiting that had kept his people in suspense for so long. To this end, it is clear that the best would be to have recourse to the ancient formula of secular games, if only because of the name they carried, which now would have such a prestigious sound: *Aurea condet saecula*. The year 18 was passed by the college of quindecemviri in studying, recopying, and culling the collection of Sibylline books. These magistrates, profiting from the obscurity that enveloped previous celebrations, thus rediscovered games in 126 and in 236 that could be vaguely connected with the ceremonies once planned for the first official celebration of a secular festival in 348, since from 348 to 17 there were three centuries of 110 years each.

The ritual of the festival was composed of very diverse elements. It was not the games properly speaking that gave it its most original character: theatrical presentations, and no doubt hunts, chariot races, and performances by balancers, fighters, and gladiators—these entertainments were to be found in all Roman festivals. They were important, too, to the extent that they magically exalted the vitality of the people and delighted the gods, those spectators and objects of the festival. Prayers and sacrifices indicated their specific intentions. Originally these were addressed for three nights, in the place called Terentum, near the elbow of the Tiber, to a divine couple— an earth mother and a god, who was both celestial and Chtonian, a pair who had been identified since the third century with

Dis and Proserpina. In that same age there had been added
to them, but in a somewhat subordinate position, some completely Hellenic figures, the Moirai and the Ilithyiae, goddesses
of destiny and of birth. The quindecemviri, presided over by
Augustus, retained the nocturnal ceremonies, dedicating the
first night to the Moirai (Horace calls them the Parcae), the
second to the Ilithyiae (or to Ilithyia; Horace preferred the
singular), the third to the Earth Mother. But their most important innovation was to double the cycle of three nights by
adding a cycle of three days in honor of Jupiter and Juno (day
avatars of Dis and Proserpina), then of Apollo and Diana, together with the Palatine temple. It is probable that at this
distance many elements escape us that justified, facilitated, or
even suggested these innovations. They indubitably had the
effect of giving the ceremonies a character that was more agreeable, less strange, less archaic, and more universal, by associat-
ing with them the great gods of Rome and the great sanctuaries,
the Capitol and the Palatine, under their familiar names. Thus
the secular games, adorned with the prestige of the most mysterious past and the most secret divinities, would be illumined
by the glow of a great historic destiny, which was to be sought
under the eyes of the gods on high.

We see immediately that Horace, made responsible for expressing the spirit of the whole festival in his hymn, had to try
to unify all these diverse inspirations. Disparate elements, which
might be harmonious in ceremonies carried on for three days
and three nights and in different places, would have been
shocking if, in a hymn of some three hundred words, they had
resulted in a juxtaposition of anomalous stanzas and themes.
In fact, Horace overcame this difficulty so adroitly that until
the discovery of the *Acta* it was almost impossible to discern
not only the structure of his poem but even, in more than one
case, the true nature of the divinities of whom he was thinking.
We can now understand that he successively invoked all the
divinities of the festival, Parcae, Ilithyia, Earth, Jupiter and
Juno (unmistakably indicated in lines 45–52 by the mention of
the white victims who were offered to them), and finally
Apollo and Diana (with the sun and the moon which are their
cosmic emblems). Careful to avoid any confusion, he named

those divinities only (Ceres and Jupiter in lines 30 and 32 are metonymies; Venus in verse 50 appears only in a narration). Some retouching was done to make sure of a unity of tone. When the poet transforms the Moirai into Parcae and makes Lucina appear behind Ilithyia, it is easy to believe that he wishes to extenuate the exoticism of the rites and bring the Romans back into the framework of their city and their national tongue. His poem is not less Greco-Roman than the ritual of the festival, but the somewhat esoteric Hellenism of the mysteries is replaced by poetic Hellenism, whereby Apollo becomes Phoebus, and the legend of Trojan origins assures the Romans of the favor of the gods.

It is by that unity of tone that the very simple and very harmonious structure of the poem is made possible:

3 stanzas (ll. 1–12) for Apollo and Diana
5 stanzas (ll. 13–32) for the nocturnal divinities
1 stanza (ll. 33–36) for Apollo and Diana
6 stanzas (ll. 37–60) for the Capitoline divinities
3 stanzas (ll. 61–72) for Apollo and Diana
1 stanza (ll. 73–76) epilogue dedicated to all the gods

We find again here the embracing arrangement that is so typical of Horace's art.

Although each series of divinities is honored by approximately the same number of lines, there is nonetheless a perceptible imbalance with reference to the ritual, in which the Palatine divinities occupied only one day and those of Terentum three nights. It is further increased because the presentation of the nocturnal divinities has been made, as we have seen, in an Apollonian vocabulary. Finally, Apollo and Diana, invoked at the beginning, the middle, and the end of the hymn, are much more clearly and affectionately individualized than the other gods. This apparent disproportion is no doubt explained by the fact that Apollo is not only one of the divinities of the festival but also the master of the whole ceremony, thanks to his connection with the quindecemviral college and to the Sibylline oracles: so that what emerges from the hymn is not a preeminence of Apollo, but the universal invocation of this god to introduce the prayers of men to all other gods. This theology of an Apollo-mediator, rather solidly based in the Roman tradition, is also to be found in the *Aeneid,* and it is perfectly possible that Augustus made it his own. Horace is also happy in it, for the Apollo of whom he is thinking is the god of poets and of the Muses (l. 62): in a certain sense he is poetry itself, never out of place, a mediator between men, heroes, and gods (*Od.* I 12), the principle of that wisdom which gives immortality (*Od.* III 4, 37–42). This extremely beautiful idea of mediation by poetry, which is identified with light, speech, and wisdom, is one of those that sustained the religiosity of the time, for it invited authentic philosophical support—we are not far from the Platonic *logos*—and could call to its aid the religious presentations and traditional images by which all hearts were moved.

It is certain that in the minds of the organizers one of the principal ends of the festival was the announcement and opening of a new age. And there was a danger that precisely that point might not be too clearly made by ceremonies inherited from a time in which there had been little speculation about the succession of ages. The hymn had to be more explicit here than the ritual. With all the prudence of form that was appropriate to an official text—the words "golden age" are never spoken, even when the reality (ll. 57–60) is directly called up— Horace did not fail of this obligation. He fulfilled it in the new spirit manifested by the changes made in the liturgy; he wished all to be light and hope. A century that begins is also a century that ends: to found a new era is also to bury the impurities of the era that is ending, and *condere lustrum* has that double meaning. Horace speaks only of the future: not a word of the purifications, although they held a very important place in the festival; a single reference—and at that, the mere phrase "pleasant nights" (l. 24)—is made to the rather oppressive expiatory ceremonies that took place in the darkness of Terentum. Nothing on the past, that past of civil wars and disorders, which it would have been so easy to call up for a last time in order to dismiss it forever. The dimensions of that hope that Horace wishes to arouse are clearly marked by geographical and chronological boundary signs. Rome is in the center, but the horizons are the very limits of the world. The security for the hope goes back more than a thousand years, being founded on the promises made in Troy of Asia: a new offspring of Venus and Anchises is bringing the benedictions of the past to the race of Romulus. The prince—whose name itself is not pronounced—appears only for a moment, in his liturgical functions, sacrificing white victims to Jupiter and Juno. Everything is committed to the good offices of the eternal gods. It is the spirit of the *Aeneid* that floats over these stanzas, where Horace in his own way (ll. 51–52) takes up the famous phrase "Honor the vanquished, crush the rebellious" (*Aeneid*, VI, 853), and then transposes the very lines in which his friend had prophesied the founding of the new age, and the expectancy of an earth stupefied before the growth of Rome (*Aeneid*, VI, 798–800).

With his love of life, Horace was no less at ease in faithfully and expressively rendering the most ancient intent of the secular liturgy: to avert the dangers that threaten biological equilibrium and the flourishing of everything that comes to light. Hence his wishes for the fertility of the earth, the healthfulness of waters and winds, the happiness and fecundity of marriages; hence his prayers to the goddesses of childbirth, and his recollection of an Apollo who was a doctor for the body (ll. 63–64), perhaps the first Apollo of the Romans. All this is linked, further, with the most current preoccupations of the imperial administrators, who had promulgated laws the year before for the reform of social customs and population increase. On these laws, too, the poet calls down the benediction of the gods.

But what constitutes the rarest success of the hymn is the contribution that Horace was able to draw from his choristers. These young boys and girls were no doubt given him, even imposed upon him, by the ritual. The words *pueri, puellae*, return constantly, but for Horace the young people were not merely performers responsible for uttering phrases: the solemn hymn was adapted to their age. He translates the naïveté of childhood: "O Sun, in your journey may you never see anything greater than Rome"; its bashful wonder before the mysteries of life, in which the singers will soon be involved: "You who cause the gentle opening of ripe fruits, protect mothers, Ilithyia;

goddess, let our descendants by many, give success to our Fathers' decrees upon women about to be linked in the yoke of Hymen, and the laws that will join us for the creation of new children"; its innocent pride: "Jupiter and all the gods join with these sentiments, I feel within me a happy and sure hope of it, I, the chorus taught to say the praises of Phoebus and Diana." It was through the eyes of that youth that Horace wished to see the great renovations of the city. The *saeculum* loses here a little of its apocalyptic grandeur. The poet does not wish to tie it in with those celestial mechanisms whose evocation gives so much solemnity to the beginning of the fourth *Bucolic*. His own "age" is a celebration of the youth and innocence of the race. It is not astonishing that in living with them during the rehearsals he forgot the civil wars and the dark days of the past, those days of which they were pure.

Mille puellarum, puerorum mille furores, the austere Damasippus had grumbled (*Sat.* II 3, 325), and after that we had Chloe, Lalage, and so many charming odes. While we hear the seven hills resounding to the virginal stanzas of the *Carmen saeculare*, it is rather beautiful to find in it again, in another form, the same tender preoccupation with the freshness of the newly born and growing.

THE LAST LYRIC BOOK

After the *Carmen saeculare* Horace did not return to his retreat. He wrote and published the fourth book of *Odes*, in which the reader who has made an effort to live with him step by step will find more than one surprise.

First, there is the very existence of the book. During the preceding years, the poet had continually repeated that he had finished forever with the trifles of the lyre, and that he must now devote himself entirely to the too much neglected care of his soul. What happened, then, that he should have been willing so lightly to give himself the lie, without seeming to remember the resolutions that we had thought to be so serious? We might at least expect to find in this reborn lyricism an echo of his recent readings in the company of the philosophers. Even before he was completely converted, Horace had often celebrated a poverty contented with what it had, and the indifference and careful reserve of the wise man in the face of wealth and power; but none of these themes reappears here. The picture that we had had was that of a slightly anxious sensitivity, quick to be wounded and to take offense. We have seen our poet withdraw into himself, disdaining to be read by the "crowd with its sweaty hands" (*Sat.* I 4, 72), wary of the vulgarly envious (*Od.* II 16, 39), and even more wary of the approaches of other literary people (*Ep.* II 2, 87–105). Here we see him expanding in his social success, congratulating himself on being pointed out in the street, and receiving the praise of his colleagues with satisfaction (*Od.* IV 3). These feelings in time of success are too natural for us to hold them against anyone. Our surprise here is not of a moral nature; it is on a literary plane: why use this naïve vanity to make a poem?

All this is not to make us cease loving Horace, but rather to make us have a better understanding of the mobile and unforeseeable nature of his genius. It would be stupid to accuse him, for this, of being superficial. Was Goethe superficial because he went on living after *Werther*? A genius such as Horace's, at the moment in which it is lending itself—it believes then, or pretends to believe, that it is giving itself—to a spiritual attitude, one that tomorrow or next year will no longer belong to it, does not stay on the surface; in one stroke it goes all the way to the bottom. That is why Horace's discoveries, even though glimpsed as in a flash of lightning, yet enrich the human patrimony more than the wearied, wearying, and careful fidelities of so many others.

Horace, then, had become an official poet, and was very pleased to be one. This aptitude for turning himself into a personage so different from those we had thought he could be makes us understand more readily why, during the preceding years, those who wished him well, Augustus and Maecenas, had thought of a public position for him. Their proposals had come at a bad moment; but in reading the pieces in which he so warmly claims his independence and his desire to devote himself only to his soul, we must not hasten to accuse his friends of incomprehension or coarseness. They knew and loved their Horace better than we can. After the poet, to man's eternal profit, had made good use for some time of a precautionary solitude, final events showed that Augustus and Maecenas had been right, since their hermit was so pleased one day to come out of his retreat. Later we will note an analogous metamorphosis, when our poet would assume hopes that he had once vigorously brushed aside: the same Horace who, in the *Epistle* to Augustus, felt the resurrection of a Latin theater to be inconceivable, would write the *Epistle* to the Pisos to say how work should be done there; and perhaps at that time he would be thinking of placing himself there personally. That versatility, which made a Yes succeed a No with the same inflexible resolution in both cases, was also at the origin of the events that I believe I have established in connection with *Epistle* 7: Horace accepts a situation prepared for him in Rome by Maecenas, *mersor civilibur undis*, then, after an attempt of some months, speaks only of letting everything go, *cuncta resigno*.

These reflections, imposed upon us by the reading of the new book of *Odes*, help us along the road of understanding how it happened that at one moment in his life, when he was writing his first lyric collection, Horace felt in an exceptionally keen, even anguished, way the fragmentation of continuity. The sense of being settled, which others find in themselves from the simple experience of their own inner continuity, was lacking in him. His haunted preoccupation with Fortune, with the incident that could throw everything into jeopardy, was in good part an external projection of that inner instability.

The composition of the book does not emerge very clearly: there is no real prologue (it is impossible to imagine that the book is dedicated to the Paullus Maximus who arises in the first piece); no real epilogue. One immediately distinguishes the two songs of victory (*epinicia*) which respectively celebrate Drusus (4) and Tiberius (14), each followed by a poem in a more personal tone addressed to Augustus (5 and 15). One also recognizes a group of light pieces: 11 and 12 are two invitations to dinner; 10 and 13 symmetrically evoke the afflictions with which age strikes young boys (10) and young girls (13); other odes—none of the preceding books contained so many—celebrate the power of poetry (2, 3, 6, 8, 9).

One piece, in the very center of the book—it is the seventh, *Diffugere nives*—will not fit into these groupings. It appears difficult to place with the light odes a piece that, without any counterargument, raises rather strikingly before the reader the perspective of definitive annihilation, total and perhaps imminent. Eduard Fraenkel has proposed, it seems to me with much plausibility, that this piece—assuredly one of the most beautiful that Horace ever wrote—should be given extreme importance, and seen as the spiritual seat of the whole book. If we group it with the preceding poem and the two following, integrating it in the cycle of the miracles of poetry, it will appear that Horace equilibrates the sadness of death with the perspective of an immortality conferred by poetry on those beings and objects, however frail, that it has touched. That this idea was in fact very important for Horace may be concluded from the careful manner in which he develops it progressively at the beginning of *Ode* 9. The thesis is this: epic poetry can immortalize its heroes, its great captains or great political leaders; but lyric poetry, too, has that power over the objects that belong to it: a sigh of Anacreon, a blush of Sappho cross over thousands of years, and so may the name, the person of a friend or a beloved on whom poetry has for a moment rested. The idea, which seems rather natural to us today, had not, in fact, appeared before. What Horace had formerly claimed with pride was the immortality of his name, the name of a poet, and of his work. He did not then explicitly take pleasure in meditating on that cortège of living figures that he carried along with him, who had also, thanks to him, become immortal for eternity. Neither in Catullus nor in the elegiacal poets—from whom it might have been expected that they would promise immortality to their mistresses—do I find anything similar, though the idea cannot have been far off. But it fell to Horace, so gifted in that direction, to be the first to have full awareness of it—awareness of the eminence of aesthetic dignity and of the possibilities of eternal consistency existing in what we would call today the life of a "person," the life of feelings and emotions.

It is possible that the success of the *Odes*, the brilliance with which that poetry, already so personal, had shed its light, had astonished Horace himself and had been a sort of revelation to him. Some years later, the choice that Augustus had made of him to write the secular hymn, and to write it in the very forms that he had just been making illustrious, must surely have seemed to him a consecration of all stanza lyricism. What he had written was, then, even much more important than he had thought. He would not only be immortal in his work; he too, like the greatest, had immortality to give. If this is a sort of discovery, a grasping of new possibilities springing up before the eyes of the poet, we understand better, perhaps, what seemed before to be merely a flare-up of vanity. We understand that he was animated by new hopes to write new *Odes*, and was determined, in this new collection, to carry even further his effort to set aside all convention and all apparatus, and to fix the most fugitive outlines—at first sight those least made for art —of what he had seen, loved, and felt, that they might be eternal too.

This new orientation that we are postulating is, I think, particularly perceptible in the tone that Horace henceforth chose to adopt to speak of Augustus and his work. In fact he expressed himself very clearly on the subject in *Ode* 2 (*Pindarus quisquis*), which is a sort of range taking vis-à-vis Pindaric lyricism, of which he had so successfully given samples in the *Roman Odes* of Book III and in the present book as well, in honor of Drusus and Tiberius. The very circumstances in which that second *Ode* was composed are extremely instructive on the present problem. We are in the year 13, at the end of the spring; Augustus is about to return from Spain. Everyone is thinking of the solemnities that will celebrate his return, and doubtless more than anyone else the praetor Jullus Antonius, to whom the ode is dedicated. It was natural that the idea of a lyric poem composed to the glory of the prince and republishing the success of the *Carmen saeculare* should occur to the minds of the organizers. Horace declines to take the task upon himself, and advises his friend to compose the poem himself. But in what form? Not a Pindaric lyric, whose dangers he calls up: "Whosoever attempts to compete with Pindar will know the fate of the son of Daedalus [Icarus] and will give his name to some crystal sea." Whatever has been said on the subject, it seems to me to be certain that Horace is thinking here not of the glory of the undertaking ("he will give his name"), which could not be promised to everyone ("whosoever"), but rather that inevitable catastrophe, which this time is certainly promised to everyone, that attends presumptuous undertakings. These words alone are therefore enough to assure us that Jullus Antonius is not being invited to Pindarize. Besides, how could Horace pretend that in that difficult art the young man would succeed better than he? Further, as most commentators have observed, Horace does not declare himself and no one else to be incompetent, withdrawing modestly before another lyric poet; he is denying the possibilities of lyricism. He advises that the poetry for the ceremony be of a more solemn tone, surely a poem in hexameters such as those through which, the scholia tell us, Jullus Antonius had already made himself illustrious. The situation is somewhat the same as in *Ode* I 6: when Horace is asked for a solemn poem, he sends the suitor off to a maker of "epics." For a set poem, answering to that rather special aspect of Pindaric art, the hexameter is most appropriate in Rome. Lyricism has other tasks.

Let us be sure to understand our poet: he did not think that his poetry was insignificant. He had been promising it immortality for a long time now. *Exegi monumentum aere perennius.* And perhaps it is at this very time that he had just discovered that it, too, could immortalize. But to attain these magnificent ends it must remain what it is, that is, a poetry of feeling, of personal expression. If a poet wished to raise its tone, Phoebus himself (cf. *Od.* IV 15, 1–2) would oppose him. But on the other hand this poetry, in its proper role as poetry of daily life, personal relations, and friendship, could be equal to the greatest subjects, among them the praise of Augustus. While Jullus Antonius would salute the return of the prince in a studied poem, Horace would not be mute: he would speak in his own name, mingling with the crowd and feeling the feelings of all the Romans who were not officials and who were expressing their gratitude as men, or their vivid joy: "Oh the beautiful, the admirable day!" It has been noted that these happy exclamations into which the poet would put his whole heart, joining in the spontaneous joy of the whole city *(civitas omnis)*, constitute the first hemistich of one of those trochaic seven-foot lines that usually lent their rhythm to popular enthusiasm: *O Sol pulcher, o laudande!* Let us remember here that even in the

Carmen saeculare Horace could not resign himself to the rather cold solemnity in which an official cantata should have vested itself. He turned it into a prayer for young boys and girls, that is, to a degree, into a piece of personal expression.

The perfect realization of this type of poetry is found here, in *Ode* IV 5 (to Augustus), which constitutes, from the point of view that interests us at the moment and from which the whole book probably takes its sense, the peak of Horatian lyricism. This ode is, unfortunately, one of those whose interpreters have been most led astray by the imprudent use of textual comparisons. What could one say to a prince, in the order of gratitude and affection, that had not already been besmirched by the impudence of flatterers? "When you are there," wrote Horace, "the day is gayer, the suns have more brilliance." Alas! in the same age, under other skies, official orators, priests and ambassadors were saying much the same thing and even much more, since for certain enslaved peoples there has never been a tyrannical master or tax collector whose face did not seem to shine like the sun. But this very point was one from which the rest of the universe, and especially Horace, as we can see in *Satire* I 7, could derive amusement. Should we believe that over the years the rapidly deteriorating Romans, especially Horace, had also lost the honor of language? Healthy criticism must interpret words in their context, and that context in the work of a whole life. When he wrote that appeal to Augustus not to put off his return too long, Horace in truth was expressing the feelings of personal affection that, in a healthy state, unite the leader with all citizens and make the fate of the one who has responsibility for all a part of the private life and, so to speak, the soul of all. The country thought of Augustus as a mother thinks of her most valiant son, whose absence worries the household and holds everyone's job in abeyance. Everyone thought that he would be happier, less anxious, if he were sure that Augustus was well and would soon return. It is not that they were awaiting some decision from him, or indeed anything in particular. They simply breathed better when he was there. Everyone passed the day in the hills or wedded the vine to the widowed trees. In the evening at the table, before the pot, they thought of him, mingling his divinity with that of the Lares.

Rural life, the relaxation of a celebration of friends, the effusion of sentiment, and national inspiration are here bound in a single sheaf. Horace was not wrong when he thought, as we have seen, that he had invented or discovered a new mode of immortality that was applicable to new objects. Augustus is immortalized in the *Aeneid* in his historic dimensions, through the admiration inspired by his genius, his infallible wisdom, and his happiness. One must be something of a philosopher to have access to this plane; and do we find Augustus there in his entirety? After two thousand years, Horace still makes us feel in an immediate way what the radiance of the prince can have been on a personal plane, and the attachment that the Romans felt toward him who was their salvation.

In this book, in which Horace was determined to have recourse to a medium tonality in dealing with what was closest to his heart, the works and the person of Augustus, he was also determined to show the maximum that the Pindaric form could accomplish for events and persons who were less close to him. Pieces 4 and 14, which celebrate the victories of Drusus and Tiberius, are obviously just as sincere in their inspiration as anything that he ever wrote; but in comparison with those most recent experiments that we have just been describing they seem rather to be "masterpieces," virtuoso performances. More than one artist has taken pleasure in thus learning just how far he could extend himself. The same judgment cannot be applied, however, to the last ode of the book, the fifteenth, to Augustus. It is obviously much more solemn than the other, the fifth, of which we have been speaking. Composed in Alcaic stanzas, it resembles in that the epinicia to Drusus and Tiberius; but, like *Ode* 5, it develops the central Horatian themes, praise of the peace and the active leisure instituted for everyone by the mere presence and person of the prince. The technique is also very different here: no longer Pindaric disorder, but the beautiful regularity of the Latin poem of praise, with its anaphoras which are supported and separated from prose by the tension of the metrical rhythm and the boldness of the enjambments. With its visions of fecundity, procession of infants and mothers, evocation of the Trojan past, illumination of a liberated world, and impression of a contained felicity, the poem somewhat corresponds to what plastic art gives us in the contemorary reliefs of the *Ara Pacis.*

Illustrated by the theoretical explanations that the poet gave us himself at the beginning of *Ode* 9, the *Odes* to Augustus suggest to us, then, that we should seek in this fourth book, as that which constitutes what is properly speaking new in it, a more complete and consciously willed fusion of all the elements of Horatian lyricism: a fusion, a synthesis, which the poet will realize in making himself more closely and constantly present in all that he writes. We can now see that it is in that sense that this book, so different from the *Epistles,* yet continues its central inspiration: a promotion, once and for all, of personal poetry. Some small details are significant: in the *Epodes, Satires,* and *Epistles,* Horace did not hesitate, when speaking of himself, to use his own name; he had never done so in the *Odes,* apparently feeling that it would be contrary to the dignity of the genre. In the same way, a purely personal memory like that of the good Cinara, a once-beloved mistress, had until now been evoked only in the *Epistles.* In the *Epodes,* in the *Satires,* and again in the *Epistles,* the poet had more than once confessed his weaknesses. Nothing of the kind had found its way into the *Odes.* In a more general way, a certain familiar poetry, made of day-to-day details, had continued to be excluded from the lyric works. In the fourth book of the *Odes,* all these barriers fell at once: the names of Horatius and Cinara appear in the open, without veil or pseudonym, in Alcaeus' stanzas; Horace confides to all his readers his sadness before his dying heart, the tears that fall drop by drop on the cheeks of the aging man who has become incapable of making himself loved. Literary fancy, they say. Let us state simply that in the preceding books the poet had never been taken by that "fancy" of apparent confession: one needs only compare the last lines of *Ode* IV 1 with a piece on an analogous subject like *Ode* III 26. In the first collection we had often read invitations to dinner, but it is only here (*Od.* IV 11) that the poet includes a picture of the preparations for the reception: servant girls and scullions busying themselves, and the spirals of black smoke (*sordidum*) rising from the stoves. Indubitably all this bears witness to an intent of using lyricism to raise to the final consistency of art many little things that until then had appeared only in the *sermo* and in poetry of the most fugitive kind, intended to amuse no one but its recipient and to be quickly forgotten.

In this perspective, we see that it is necessary to reverse certain rather hastily formed judgments having to do with alleged flaws of taste that supposedly disfigure this book. A flaw of taste, the confession of the poet's feelings for Ligurinus, and the impotent distress of the old man (fifty-two years old) in love? A flaw of taste, the display of his author's vanity, a Horace pointed out in the street and delighted to be directing the rehearsals of his hymn? The facts are to be taken otherwise. Arrived at this point in his literary development, Horace became aware that in the end, and from whatever slant, everything that is deserves to be; and consequently to be eternal; and hence to be said. It is another side, or a logical sequence, of the metaphysical liberalism that we have noted in the *Epistles*: all is true.

We can now approach, in conclusion, one of the most famous difficulties presented by this book: Who is the Vergilius to whom the invitation of the twelfth *Ode* is addressed, and how should we take this poem? We can be fairly certain that it is the author of the *Aeneid*, and not a homonym: C. M. Bowra has demonstrated that the piece is composed from one end to the other of borrowings from Vergil, adaptations of words and turns of phrase that are peculiarly Vergilian; this pursuit would be incomprehensible if Vergilius were not Vergil. Difficulties remain to be solved which would be there even if the person for whom the *Ode* is destined were someone else: a perfume seller, the scholiasts tell us. Horace advises his guest to put aside for a moment his concern for gain; a client of young noblemen, he is always preoccupied with feasting at the homes of others without opening his purse; but this time, beware! Horace will not welcome him at his table unless he brings his share, the perfumes needed for the feast. If that is said seriously, it cannot be very agreeable to hear. If the poet is joking, I would find it easy to believe that this is precisely the type of joke that one must not make to a merchant. Can one conceive of an invitation to dinner that is a satire on the person one is inviting? This sort of jesting, if it is not to run the risk of wounding, must assume a guest who is precisely *not* notably a prey to either the *studium lucri* or the taste for good fare. One can suppose that our Vergil fairly well fills these two conditions. Horace can, without danger, pretend to believe that if his guest hesitates to go out it is in order not to have to share expenses with other diners, in order to accumulate even more money by his unrelenting labor.

People have spoken of indecency, even of bad feeling. Surely we can exclude bad feeling: the echoes of the *Aeneid* in the *Carmen saeculare* and in the last stanza of the last ode of the present Book IV express clearly enough the admiration of Horace for the greatest poet of his time. Only—is it then so difficult to conceive of it?—Vergil for Horace was not only the greatest poet of Rome, he had also been his friend. If the originality of the lyricism in this last book of *Odes* consists precisely in fixing forever what formerly neither Horace nor others had thought could be made eternal, why would Horace not have wished to keep for us a picture that only he could draw of his friend and their long friendship? Far from thinking that he treated Vergil badly or lacked respect for his memory, Vergilians should rather be grateful to him for this little, unpretentious, but exquisitely written, piece, which is all that we have to allow us to catch a glimpse of the great poet in the last years of his life, seldom going out, walled up in his work, needing to be told by others that spring had come to the earth; but not absolutely alone, surrounded by distinguished young people who admired him, and still capable of laughing at the jests of an old friend who sought to amuse him: "Mingle with your serious thoughts, when you still can, a short folly; it is sweet to be mad on occasion."

At the concluding moment of his last lyric work, Horace restores, by grouping together *Odes* 11 and 12, the proximity of those eternal friends Maecenas and Vergil, one dead, the other still there, whose two names in *Odes* I 1 and I 3 had opened his first collection. This little man, volatile and variable, who always had so much trouble in grasping his own inner continuity and building a true moral adventure on that certainty, had in his friendships—and much more than Vergil—a genius for fidelity. Vergil soared; he saw things from too high for ephemeral beings really to exist before him. Did he himself exist in his

own eyes, while Roman destiny, and centuries contained within
one another and symbolizing one another, appeared to him,
reflecting one another to infinity? Horace, on the contrary,
because he installed himself on the level of his own life, was
also capable of seeing others and interesting himself in them.
He remained more faithful to them than to himself, and who
can be surprised? It is in ourselves that we experience the flight
of time and our almost irremediable fragmentation. Our friends
change too, but we see it much less. The sense of the reality
of their existence reassures us a little on the solidity of our own.
They are a marking post for us. They send us back the image
of what we ourselves once were, "under the reign of the good
Cinara" (*Od.* IV 1, 4).

THE LETTERS ON THE THEATER

While the *Epistle* to Florus (*Ep.* II 2) belongs to the same
vein as the first book of *Epistles*, being made up of personal
confidences and expressing Horace's ever livelier taste for retreat
and philosophy, the *Epistle* to Augustus (*Ep.* II 1) and the
Epistle to the Pisos (*Ep.* II 2, or *Ars poetica*) describe other
concerns and bring up very different problems: the present
position of poetry, and questions relative to dramatic art.

The *Epistle* to Augustus can be dated with some precision:
lines 252–53 repeat textually, by a voluntary allusion whose
intention is made clear by the context, lines 11–12 of *Ode* IV
14. This established connection makes us perceive others, either
with the same *Ode* or with *Ode* IV 5. Now, these two odes were
composed in the year 15 (or 14) and in 13. The *Epistle* to
Augustus must have been written in 13 or in 12. No doubt it
would be imprudent to go further back: the allusion that we
have mentioned would lose much of its interest if it went back
to a poem that was already old. Besides, in lines 111–13, Horace
presents himself as being then occupied with writing verse; we
will find it easy to believe that he refers to the fourth book of
Odes, which was apparently published in 13. We can thus
wonder whether the *Epistle* to Augustus was not, among other
ends, intended to introduce the fourth book of *Odes* to the
prince, as *Epistle* I 13 had, ten years earlier, indirectly presented
the first lyric collection. Only, since then Horace had become

bolder: he who had always been so careful not to importune
the prince with his verses (cf. *Sat.* II 1, 18–20; *Ep.* I 13) would
dare this time, after having defended himself a little (ll. 1–4),
to dedicate to him an epistle of 270 lines.

Often in our poet an epistle begins with pleasantries that for
a while will amuse the reader, who is curious to know where he
is being led. Horace's gaiety takes pleasure in it, and also his
desire to have his epistle retain the spontaneity of a familiar
letter. Here there is nothing of the sort, and that initial austerity,
which gives the piece something of the firmness of a report,
will not be contradicted by what follows: the prince is not a man
to be amused. The whole epistle, even when a smile slips into
it, evokes the presence of Augustus before us. But let us follow
the text step by step.

It is through the compliments of the beginning that Horace
will introduce the subject that is close to his heart: Augustus,
happier than the legendary heroes whose merits were often not
recognized until after their departure from this world, is during
his very lifetime an object of love and respect. In regard to him
the Romans have not felt the attraction of that blind envy
which, in all other cases, leads them to diminish the greatness
with which they live in order to honor the past. For in literature
as well, they wish to know only the works of the past; it is a
fixed point of view, a prejudice, shared equally by the critics
and the crowd that presses into the theater (ll. 5–62). How
wrong they are! Even in Greece, those masterpieces that we admire were the fruits of innovation. Everything changes; the
Romans of the past were chicaners, greedy for gain; now they
make verses; an innocent madness which, in the end, profits
the city (ll. 63–138).

Our ancestors were peasants, and their first amusements were
so gross that the law had to intervene to put down their excesses. Greece, at last, civilized us, but we retained for a long
time, we still retain, more than one mark of our original rusticity.
It was already very late when we applied ourselves to the study
of the Greeks and especially the tragic poets; in that domain we
would have come off fairly well if we had made more demands
upon ourselves. Among us it is believed that comedy requires
even fewer scruples, less art. What a mistake! The plays of

Plautus frequently do not stand up. It is quite another effort, infinitely more costly, to which a poet must consent if he really cares about his reputation: but what can one do with such a public (ll. 139–207)!

Do not think that my reservations about dramatic art arise from the paucity of my desire to try myself at it. On the contrary, I admire the success of a true man of the theater as a tour de force, a miracle of magic. But if you wish to fill your library with works worthy of Apollo, do not forget those poets who, repelled by the caprices of spectators, prefer to dedicate their books to attentive readers. They have sometimes bored you, and yet it is to them that you must commit the care of your glory. A Vergil, a Varius— those are the names that honor your choice. Forgive the lowliness of my inspiration, which prevents me from equaling them. [ll. 208–70]

Two themes appear very clearly in this letter: an apology for contemporary literature, better than that of the past; and an apology for a literature that addresses itself to readers and that, in the most favorable conditions, is better in quality than dramatic literature. But these two themes unite: in Rome, the ancient literature was a dramatic literature, with Naevius, Ennius, Pacuvius, and Accius, while the modern literature is addressed to readers. There are therefore, in fact, two literatures: that of the past, which is a literature of the theater and is not worth much; and that of today, which is a literature of the study and which is excellent. Subsidiary developments help to reinforce this contrast: at the heart of the *Epistle* (ll. 126–38), a magnificent passage in praise of poetry concerns, according to all the evidence, lyric and moralizing poetry, that which forms the minds and hearts of the citizens, that which intercedes with the gods; in contrast, Horace compares the spell of the theater with the successes of the ropedancer and the magician. The passage on the coarseness of the Roman public (ll. 177–207) is also extremely important, since, even outside of any judgment on the repertoire, one concludes from it the impossibility of creating a dramatic literature of quality in Rome. It seems that the twice-drawn picture (ll. 103–107 and especially 139–60) of Roman rusticity is intended to prepare and confirm this thesis, as is the contrast established between the heaviness of the Romans and the airy lightness of the Greeks (ll. 90–117).

Coming from the pen of Horace, none of these ideas can surprise us. Esteem of Greek literature, disdain of the ancient Latin literature as peopled by careless and prolix pieceworkers, a resolute defense of the literature of today—all this was already in the *Satires*, as was the antipathy toward dramatic literature and all forms of popular art. We already knew that Horace had no taste for writing for everyone, that it was chosen readers and friends whom he proposed to please. We have seen that his quarrels of that time had been precisely with entrepreneurs of public amusements and official organizers of performances. At the time of the writing of the *Odes* this aristocratic attitude seems to have grown even stronger. Later, it is true, the part that he was given to perform in the celebration of the secular games and, correlatively, a better knowledge of the range of influence of his earlier work opened his eyes to what we would call the social mission of a poet. But if these new concepts had led him to see the ends of lyricism in a slightly different light, there is no reason for his views on the theater to have changed.

Thus, the problem here is not one of Horace's doctrine. The problem is to know why, after more than twenty years, he thought it important to take up these themes again, on this unique occasion when the prince gave him so long an audience. We must admit that the reasons do not appear immediately. In the *Satires*, the proclamation of these themes had to do with an opportunity for a personal apology: a young writer, representing a new school, affirmed his rights in relation to the ancients. But the Horace of the *Epistle* to Augustus had arrived at the peak of his glory. We would understand his defending himself against the reservations or criticism of younger men, as Cicero had had to do. But no: after the brilliant triumph of the moderns, Vergil, Varius, and himself, it was still the ancients who preoccupied him.

Or again: we can understand that in the *Satires* he might have denigrated the ancients in order to reach Lucilius, since he met that great name on the very ground on which he himself proposed to build his work. But why should the poet of the *Odes* feel such a lively disquiet over the prestige still enjoyed by Ennius' tragedies and Plautus' comedies? Finally, if the only matter at hand was to defend the moderns against the ancients, why this insistence on speaking of the theater? Why not have carried the debate to a field in which there could be competition and comparison, for example the epic? Why is it the tragedy of Pacuvius rather than the *Annales* of Ennius that is made a case in point? Why the insistence on supporting the thesis that even today the coarseness of the public makes the creation of a theater of quality impossible? The essential problem of the *Epistle* to Augustus is that everything in it seems to gravitate around the question of the theater, particularly the tragedy.

This problem can at least be clearly stated from a text like the *Epistle* to Augustus, which is relatively easy to interpret and dated with some precision; it seems to come up again in the *Epistle* to the Pisos, but under much more complex conditions. Yet the two works shed light on each other. There is no doubt that they are closely related; they were written at much the same time, and by a Horace who was remembering the first as he wrote the second. In editions of Horace we find an extended list of corresponding details that can be established as existing in the developments of the two poems. In each, the central point is dramatic art and its problems: but in the *Epistle* to the Pisos Horace gives his advice on how to judge the quality of works and, eventually, how to write good ones, while in the *Epistle* to Augustus he seems to exclude the possibility that the genre is a viable one for the Rome of his time, precisely as an art form. The contrast, very sharply marked in the *Epistle* to Augustus, between dramatic poetry (meant for the people) and poetry to be read (meant for persons of taste) does not appear in the *Epistle* to the Pisos; here, on the contrary, the advice given to the future dramatist is sometimes illustrated by examples from the epic. The contrast between ancients and moderns also has less place in the *Epistle* to the Pisos, where, on the other hand, we find broad considerations on the unity and propriety of a work of art.

How should these two works be situated chronologically? If we were to imagine the *Epistle* to the Pisos to be anterior to the *Epistle* to Augustus, would it not be strange that Horace was dedicating to the prince a work that would then appear to be a reworking or an abridgment, and that, furthermore, condemned and annulled those hopes of a dramatic revival so seriously contemplated in the *Epistle* to the Pisos? But if we put the works in the opposite order, it is much more readily understandable that the themes, first developed for Augustus in a new and original fashion, were now being taken up again for less important personages, in another work of a much more ample and somewhat didactic character; and here, naturally enough, the categorical and pointed character of certain judgments is more clearly implied. One generally writes the essay before the treatise, and it is the first work that gives the most spontaneous reactions, those that are most in conformity with what one has always thought.

To these general considerations it is possible to add other, more particular, ones deduced from history. There is no doubt that the revival of the Latin theater was a subject that preoccupied Horace's contemporaries. In the list of good poets that he slipped into *Satire* I 10 (ll. 40–45), it is the comic poet Fundanius who is at the top, "unique among the living in your pleasant talent for jesting in your light works with the ruses of a courtesan, helping Davus to dupe old Chremes"; then comes Pollio, the author of tragedies that Vergil had already (*Buc.* 8, 9–10) held to be equal to those of Sophocles; Varius, with the epic, and Vergil himself with his *Bucolics* appear only after these. Very fortunately, Octavius took an interest in these first attempts and encouraged them. At the time of his triumphs of 29, he had a modern tragedy, the *Thyestes* of Varius, figure in the program of the festival, and he honored the author with a million sesterces. He himself had undertaken to write an *Ajax* which he never finished (Suet. *Aug.* 85). We know that he had a taste for entertainments; he took pleasure in them and never made any mystery of the fact (*ibid.* 45); he even enjoyed the works of the old Latin comic authors, whom he frequently had performed (*ibid.* 89). As the years passed and the success of the Vergilian epic, Horatian lyricism, and the elegy of Tibullus and Propertius was established, it was easy to observe that the Romans were now equal to the Greeks, with the single exception that they still did not have a great theater.

And yet plays occupied a very important place in Rome, as

they did in Athens. Perhaps they were even more important in Rome, now that the great spectacles in the Forum were suspended and there was no more political eloquence, no Gracchus or Cicero, to arouse the crowds. It was now in the theater that the Romans lived their social life and what was left of their political life, as we so often see in Suetonius. Remembering what the theater had been in Greece, how could the Romans fail to have pretentions of emulation? Now that Rome, reborn under Augustus, had given herself a great literature, was it not paradoxical that in her collective festivals she should have to content herself with miserable entertainments, and that no artist should be found to orient these traditional spectacles toward a better future? A theater worthy of the name, addressing itself to the mass of Roman people, could have established spiritual bonds for all, a union of high quality: it would have been the temple and the school of the city. In any case it is clear that, in this opening out toward the broad public, poetry would also have gained, in robustness and in simplicity: when Horace almost exclusively defended the rights of the poetry that is meant to be read in private, when he allowed himself to believe that only that kind of poetry was real poetry, he did not take the measure of the dangers that, in the next generation, would appear so redoubtable and would eventually triumph.

Truly, it is only by making the hypothesis of plans and hopes of that kind that we can explain why the problems having to do with dramatic art hold so large a place in our two *Epistles*. To claim, as has often been done, that in discussing dramatic poetry Horace only meant to state principles that are valid for all poetry is to go directly in opposition to what emerges from the *Epistle* to Augustus, in which dramatic poetry is clearly contrasted with what for Horace is the only true poetry, poetry to be read. It is true that Aristotle wrote his *Poetics* with very special reference to theatrical works; but this is because he was writing in a period when the masterpieces of the Athenian stage eclipsed all other kinds of poetry. To imagine that Horace would fall into his footsteps without noticing that the Rome of the first century was not the Athens of the fourth, and specifically that it had no theater, is, it seems to me, to do little

credit to his judgment. Besides, even in this way everything is
not explained. For Horace to have spent so long in talking about
the theater, we must assume that the problem of the theater had
arisen.

We now see how strange it would be if Horace had first, in
the *Epistle* to Pisos, benevolently examined those hopes for a
renovation of the Roman theater, and even defined the conditions for their success, and then had written to Augustus, perhaps one of those most interested in the enterprise, to assure
him that it had no future. On the other hand, we can understand much better how Horace may not have clung to the
initial and negative position that he had defended in the
Epistle to Augustus. Do we not often first spurn enterprises
and then rally to them, even to the point of collaborating in
them? It is much rarer to declare an enterprise to be without
a future when we have taken some pains with it and even
lent it our name. The Horace of the *Epistle* to the Pisos is a
Horace who had in part rallied to the hopes that he had
formerly criticized. Doubtless he was not yet really considering
writing for the stage. Yet the possibility that he would come to
it one day is not excluded (cf. ll. 234–43), and in the meantime
he is prodigal of advice to those who are younger and bolder.
The *Epistle* to the Pisos comes after the *Epistle* to Augustus.

The chronology that I am defending—and which is so important to the interpretation of the two pieces—is, furthermore,
the only one which satisfies the indications of outside criticism.
Porphyrio tells us that the person to whom the *Epistle* to the
Pisos was chiefly addressed was L. Calpurnius Piso Frugi the
pontifex, a consul in 15, son of Piso the Epicurean, Philodemus'
protector. This information is in all likelihood authentic. It is
not without importance that a link is thus established between
the *Epistle* and Philodemus, who had been a great theoretician.
Further, we know that Piso the pontifex honored poets. Many
epigrams in the Anthology still celebrate his memory because of
this. Now, this person was born in 49. It is difficult to suppose
that in 14 he had two sons old enough to take a personal interest
in literature. The nearer we place the *Epistle* to the end of
Horace's life, the less trouble we have in satisfying the data of
this little chronological problem. We can suppose that it was

written around the year 10. The arguments that have been
advanced to support an earlier date do not seem to me to be
very solid: Horace's silence on the epic—this argument supposes that Horace had to speak about the epic—would be explained by the fact that the publication of the *Aeneid* was
expected at any moment; it would then be 18. Or again,
Suetonius tells us that Horace wrote his *Epistle* to Augustus
after the latter had complained that no *Epistle* had been dedicated to him: M. Rostagni has felt that Augustus' complaint
would make sense only at a time when Horace had already
undertaken to compose long epistles (the *Epistle* to Florus . . .
and hence the *Epistle* to the Pisos) that would be truly worthy
of a prince.

The links and the order of succession that we have recognized
between the *Epistle* to Augustus and the *Epistle* to the Pisos will
be of singular assistance to us in interpreting that long *Epistle*.
As a matter of fact, most of the difficulties, often insoluble, that
have been raised in this connection arise from the presupposition
—in my opinion, entirely illusory—that Horace had intended to
write an Art of Poetry. To one who believes that, it was necessarily astonishing that he did not say a word about lyric poetry
and hardly mentioned the epic, and that everything seemed
oriented toward analysis of the virtues or the faults of the
dramatic poem. Everything created difficulties: everywhere
there were omissions, disproportions, and irrelevancies. It was
even worse when the *Epistle* was searched for a plan that could
be that of an Art of Poetry. Hypotheses and interpretations in
this regard have multiplied, especially since the publication in
1918 by the papyrologist Chr. Jensen of a fragment of Philodemus (found at Herculaneum), in which this learned theoretician criticized definitions of the words "poetry," "poem," "poet,"
and "poetic" given by one of his predecessors, Neoptolemus of
Parium. We already knew this person: Porphyrio had told us
that in the *Epistle* Horace adopted a certain number of precepts
given by Neoptolemus: "not all, but the most important."
Observing that after line 294 the *Epistle* ends with advice relative to morality and the literary hygiene of the poet, some
persons have imagined that Neoptolemus' treatise was divided

into three or four parts, each one having a title consisting of one of the terms whose definition was criticized by Philodemus; and it is this plan that they have tried to find again in the *Epistle* to the Pisos.

Of course, everything in this enterprise was illusory, since the point of departure was to bring in Porphyrio—who had spoken of borrowings of details—for authorization to seek in Horace the plan of a treatise by Neoptolemus. Add to this that it has never been possible to know with certainty what Neoptolemus placed under the words "poetry" and "poem," for we know his definitions only by some snatches of text and through the medium of the discussion of a critic (Philodemus) who was making every effort to make them look absurd and, especially, intrinsically contradictory. It is particularly difficult—and this has some importance, since the question is one of rediscovering a plan—to tell whether "poetry" came before "poem" in Neoptolemus, or the reverse. Finally, nothing suggests that the words "poetry," "poem," "poet" (in whatever order the first two must be placed) introduced the three parts of Neoptolemus' treatise. Philodemus does not say so, and in antiquity no other analogous treatise seems to have been so constructed. All this, therefore, collapses and sheds no light whatever on either the composition of the *Epistle* to the Pisos or Horace's intentions.

But these labors have not necessarily been in vain. It is often in pursuing the illusory that one discovers the real. So many texts exhumed, compared, and sifted, and the effort to restore the history of literary criticism and of literary theory, now bring to the reader of the *Epistle*—if we speak only of those results that concern Horace—a considerable number of clarifications of detail. We gain a better idea of what the critical and theoretical tradition was in which Horace had come to take his place. We have a better view of the diversity of influences to which he exposed himself. It is precisely as, year by year, the fan spread out more and more widely before the philologists' eyes that comprehension dawned: in the *Epistle* to the Pisos the central personage, the organizing intelligence, cannot have been Neoptolemus, or Heraclides of Pontus, or Aristotle, or Panetius. In the end it was to Horace, to the work itself constructed as a work, that it was necessary to return.

The *Epistle* to the Pisos opens with a grotesque picture of a poem without unity: a human head on the neck of a horse, a woman with the body of a fish, the marriage of a tiger and a lamb (1–13): it concludes with the burlesque portrait of the "inspired" poet, clinging like a leech to everyone that he hopes will listen to him (453–76). These pleasantries give and confirm the tone. This is not to be a formal treatise, but a conversation from which all pedantry is to be banished, and where musing, even some wandering, will be allowed. But a good joke always has a meaning. What Horace wishes us to understand from the very beginning is that the work of art must constitute a whole. That means that beauties of detail are justified only by their harmony with the ensemble (14–21). The beginning of a poem must correspond to its end (21–23). Here the best is the enemy of the good, if the perfection of a detail is to retain the reader's attention unduly. What is important is the general effect (24–37).

After this introduction, a more pressing imperative clearly marks a joint of the development: we are entering the heart of the first part of the *Epistle* (38–152): choose a subject that corresponds with what you are, and you will find easy expression and order (38–41). *Materia, facundia, ordo,* these are the three themes that are developed in succession. Only a few lines are devoted to order (42–45). We pass almost immediately to the section on expression (*facundia*), which will continue for some time (46–118) and is, so to speak, divided in two. It is not difficult to follow: form is considered first in itself (originality of vocabulary, effective use of ordinary words, neologisms, revival of old words (46–72), then in its application (to subjects, 73–92; to feelings that one wishes to express, 93–113; to the condition of the heroes whom one causes to speak, 114–18). There remains the *materia* (the word, in line 131, recalls the division announced in line 38). *Materia* can be found in two ways: either by establishing contact with literary tradition, *fama*, in which case the characters of the personages are already drawn and it is enough to conform to them (119a, 120–124); or by creating an entirely new fiction, in which case the only rule is the inner coherence of the personage; but Horace advises against this procedure as too difficult (125–30). What one is to do, then, is to dip into the common treasure of the legends, and there several dangers appear (131): becoming engulfed in matter that is amorphous and too drawn out (132); following an earlier work too closely (133); constricting oneself in too narrow a framework (134-35); and finally professing exaggerated ambitions (136-39). These four perils, introduced by a quadruple anaphora, are really only two: the second and third are obviously connected, and the fourth (with *cyclicus* 136) recalls the first (*patulum . . . orbem*).

A eulogy of Homer (140-52), brought in naturally by the evocation of that *fama* into which all poets dip, and by the words *Iliacum* (129) and *cyclicus* (136), gracefully concludes the whole first part. This passage is valid not only with reference to the lines that immediately precede it; it is so conceived as to gather up all the themes developed until now. It is clear, notably, that line 152 refers to the very first lines of the *Epistle*.

In line 153, Horace expressly announces to us that he is now going to concern himself with the theater: "Listen to what I desire, and what the public desires with me, if you wish to find enthusiasts who will wait for the curtain and stay in their seats until the leader of the troop says, 'Applaud!'" (153-55). It is the beginning of the second part of the *Epistle* (153-294). In fact, Horace has been speaking to us of the theater for some time now, without having announced the fact, and under the guise of general poetics; a kind of drift toward dramatic literature is perceptible in the first part from line 89 on: the principles he is defending are valid for any poetic work, but the illustration of these principles is regularly borrowed from the theater. In an analogous manner, the second part flows out of the first: Horace will arrive only progressively at the examination of the technical problems proper to the theater. The introduction of the second part has a transitional character: how to create a personage for the stage and make him live (146-78); these reflections, so far as the principle is concerned, could have equal validity for any literary work.

The three developments of the second part are easily discerned: the distribution of dramatic material (scenes to be played and scenes to be recounted; the laws of five acts and three actors; the function of the chorus and the encroachments

of the musicians, 179–219); Satyric drama (220–50); the problems of metrical form and the old Roman dramatists (251–74).
The difficulty arises from the presence, in the middle of parenetic
developments, of two sections that seem to be historical and
hence heterogeneous to the rest, one on the evolution of stage
music (202–19), the other on the history of the Greek and
Roman theaters (275–94). As a matter of fact, these are not
extraneous sections. Each of them makes a tight unit with the
preceding development. The section on music is in rapport with
what can be expected of the chorus: Horace's idea is that the
musicians have arrogated more and more importance to themselves, corrupting the simplicity that is appropriate to the com-
ments of the chorus, which have as a result taken on a swollen
and torrential quality; it is up to the poet to react against this
trend, to defend himself against the musician and bring the
chorus back to its authentic function. Thus lines 193–219 form
a whole.

The coherence of lines 275–94 with what has preceded them
is less evident. This is because we are approaching the end of
the second part, and Horace is allowing himself here, as in the
eulogy of Homer at the end of the first part, a little liberty: a
brilliant tableau occurs which has a conclusive character, acting
as a boundary mark for the reader. Yet—and this was also true of
the eulogy of Homer—these lines are in fact connected with
what has preceded them. We must not see it as a tableau contrasting the Greek theater with the Roman theater; the distinction between the genres within the dramatic literature of the
Greeks (275–84) makes sense only in relation to line 285:
"There is nothing of all that that our poets have not tried" and
then have even invented new genres (286–88); their only
weakness is their indifference to form (289–94). Thus these
lines as a whole, at the same time that they brilliantly conclude
the whole second part, add correction and confirmation to the
last of its three developments, the one that has to do with
metric form in poems and the old Roman dramatists. We have
noted that at the beginning of the second part of the *Epistle*
(devoted specifically to dramatic problems) Horace handled the
transition from the first (devoted to the more general problems
of literary works) by progressing from a problem that still

touched upon general aesthetics (the delineation of characters) to more special problems (the five acts, the chorus, and so forth). Now we will note that at the end of the second part, the passage to the general considerations that will take up the third part of the *Epistle* (the poet) is also handled by the generality of the views into which the development devoted to theatrical metrics flows. In that itinerary, which leads us from general problems to dramatic problems (the heart of the work), and then leads us back to general problems, the intention and meaning of the *Epistle* to the Pisos become clearly visible: the subject is not the art of poetry in general, illustrated by examples borrowed from the theater; it is dramatic poetry as it must be if it is to answer to the general exigencies of poetry.

The second part of the *Epistle* had ended on a warm note of optimism and confidence in the natural aptitudes of the Romans: "Latium would not be less powerful in its language than in its valor or the glory of its arms if for all its poets the slow labor of the file were not a stumbling block." The third and last part (295–476) will begin in a contrasting fashion, using for an introduction (295–304) the grotesque portrait of a poet so smitten with the determination of preserving the integrity of his inspiration that he becomes unsociable and neglects his beard and his bath. All the third part will be treated in the same tone of fine humor. But the object is nonetheless serious. It is the problem of the poet, and more precisely of the efforts to which he must consent if he is to create a work of value.

As in the first part in lines 38–41, here too Horace announces a plan (306–308). Again three developments: "Whence come the resources of talent, what makes a poet grow and forms him (ll. 309–46); what is fitting, and what is not fitting (ll. 347–407); where good judgment or error leads" (ll. 408–76). The first development is devoted to the statement of two principles: one must think well, and for that one must study moral philosophy (we find this "think well" in a play in which general ideas shine, 319; which brings something to life, 334; which old men will approve of, 341); but at the same time the play must have grace and art (320), it must be pleasing and agreeable (333–34); this is attained chiefly by conciseness and plausibility (335–40); then it will have a chance to please the young as

well (342). The conclusion is that to be perfect one must mix
the useful and the agreeable (343–46). The comparison between
Greeks and Romans, which intervenes (323–32) in the middle
of this development, is to be interpreted in relation to that
duality: the Greeks have an innate sense of harmony, that is,
of what is agreeable; the Romans are especially wedded to the
useful. The second development (what is fitting, what is not
fitting) has to do with the degree of imperfection to which the
poet may resign himself; Horace starts with a few words of indulgence (347–53), but he soon becomes very demanding: half-
successful poetry, which has a charm that evaporates when
one looks at it closely, and which cannot stand up to being
revisited, is unsuccessful poetry (361–65); there is no difference
of degree between the mediocre and the worst (366–90); a brilliant depiction of the grandeurs of poetry (391–407) will no
doubt convince the apprentice-poet of the seriousness of the task
that he has undertaken. On the threshold of the third development, Horace brushes aside with a word the distinction between
craft and natural gifts; one must have both, and that supposes a
great deal of work; the true contrast, as he had announced in line
308, is the one between *virtus* and *error*: courage and letting
things slide. Here he discusses the necessity for effort (412–18);
the danger of the flatterers who will persuade the rich amateur
that he can dispense with work (419–37); and the good services
that a demanding critic can render a poet (438–52). Horace
brings in a very amusing picture of the poet who is delivered
to his genius alone because he had discouraged all criticism
(453–76): he is a counterpart of the picture of the grandeurs of
poetry (391–407), a reminder of the dirty and ill-shaven poet
who opens (295–304) the third part of the *Epistle*, a reminder
of the incongruous monster of the very first line of the *Epistle*.

We noticed in the first part of the *Epistle* a sort of drift,
becoming more and more marked, toward the problems of dramatic art, to which the second part is devoted. In the third,
it is the reverse: in line 316, Horace is speaking of creating a
character; in line 320, he is thinking of a play; *fabula* in line 339
could be equivocal; but after that he is speaking of poetry to be
read (*lectorem*, 344); the praise of poetry (391–407) does not
especially concern dramatic poetry, for the great names are

those of Orpheus, Amphion, Homer, and Tyrtaeus; the burlesque scenes on the dangers of flattery obviously have no meaning unless the poetry is one that is to be savored in a circle of
friends; and finally, the maniac poet who gesticulates in the
last lines of the *Epistle* is not a poet hissed by the audience, it
is a simple madman.

If we take the *Epistle* to the Pisos for what it has every
appearance of being, namely a letter on dramatic art illuminated
by principles of general aesthetics, it no longer seems to be
the chaos of bookish recollections and repetitions that one can
hardly fail to consider it if one takes it for an Art of Poetry.
There are three very exactly equilibrated parts: the work of art
(1–152); the dramatic poem (153–294); and the poet (295–
476). Each of these parts is composed in more or less the same
manner, with an introduction and a brilliant conclusion that
each time enclose three developments which are also in ap-
proximate equilibrium. Just as it is the second part that is the
most important and a sort of raison d'être of the rest, so perhaps
the second development of each part has a particular importance
in the eyes of Horace: the suiting of matter and form; Satyric
drama; unbearable mediocrity. From one end of the work to
the other, there is a directing thread: we leave the most general
principles of aesthetics to come to the most particular problems
of dramatic technique; whence we return to general problems
of aesthetics. In fact, it would have been surprising if Horace,
after having made fun of a work made of bits and pieces, had
exposed himself to the same derision. Let us merely recognize
the fact that, in most editions, paragraph breaks and punctua-
tion do not always facilitate the task of the reader.

In spite of the simplicity of line and solid unity that we have
tried to demonstrate, the *Epistle* to the Pisos is a work of extraordinary richness and diversity; for Horace was full of ideas,
his mind was nourished by the most diverse reading, and he
enjoyed taking sides and having his say about everything that
he happened to encounter. Innumerable studies of detail and
admirable commentated editions (Immisch, Rostagni, Steidle)
have taught us how much substance and intent can be discovered behind a development of a few lines or a simple phrase.

Hence the impression that the *Epistle* is also a sort of compendium into which all the currents of ancient literary doctrine flowed together to be approved or criticized. It is the more legitimate to study it as such in that Horace's allusions often give us very valuable aid in reconstructing theories and bodies of doctrine of which direct reports no longer exist. I cannot go into that subject here; yet, without going too far astray from the central intentions of the present work, it may be useful to define and place, more clearly than it has been possible to do in the foregoing analysis, the broad lines, or some governing ideas, of Horace's doctrine on poetics and on the theater.

So far as knowledge and appreciation of his aesthetics is concerned, the reader too often allows himself to be led astray by an illusion of self-evidence: the principles defended in the *Epistle* seem to him to be obvious; and it then becomes impossible for him to consider them as being of any real interest. This impression is fallacious. It usually comes from an insufficient effort to recognize what the celebrated phrases, too often quoted, repeated, applied, and extended without too much attention to Horace's true sense, really implied and excluded. Everything that we know of him makes it seem rather unlikely that he can have taken pleasure in laying down the law in a vacuum. Nothing banal, we may be sure, nothing dim or insipid can have come from the pen of a man who was so vital and so active. He would have been more likely to sin by gaiety, or by love of the paradoxical. When he stated a principle, we can be sure that he was thinking of something precise; in fact, to all appearances he was thinking of someone, if not indeed against someone. But on the other hand, he gave matters so much thought that very often a criticism or statement went beyond its particular object to define his position in one of those great debates of which aesthetic history is made.

The *Epistle* begins by stating that every work must have unity. Horace felt that this was not a thing that was evident to everyone. As we see from the examples that he cites, he first criticizes unformed works in which the raw material furnished by either legend or experience has not been sufficiently elaborated: cyclical poems that go from episode to episode without any system; *annales* to which the poet keeps adding extensions because the story that he is versifying is continuing in real life; and unrhythmical works lacking a dynamism proper to them. It is not very difficult to imagine that if Horace had lived in our time he would have had a low opinion of those auto-biographies and disguised reports that are presented to us as novels. He would have defended the rights of imagination and creation. Life always remains open; it produces nothing but the imperfect, nothing but the ambiguous. Only art concludes and perfects.

When he insisted so strongly on the unity necessary to a work of art, Horace was trying to forestall other misconceptions as well. Literature, in the coming years, would soon consist of sewing brilliant patches together, so that the works resembled harlequin cloaks. We have an indirect report of this tendency from Seneca the Elder, and one from Tacitus that is entirely explicit (*Dial.* 20): a work was appreciated to the extent that one could extract from it "something brilliant that deserves to be kept; the young people repeat to one another, and often write down in their colony or province, thoughts to which a subtle and brief stroke communicates a resplendent light, or commonplaces illuminated by an exquisite and poetic form." It is the tendency toward a pointillist taste, a taste for the perfect detail and for concentration, which arises periodically as litera-tures develop. Horace affirms the superiority of the organized work, which can extend to great lengths without becoming pallid and have life through the concurrence of all its parts.

In our time Horace would have been against the doctrine of art for art's sake. It seemed to him to be obvious that art has a social influence in which the poet cannot be disinterested. Concerned with the whole man, he was too deeply attentive to the preoccupations of a Maecenas or an Augustus to be unaware that in society art is normally a factor of drawing together and cohesion; in particular, it is up to literature to give the citizens a common language, and to place the right words on still in-expert lips. But with us, those who thus place the poet in the heart of the city lean toward the idea of poetry-inspiration: think of Victor Hugo and his *Mages*. Horace, on the contrary, is for poetry-construction, and on this problem we would find him in league with Edgar Poe, Mallarmé, and Valéry, poets who in general gave very little thought indeed to contributing their part to the health of the city. This is a curious split between Horace and the moderns. He would no doubt tell us that poetry can be educational only to the degree that it is constructed, adjusted, and planned: what good is to be hoped from an inspiration or an impulse that is uncontrolled, even if its disorder is a generous one?

Some of his judgments more especially concern the society in which he lived; they are the ones that chiefly interest historians of civilization. Thus he was against amateurism in poetry, precisely because of the high idea he had of the demands of the craft. He had not always felt the same way. In the *Satires*, it was the amateurs, a Calvus, a Catullus, who were the good poets; the professionals were public entertainers without artistic scruple. His new attitude reflected a transformation that had taken place in the social condition of poets during the last twenty-five years. At the time of the *Epistle* to the Pisos, there were still professional entertainers; there were still amateurs to continue the tradition of the refined great lord who prided himself on his writing, as Calvus had done. But between the two a new category had sprung up, for whom poetry was their whole life: a Vergil, a Horace, a Propertius, inconceivable in the preceding generation. It is with them that poetry, once a simple diversion—whatever its artistic quality had been—began in Rome to become a completely serious activity, a sort of religion.

But the most original judgment is certainly the one that, in that ultimate work, he felt justified in pronouncing on the literary aptitudes of his fellow-citizens. We all know the required *topos* that consisted of deploring the prosiness of the Romans, their lack of imagination, their utilitarianism, and the unfortunate and incurable heaviness of their national idiom; all of that was conceived as one panel of a diptych in which the Greeks, on the opposite panel, were exalted. The diptych did reappear in Horace, but the opposing argument that he put forward was very different: the Greeks had had the natural gifts, everything with them had bloomed spontaneously; it was up to the Romans to become poets through the example of the Greeks and through work, *limae labor et mora*. It is clear that

this contrast (*ingenium: ars*) is to be interpreted in the light of
Horace's whole aesthetic: in his eyes it was the file, much more
than inspiration or facility, that made the poet. Let us listen,
furthermore, to the conclusion that he drew from that confron-
tation, and his final judgment:

There is nothing that our poets have not attempted [*nil intempta-
tum nostri liquere poetae*—note the solemnity of those heavy
spondees], and their merit is not the less for having dared to
abandon the footsteps of the Greeks and celebrate national events,
placing personages on stage in the *praetexta* or the *toga*. Latium
would be no less powerful in its language than in its valor or its
glory in arms, if for all its poets the slow work of the file were not
the stumbling block. [285–91]

Far from attributing a narrow and dry heart to his compatriots,
Horace saw them as having a taste for literary courage and
audacity. They lacked only the power to discipline themselves:
if they wished it, the highest success was within their reach.

However interesting these judgments may be from the point
of view of literary history or of general aesthetics, the principal
object of the *Epistle* was obviously the reform of the Roman
theater. Horace did not content himself with laying down
principles: we have seen that he entered into details of execution. It was necessary to arrive at a correct and regular division of
the play (the five acts); to change the choruses into ones that
would take part in the action and whose songs would have
moral content; to create a Roman Satyric drama; to give the
new theater a form and, especially, metrics that were worthy of
it. Here many exegetes have difficulty. They do not know how
to take all these precepts; they see them as padding, as erudite
"pericopes," so reluctant are they to attribute to Horace the
idea—absurd in their eyes—that the Roman theater might have
revived. Yet it is not very difficult to ascertain that such a hope
would have had nothing unreasonable about it: one needs only
to observe that sixty years or so later the program drawn up by
Horace was realized in full (with the exception of the parts
about the Satyric drama) by the tragedies of Seneca. And from
Seneca, as we know, the whole theater of modern Europe de-
pends. It is not very often, I must say, that the precepts of a
theoretician, the ambitions expressed in a doctrinal piece of

writing, bear such literary fruit. Is it not paradoxical that on the very point on which Horace's efficacity was the most striking, he can have been accused of considering something that was impractical?

This ambitious and reasonable program was also original. In all the literary tradition of the ancients, Horace was the first to make formal statement of the five-act rule. Certainly he did not invent the necessity for coherent divisions of the action; in studying Greek classical tragedy, we can see that the choral interludes divided it into parts. But that division, as we can still judge, was not always very clear or striking; and above all it did not always distinguish five parts rather than four or six. It is doubtful whether in the Alexandrian period, when the disappearance of the chorus was orienting the dramatists more toward the creation of a continuous action, this problem was subjected to any more rigorous definition. If any attempt had been made in this direction we would surely know it from the scholiasts of the tragic poets, but they tell us nothing of the sort; it is apparently a question that they never asked themselves. All the discussions of five acts go back historically to the text of the *Epistle* to the Pisos.

The development on the restoration of the chorus begins by a reminder of Aristotle: "The chorus must be considered as one of the actors, be a part of the whole, and contribute to the action" (*Poetics* 1456a). The philosopher's intent was to protest against the prevailing tendency to use the chorus only for lyric interludes or musical entertainments having nothing to do with the "fable." This intent cannot have been displeasing to Horace. Yet we see without difficulty that his thoughts were not oriented in quite the same direction. Did he really wish the chorus to assume the role of an actor?

The chorus should side with the good and give the counsels of a friend, moderate those who are enraged, and love those who dread transgression; it should praise the dishes of a frugal table, the benefits of law and justice, and peace, which opens the doors of cities; it should keep secrets and call upon the gods, praying to them to make Fortune turn again toward the unhappy and forsake the proud. [196–201]

We cannot doubt that this is Horace speaking for himself: we recognize the principal themes of his moral poems and his

Odes. In tragedy as he would like to see it, ideas dear to him would have their place and would be expressed by the chorus. Our own time has rediscovered in Claudel and T. S. Eliot how much power a dramatic action can gain from a lyric commentary by elements that are intermediaries between the actors and the audience. It is therefore possible that our age is better able than any other to understand Horace's intentions and the richness of the form that he worked out.

The observations on dramatic metrics do not have the same universal interest, but they were important for the Romans. They are personal to Horace; it is clear that no Greek theoretician can have slipped them under his pen. They were no doubt called forth by a malaise that the Romans had now been feeling for some time. Cicero had complained in the *Orator* (184) that in the ancient dramatists it was difficult to find any rhythm, or even a perceptible verse line. The restitution of a more rigorous prosody was to be expected, and an evolution in that direction had begun well before Horace. In any case, it was he who brought the evolution to pass in one stroke: for four or five hundred years at least, these few lines in the *Epistle* to the Pisos put a stop to the old liberties, some traces of which lingered for a time only in Phaedrus or the mimographers. Here we find again the disciple of Catullus, the meticulous technician of Archilochean iambics, the strict metrician of the *Odes*.

The lines on the Satyric drama have been the subject of much discussion. But in a work that has so much to do with Horace himself and with the reality of his time, how can we imagine that these lines are a mere parroting of a fragment of Alexandrian erudition? It is notable that in this passage, which by the way occurs in the exact center of the *Epistle*, Horace enters personally, and in a very direct way: "Not for me, Pisos, if I come to write Satyric plays" (235). It seems reasonable, therefore, to assume that Horace was envisaging, as realistically as the reforms of the chorus and of metrics, and in the most positive manner, the creation of a Satyric drama in Rome. Besides, it is not very difficult to see what it was in him that would give rise to such an idea: the desire to enrich Latin poetry with a genre that was still lacking—this sort of ambition was dear to all Latins, and Horace would soon state it with particular fervor—

and also the desire to insert a middle genre between tragedy (sublime) and comedy (simple) so as to accomplish the tripartite form that had become traditional. But, as we just saw, in the passages on the chorus and on metrical reform Horace was unquestionably remembering that he had written the *Odes* and accustomed Rome to Archilochus' iambics. In this passage, how can he not have been thinking of his *Satires?* The plays that he would write would have the same apparent but artful facility, which had once deceived some readers: "Some think that one can write a thousand lines like mine a day" (*Sat.* II 1, 4); here, "I should fashion my lines in such a way that everyone would hope to do as much, but would later sweat and toil in vain if he ventured into the same undertaking" (240–42).

The Satyrs, furthermore, were not unknown in Rome. They had their part in the traditional processions described to us by Dionysius of Halicarnassus (VII 72), "joking and, by word and gesture, transposing what the other participants were doing and saying into buffoonery." In a word, for a long time they had already been practicing that *vertere seria ludo* that would be Horace's motto for his future theater—a motto that would have been a very fitting one for the *Satires*: we remember what Stoic preaching became in the mouth of Damasippus (*Sat.* II 3). But Rome knew literate and well-spoken Satyrs as well as the rather gross and disrespectful ones: Horace speaks of them (245–46), and Vergil had chosen old Silenus, their dean, to sing of the genesis of the worlds (*Buc.* 6); Satyrs were also found in bucolic poetry, which we are assured had links with the theater. All these were elements that were to be incorporated into the future Satyric drama; they would have rooted it in living traditions. Finally, Horace cannot have been unaware of the Italian public's taste for parody. This public, which was now cool to too sublime tragedy and to indifferent comedy, had once been amused by the *hilarotragoedia* of Rhinthon. By this time it was being offered nothing but Atellanae and mime, which were equally mediocre. Perhaps with Satyric drama it would be possible to find a dramatic formula that would resolve all the problems of the Roman theater, which would become popular, artistic, and educational all at the same time.

It would be doing less than justice to the *Epistle* to the Pisos if it were not to be seen, on the expressive plane, as a work of art. But this breviary of classicism hardly corresponds to the common idea of classic taste. Even in the freest *Satires* and *a fortiori* in the *Epistles*, Horace had never been more gay, more saucy, and sometimes more droll, prancing and flatulating like a snorting Satyr. How many "low" words! and how many "low" images, since he is speaking of mange, of louts, of fried chick-peas, of Simon who has just had his nose blown for him, of an unfortunate who is cooking human entrails on stage, of another who has urinated on the ashes of his father! How many jagged or even shocking lines: in line 41 the third foot is formed by a single word; in lines 63 and 263, what similar aberrations! However, we may be sure that Horace's conscience was untroubled: the style that he had adopted was the "median" or intermediate style, which was also called "mixed," the style of the *Satires* and the Satyrs. Thus he had the right to be so diverse and to mix various tones together, for we have seen that at the same time he was able to be serious and solemn. The *Epistle* has aspects that are baroque and even burlesque— a joyous and gratuitous fancifulness.

We can be grateful that we are free today of some prejudices of the Romantics. I suppose that no one any longer doubts that in the hands of a Lucretius or a Vergil a manual of physics or of agricultural economy can be transmuted into a very great poem. If we open our eyes and learn to read again, if we shake off classical banalities as well as romantic ones, if we are willing to amuse ourselves sometimes, taking pleasure in a colorful art that is also a bit clashing, an art of many dissonances—then perhaps we will rediscover that the *Epistle* to the Pisos, that literary manifesto and program, is also a true poem.

6 · Posterity

Augustus' and Maecenas' friendship surrounded Horace to the end of his life. The *Epistle* to the Pisos was not written by a misanthrope: it gives us the picture of a man who was gay, full of plans, manifestly without anxiety as to what might be thought of him, and very much at his ease in giving his advice on anything. The very circumstances in which we must place the *Epistle* show us a Horace who had been converted, at least in his imagination, to outdoor literature: perhaps this astonishing, ever-resilient man might, if he had lived a few years longer, have given us some works for the theater. Besides, although it is difficult now for us to visualize the addressees of the *Epistle*, the manner in which Horace wrote to them gives every indication that in those last years our poet was continuing, as in the time of the first *Epistles*, to be surrounded, made much of, and consulted by younger poets. It has been supposed, not implausibly, that in writing the *Epistle* to Augustus he had intended, among other things, to recommend these young hopes to the prince.

Yet when he died on November 27, 8, suddenly and abruptly, in the impulsive way that had always been characteristic of him —certainly the slow agony that Hermann Broch has made us relive at Vergil's bedside would have assorted ill with Horace's nature—we become conscious that a period was closing in literary history and that for several years now the foreground of the stage had been occupied by other actors. Vergil and Tibullus must have died around 19, Propertius in 15. Maecenas had died some months before. A young knight from the Sulmo area, Ovid, was causing much talk; it was ten years ago now that he had published his *Amores*, a sort of poetic novel, and his *Heroides*, which are letters exchanged between famous lovers, Ariadne and Theseus, Helen and Paris, Aeneas and Dido. All this was hardly calculated to please old Horace. He had never approved of cerebral loves, those complicated passions that invade everything, both life and books. He had often mocked and teased elegiacal poets. And with Ovid it was indeed the elegy, under only a slightly new guise, that was again seducing the public with its subtleties of sentiment.

Furthermore, that style of poetry manifested from the first an extraordinary aptitude for becoming fashionable. It was unvigorous and diffuse—in a word, within the reach of amateurs: here again was a reason for antipathy. Ovid may have heard Horace accompanying his well-wrought poems on the lyre. He admired Horace's metrical virtuosity (*Tristia* IV 10, 49), and more than one echo of Horace came from his pen. But what he really thought of Horace, and what the others around him thought of his form of art, is clearly seen from the fact that none of the young elected to follow him: Horace's writing was too dense and technically too difficult; it did not commend itself to persons who were in love with brilliant developments. When Ovid composed a library for his feminine readers (*Ars amatoris* III 329 sqq.), he included Callimachus, Philetas, Anacreon, Sappho, Propertius, Gallus, Tibullus, Varro, and the *Aeneid*; he did not include the *Odes* of Horace. To what avail had our poet once broken so many lances for the "new poets" and Alexandrian taste? Now that the school had triumphed, he himself was set aside. He was expiating now his mockery of the elegiacal poets, and especially that kind of classicism toward which, ever since Actium, he had inclined.

It was not only the taste of the men of letters that had changed; with the years the society itself had changed as well. Vergil, born in about 70, and Horace, born in 65, were of the generation of Augustus, born in 63. The rhythm of their life had been the rhythm of recovered health. They had known

the bloody and disgraceful disorders of the republic; they had
known civil wars. The miracle of the peace that had been reestablished and maintained marked all their thoughts: hence
their admiration for Augustus and their ease in understanding
him. Born in 43, Ovid was twelve years old when order returned
to the universe. Political and social equilibrium seemed to him,
as to all those of his generation, to be perfectly natural: in their
eyes, Augustus could seem no more than a good administrator.
If he was more, he could only be a restraint, a despot. Thus a
whole part, perhaps the most noble part of Horace's lyricism,
the one devoted to admiration and gratitude, was to become incomprehensible, or even repellent, to the new generation. In
fact, as M. Bardon has clearly demonstrated, starting with the
last decade B.C., Roman letters drifted bit by bit toward the
opposition. Cicero was exalted as the victim of the triumvirs;
Seneca the Elder has preserved for us a whole repertoire of
selections from the rhetoricians which speak of nothing but
cleaving tyrants asunder.

This climate of disaffection toward Augustus would last for
the last twenty years of his reign. It would become more serious
under Tiberius and Caligula. It was to obscure the fame of
those who had so greatly admired the peacemaker and the
prince. During that period the *Aeneid* was able to breast the
wave because the poem had to do with all of Roman history;
because it was a narrative work in hexameters, of the type—in
that respect, at least—of those that were in high vogue at the
moment; because Vergil had been dead so long and had already
entered into glory; and because his indifference to literary
quarrels had not surrounded him with enmities such as those
that Horace, up to the very last moment, never ceased to
awaken and stimulate. It is thus rather natural that our poet
was shipwrecked. While the rhetoricians presented to us by
Seneca the Elder were all full of Ovid, Vergil, and Catullus, it
is impossible to discern any trace of Horace in them. Phaedrus
and Manilius do not seem to have read him. Under the reign
of Tiberius, in 29, Velleius Paterculus, recalling the glories of
modern literature, would cite Sallust, Titus Livius, Tibullus,
Ovid, Vergil, and Rabirius, author of an epic very much
esteemed by Ovid (*Pont.* IV 16, 5); of Horace, not a word.

Some years later, under the reign of Caligula, it is not hard to imagine the bizarre impression that reading the *Odes* could have aroused in circles attached to the court, at a time when the emperor was forbidding the celebration of the anniversary of the battle of Actium and was seeking out the works of Vergil in order to have them destroyed.

Again, in this rather ignominious retreat we have considered only the *Odes*, the works least badly placed at that date for braving the future. One cannot hope that the *Epistles* and *Satires* would have met readers who were better disposed. Earlier we noted that the Lucilian versification of the *Satires* had, from the beginning, astonished and grieved Horace's friends. After the refinements in the technique of the hexameter that were realized by Vergil and then by Ovid—and which seem to have been considered, if we are to judge by other contemporary production, as a final and universally valid achievement—the *Satires*, even the *Epistles*, must now have seemed to be of the lowest degree of art. As for the core of the work, nothing was further from the academicism, or the grandiloquence, or the violence of the time than those pieces characterized by a direct and rather plebeian verve, in which the humor of the writer implacably foiled any fancy for rhetoric.

After the reign of the erudite Emperor Claudius, the middle of the first century (perhaps more precisely the good years (54–59) of the reign of Nero) was the starting point of a literary renaissance which would bear fruit up to the end of the reign of Trajan (98–117), if not up to the time of Hadrian (117–38). Its essential element was a return to the values of the Augustan period. Vergil began to shine again, and even more brilliantly. Horace reappeared, and it is then that the double star Vergil-Horace, the beneficial influence of which we have not yet ceased to feel, appeared on the firmament of literary history. The two names appear in association, on the plane of excellence, first in Petronius (118) and in the *Praise of Piso* (ll. 230–42), then in Tacitus (*Dialogue,* 20), and finally in Juvenal (VII 227): where we learn that the portraits of the two poets, dusted over with soot or faded by light, presided in classrooms over the labors of little schoolchildren.

In that second half of the first century, Horace also knew one

of the great strokes of luck of his posthumous history: he stimulated poets who, without exactly imitating him in a continuous
and industrious way, received their spark from him and, in
writing their own works, made him live again under another
form. There again, how different his fate is from that of Vergil!
Vergil was imitated, and his imitators took pleasure in adopting
his words; Horace's successors seem to us at the same time to
owe him everything and yet to be nothing but themselves.

The form of art, so peculiar to him, which he had created in
Lucilius' wake, had not had continuators. But around 55 a
very young man, who was to die at the age of 28 in 62, brought
the genre back to life. The *Satires* of Persius, a little book of 650
lines, have been the object of highly contradictory judgments
for nineteen centuries. The Middle Ages and the Renaissance
profoundly admired them. Renan recognized in the author "a
superior talent and the highest sentiments of a great soul." The
alleged obscurity for which Boileau made him notorious comes,
essentially, from the habit of asking the text absurdly precise
questions to which there is obviously no answer: our ignorance
of the details of daily life and the fact that we are unused to
a truly spoken, explosive, almost sound-recorded Latin explain
the rest. Unduly distraught over the premature fate of the
author, the moderns have a tendency to turn him into a little
saint or a doctrinaire, feeling free later to accuse him of not
having stated his ideas with sufficient logic. It is far better to
try to learn to feel the gaiety of this writing—he had a petulant
spleen, he tells us, and a ready laugh—and to recognize in these
little pieces an art of sketching and of direct notation thanks
to which they deserve to occupy a place in the very first rank
in general literature.

Persius defined with a rare felicity (I, 116–18) the characteristics of Horace's art: "The sly Flaccus puts his finger on the
faults of his friend, and makes him laugh at the same time;
always welcome, always clever at making fun of the world, he
disports himself heartily." But perhaps the greatest service that
he rendered to his memory was to demonstrate that after
Lucilius and Horace the genre in which they had made themselves illustrious, at the confines of the confession and the
apologue—a genre that was still ill defined and hard to distin-

guish from the *Menippea*, the conversation, or the letter, and which perhaps did not yet have a very specific name—was one that had consistency and an identity of its own. It is with Persius that the idea of satire, as we now understand it, found its complete definition. Quintilian, thirty years later, would give it its titles of nobility: in a review of the great poetic genres, satire took its place between elegy and iambics, as the special glory of the Roman muse. "Satire belongs wholly to us" (X 1, 93).

At the moment when Quintilian was writing that sentence, which was destined to become so famous, collections of satires were appearing every day in the Rome of the good Nerva. We are unable to name any of these authors. But soon the famous Juvenal would enter the arena in his turn, once more relighting "the lantern of the man from Venusia" (I 51). Juvenal belongs to a poetic type that is less unusual than that of Horace or Persius. He is better at recounting than at making us see; he is sometimes a little ridiculous because he never husbands his strength; but he has given us work well done, and solid verse. He is able to construct a tirade, and since he has amplitude and a long wind—*Satire* VI has 700 lines—he is an unequaled witness of Roman life at the begnning of the second century.

Concurrently with this resurrection of the Horace of the *Epistles* and the *Satires*, the lyricism of the *Odes* came back into fashion. Quintilian appreciated our poet's variety of figures and the happy boldness of his choice of words (X 1, 96), and, as far as the satire was concerned, he tells us that the lyric Horace would henceforth stimulate many emulators. Passennus Paulus, a friend of Pliny the Younger (*Letters*, IX 22), wrote odes "in the style of Horace." Martial (V 30) knew a Varro who excelled at sounding "the lyre of the Calabrian." Manilius Vopiscus seems to have promised himself to be a new Horace, since we see him (Statius, *Silvae* I 3, 99–104) in his house at Tibur, wholly occupied in writing epistles, satires, and odes, which he dedicated to the Fauns of the area. Perhaps we have some fragments of a lyric poet of that time, Vestricius Spurinna: their expression is dense and their phraseology vigorous, and the images are sharp and lively.

But it is in the tragedies of Seneca (written between 49 and 63) that the influence of Horace's lyricism appears in its most obvious features, and this time to result in unquestionable masterpieces. In some ways, as I have said (cf. p. 163), it is the form itself of Senecan tragedy that seems to have been inspired by Horace. But in these tragedies the choruses, in any case, exist only through him. Of course, Seneca did not think it possible to hark back to the stanza form, apparently too foreign to the traditions of Roman tragedy; but he recognized what power is conferred on the evocation of a myth or a meditation on destiny when the poet constrains himself to strict forms, to the nervous or tormented verse lines—Glyconic, Sapphic, Asclepiadian—which were those to which Horace had accustomed Rome. As Juvenal and Persius had done for the satire, Seneca confirmed forever what Horace's work had shown to be possible in the forms and content of lyricism: a poetry that would be the vehicle for the highest thoughts (we remember that in the preceding century Cicero was still declaring that if he were to live two hundred years he would never take the time to read lyrics); and metrics that, even in Latin, would be the respiration of an exalted soul, and in comparison with which the hexameter, dramatic verse, would henceforth seem incurably prosaic, or rhetorical, or bland. The Christians, when they came to make their hymns, would remember this masterful demonstration.

Nor did the philologists remain inactive. The great Caesius Bassus dedicated to Nero a treatise on metrics in which the study of Horace's meters occupied an important place; later centuries would pick up and adapt it indefinitely. It is not impossible that M. Valerius Probus undertook a critical edition of our poet; we are told so, and certain singularities of our manuscript tradition would be readily explained as the fruits of the very personal methods of this philologist. Under Hadrian, Q. Terentius Scaurus published a ten-book commentary on the entire production from which Porphyric would later take his inspiration. All these were solid works, which would keep Horace from disappearing even if the literary fashion were to change: philologists are faithful.

In spite of this radiation into creative literary and intellectual circles and among the fairly numerous literate persons whose faces now and then rise before us from the *Carmina latina epigraphica*, it does not appear that in the first century the study of Horace penetrated schoolteaching. Two facts seem significant here: not a line of Horace is recognizable in the graffiti of Pompeii, where Vergil is so often present, together with Ovid, Lucretius, the elegiacal poets, and even Ennius. Furthermore, we shall soon see that the last two thirds of the second century and the whole third century were marked by a nearly total eclipse of the fame of our poet; this phenomenon would be inconceivable if a school tradition had preexisted. It is, of course, easy to understand the reservations of the educators. Quintilian himself noted it expressly: "There are passages that I would not wish to explain before young people" (I 8, 6). Thus Horace would have been usable only in selections. It is probable that the teachers preferred to get along with him, contenting themselves with giving him in effigy (*honoris causa*, along with Vergil) the presidency of the class.

Toward 130-40, an archaistic taste, as inexorable as a tidal bore, had devasted Latin literature; here were Seneca and Lucanus consigned to the gibbet, Tacitus forgotten and in danger of disappearing forever, Cato preferred to Sallust, Vergil saved only for a few old words that were now rediscovered in the *Aeneid*. This wretched and hypocritical sectarianism—for in fact many of those ancients whom they pretended to admire were already no longer accessible, their works being lost—was severe toward Horace: he was resented for his mockeries at the admirers of the ancients. He who, a hundred years earlier, under Tiberius, had been disqualified as old hat and insufficiently polished, was now in disgrace for having been too modern in his own time. Aulus Gellius, who was so knowledgeable and had so supple a mind, refers to a word of Horace's only once or twice in passing. Appuleius seems to have had no knowledge of him. It is a little painful to see Marcus Aurelius writing in the postscript of a letter: "Speak to me no more of Horace; so far as I am concerned, I wish to he had never existed." *Mihi est emortuus* (Fronton, p. 28 Van den Hout). Let us hope that it was only a joke.

THE CHRISTIAN ERA

When all of literature, both poetry and prose, was reborn in the fourth century, the situation of culture had changed very

much again. Rome had once more crossed an ocean of misfortunes. The Romans were trying to live again, and to rejoin a
dear and brilliant past that would be a warranty for the future.
No more would there be question of the disputes that I have
just described: the great ancients, as diverse as they had been,
would from now on form a bloc, more and more consolidated
by academic tradition. It was already from them that one
learned Latin.

At this date it is the Christians who must interest us especially, for the future belonged to them. With individual differences that no doubt had to do in part with whatever their
youthful training had chanced to be—Saint Augustine, for
example, never filled the lacunae caused by a lack of schooling—
we recognize a good command of Horace in almost everyone.
Given the nature of their preoccupations, it is natural that they
did not very often have occasion to remember him or to recall
him. But our poet was, in spite of everything, never very far off.
Second-rank writers like Cyprianus Gallus (about 425) and
Commodianus perhaps bring us particularly significant evidence
in this regard: in the Prologue of the *Carmen apologeticum*, in
ten or so lines, seven more or less unmistakable echoes of Horace
have been discerned: the *Odes*, *Epistles*, *Epodes*, and *Ars
poetica* were all present in the memory of the writer.

In Saint Jerome there are not only echoes but explicit quotations, about fifty in the ensemble of his work. Jerome, furthermore, did not live on memories of his childhood alone, and
his immense reading led him, in the line of antique erudition,
to reflect on the literary act itself: a reflection of vital importance, which made him recognize that the Bible too is literature.
We should keep certain texts in mind here as being of the first
importance in clarifying the greatest literary event of the fourth
century, the *translatio* of the profane Horatian lyric into the
Christian church under the form of the hymn. The spirit in
which this occurred matters little. Jerome was an impulsive
and irascible man: "What has light in common with shadows?
What agreement can be conceived between Christ and Belial?
Is there anything in common between Horace and the Psalter,
between Vergil and the Gospels, between Cicero and Saint
Paul?" (Letters, 22, 29). "Is there anything in common . . ."

Why, yes, and this very text, believed to be denying it, helps
to make it apparent, by the three definite correlations that it
establishes. Elsewhere: "David, who is our Simonides, our
Pindar and Alcaeus, our Horace, our Catullus, our Serenus,
sings Christ on his lyre, and on his ten-stringed psaltery calls
him back from hell, resurrected" (Letters, 53, 8). Or again:
"What is more melodious than the Psalter! Sometimes in the
manner of our Horace and the Greek Pindar it causes the
iambic to run, sometimes it causes the crash of the Alcaic to
resound; it expands into Sapphics or marches in step with the
senarian" (Preface to the translation of Eusebius' *Chronicle*).
It is clear that observations of this sort—their roots are already
found in Jewish literature, and Josephus does not hesitate to
speak of the hexameters of the Canticle of Moses and of the
pentameters and trimeters of David—prepare the coming of
literary forms that will lean in particular on Horace, Catullus,
Serenus, and the Psalter, all at the same time.

Between Horace and Ambrose's hymn, there are seemingly
few perceptible links. Not a single echo or borrowed word is
perceptible. But the essential point is a deeper one: until then
the Church had known only canticles in prose, the Psalms, the
Magnificat, the *Gloria in excelsis*, the *Te Deum*. These pieces
lend themselves to antiphonal execution, but the responses
are always uneven, being based upon what are often very arbitrary divisions. Ambrose's hymn, on the other hand, is constructed of rigorously superimposable stanzas, whose prosody
makes any wavering impossible. The reader is reminded of the
earlier discussion (pp. 72–77) of Horace's originality as a
builder of stanzas. At least in the present state of our knowledge, it is difficult to see how Ambrose could have conceived
of the rhythmic form that he fixed upon unless Horace's
example had influenced him. One detail, perhaps, has its value:
Ambrose's stanza has four lines. No intrinsic necessity imposed
this figure, and experience shows that stanzas of three or five
lines are perfectly viable in Latin. Horace too, in spite of the
extreme variety of meters that he used, held himself rigorously
to the stanza form and to the stanza of four lines.

Many elements must have joined together to bring about the
perfect success of the form that Ambrose instituted in the

Church. Among others, iambic dimeter came from the poets of the second century, no doubt especially from Serenus, whose name was connected by Saint Jerome with that of Horace. But it is of interest for the posthumous story of our poet that we can discern his presence too at this very important moment. In the mold thus created, authors who were more cultivated or more concerned with belles lettres—a Prudentius, a Paulinus of Nola—would have no difficulty in reawakening more particular and precise memories of Horace. The essential point is that there now existed a Christian lyric poetry. Horace had proved capable of assuming the inspirations of the Psalter. Henceforth it would be impossible for the people of the church completely to forget our poet.

Furthermore, the school of the ancients had not collapsed all of a piece. It may have lasted in Gaul until the end of the fifth century, in Italy until the Lombard invasion (568), and in Africa until the Arabs (698). As long as it lasted, for everyone who sat on its benches, Horace survived. Only, as the political chaos increased, the number of persons who benefited from that training become fewer. Circumstances also were to lend themselves less and less to their remembering Horace once they had become adults. No doubt in their youth they would have met only a more and more reduced Horace, a few pages in an anthology. Texts were beginning to be scarce. The culture ceased to be relatively homogeneous on *Romania* as a whole. Concerning Horace, the case of Arator is particularly significant. His *Acts of the Apostles*, a vast Christian epic, was one of the great literary events of the sixth century. He himself grew up between Milan, Pavia, and Ravenna under the enlightened reign of Theodoric. His classical culture was very solid: he knew Vergil, Statius, and Lucanus through and through. He seems to have been more or less ignorant of the work of Horace: probably he had never had access to it. And yet at the same era, in Rome, the regular consul of the year 527, Vettius Agorius Basilius Mavortius, aided by the advice of Master Felix, orator of the city of Rome, undertook a critical revision of the text of our poet. From this we must assume the existence of both sufficient documentation and social circles that were likely to be interested in such a work.

The greatest danger that then menaced the survival of the classical poets came from the existence of the Christian poetry for which they had furnished the models. Arator, as we were saying, knew Vergil and Statius well; but he also much frequented Sedulius and Prudentius, and he himself would soon become a classic who would be long remembered. Dag Norberg has shown that the poets of the Merovingian period scarcely went back further than Juvencus and Ambrose to seek their models. To some persons it now seemed possible that the greatest names of pagan literature had been adequately replaced, indeed their thoughts corrected and completed, by very great names in Christian literature—that Ambrose and Augustine could absorb and at the same time departicularize a Cicero and a Varro, Prudentius, a Horace. There was a danger that ancient letters would survive only in technical works of computation, medicine, or grammar which the Christians would have thought it pointless to rewrite. A man as learned as Isidore of Seville (570–636) perhaps never had direct contact with the work of Horace; neither, probably, did his contemporary Gregory the Great (540–604).

What is the most important, then, is not those few original minds who, if the library chanced to allow it, one day found Horace and derived nourishment from him: Maximilian certainly (toward 550), and perhaps Fortunatus (530–600). We have now arrived at the time of hibernation. Some manuscripts slept in libraries, sometimes curiously awakened without our quite understanding why, as by that anonymous person of the Metz region who, during the seventh century, wrote a commentary on Horace of which very important fragments have come down to us. The little flame of life, the unbroken link to history without which there would never have been a reawakening, was maintained by the child, thanks to manuals of grammar used in the schools (which at that date were becoming more and more monastic or episcopal). These technical works, as we were saying, had not been wholly reworked. They thus continued to carry, as rules or models, the same quotations and extracts that had been offered to schoolboys in the fourth century. Saint Columban, who as we know did not regard the principles of asceticism as a joking matter, also knew some texts of Horace and willingly recalled them. Braulio of Saragossa (d. 651) wrote: "We learned our alphabet with Horace and held out our hand to the rod" (quotation of Juvenal, I 15), "and it can be said of us: He has hay on his horns, flee him!" (quotation of Horace, *Sat.* I 4, 34). This is something, but not very much; it hardly expresses an involvement. One hundred years later, Peter of Pisa thought that he would please Paulus Diaconus, one of the best poets of the Lombard Renaissance, by calling him a new Horace; but the recipient of the praise rebuffed him vigorously, stating that in his eyes pagan authors were to be compared to dogs.

The course of history changed, as we know, toward the end of the eighth century. The essential point was that beginning with Charlemagne there were once again true political powers in Europe, endowed with stability, continuity, and prestige. In fact it appears that in the Christian world the authority of political power is a condition that is indispensable to the development of those "natural" values to which the church almost always—whatever its theoretical doctrine on the subject may be—tends to refuse sufficient autonomy. In Alcuin (730–804), as well as in the contemporaneous Paulus Diaconus, it is impossible to mistake a direct knowledge of Horace. But Alcuin boasted of it and liked to carry the surname of Flaccus at court. In the following generation, Rabanus Maurus (784–856) and Walafrid Strabo (808–49), nurtured by Horace and great poets as well, wrote remarkable hymns in Sapphic or Asclepiadean stanzas. It was in the ninth century that the most ancient manuscript of Horace that we now have was executed at Fleury-sur-Loire. It was also in the ninth century that one of the foundations of the knowledge of Horace in the Middle Ages was composed, the vast commentary by Heiric d'Auxerre. Henceforth, from century to century, manuscripts, commentaries, imitations, and quotations would multiply. The thirteenth century was marked, as we know, by a certain relaxation of the bonds that united the contemporary culture to ancient letters. There is every indication that Dante had no personal knowledge of Horace. But we are no longer very far from Petrarch (1304–74), who would inaugurate a new age.

The people of the Middle Ages realized perfectly well how much of Horace's work was antipathetical to the civilization in which they were henceforth to seek survival. Whether we are speaking of Notker the Stammerer (840–912), of Conrad of Hirschau (toward 1100), or of Hugo of Trimberg (toward 1280), their reservations are clear: Horace had noble maxims, but he was elusive and inconsistent: certain parts of his work, especially the lyric pieces, could hardly edify minds that had already been formed. It was, in a word, a restatement by more skillful pens of the somewhat contradictory judgment that we read in the *explicit* of one of our manuscripts of the fifteenth century: *Explicit opus divini Flacci Venusini viri ebriosissimi libidinosi Epicurei voluptuosissimi lippi.* Furthermore, it is rather difficult to measure the true density of Horace's presence here. The texts in which his name occurs may have hardly any significance; it is not necessary to have read him in order to honor him with the title of prince of lyricists. The quotations that are made may have been taken from anterior works or come from anthologies. Often the texts in which we recognize an echo of Horace's words or approach to a passage cannot be interpreted with any certainty. Certain documents seem to give us information on the use that was made of Horace in the teaching of Latin, but we must not give their meaning too much importance: "Horace" could appear in a program of studies and be represented by only one or two pieces that were hastily or rarely explained. If we are to believe the *Ars lectoria* of Aimeric, a good classical training for a literate person at the end of the eleventh century required the knowledge of the works of Ennius, among others; was Horace much better known? We feel ourselves on surer ground when library catalogs or the results of paleographical analysis can establish that at a certain date, in a certain place, a copy of the works of Horace existed or was executed. It is very important to observe that from the eleventh century on these manuscripts multiplied all over Europe. This obviously presupposes admirers. During the eleventh century, too, it seems to have become fashionable to sing some of the lyric pieces: in fact, about ten manuscripts established as being of that time, and coming from very diverse provenances, give us neumic texts for *Odes* I 1–3, 5, 15, 33; II 2; III 9, 12, 13; IV 11. The selection is not bad; it even bears very favorable witness to the taste and rhythmic sense of those who made it.

What did they ask of Horace? Proverbs, aphorisms; so much is sure. In the twelfth century, the *Epistle* to the Pisos, which for a long time had been raised to the dignity of an Art of Poetry, served as the model for innumerable *Arts of Poetry* in which Horace's contributions were mingled with those of the *Rhetoric to Herennius* and Cicero's treatises; the influence of these works continued up to European classicism, for which they furnished a doctrine, a body of references, and, so to speak, a backbone. In all ages the *Odes* have been a model of perfection for innumerable poets who were makers of hymns and canticles, and who apparently could never manage, however abundant their production, to satisfy the needs of a piety that was forever greedy for new works. Given the difference in the narrative content of these liturgical or paraliturgical hymns and the *Odes*, it is not astonishing that it is seldom possible to establish literal correspondences between them; but what was transmitted, and is much more important, was a certain ideal of clarity and firmness, a certain manner of handling word order and the relationship of the sentence and the line; it was above all the admirable metric forms, whose difficulty might well have put the poets off in the end if they had not felt that the prestige of the great pagan poet imposed his forms, and if they had not felt themselves obliged to do no less for Christ. Vergil and Ovid would not have sufficed to inspire those intricate and rare masterpieces of truly Roman solemnity of which we unquestionably have a few finished examples in the hymns of Rabanus Maurus or Alphan of Salerno (d. 1085).

The living presence of an author cannot be measured by the number of echoes that may be discerned in his successors; works must appear that, in great likelihood, would never have appeared if it had not been for him. In the history of Roman satire, Juvenal's case is significant. The swiftest reading leaves us no doubt that he is a descendant of Horace; and yet, from one work to the next, the number of passages and groups of words that can be shown to be parallel is minimal. Medieval literature is still so little known that it is of course infinitely more difficult, without texts to collate, to try to identify this living presence of an inspiration. And yet, to take one's inspiration from an author without necessarily having to imitate him, is this not, can it not be, one of the highest forms of fidelity and one of the most priceless instruments of literary continuity?

With these reservations in mind, it does not seem too imprudent to think that in the course of the Middle Ages Horace had something to do with the flowering of certain genres that the Christian poem had not found in its cradle and that, reborn, were to have so splendid a future. First it was the satire in hexameters, which, mingled with dialogues and moralizing homilies, reappeared with the *Sermones* (in four books, like Horace's *Satires* and *Epistles*) of the Rhenish Sextus Amarcius Gallus (toward 1050). The inspiration of this poem has been ascribed to the often caustic preachings of the Cluny reformers. But in Amarcius, profoundly Christian as he is, there is much besides morality: there is the eye, the taste for form, the taste for the sketch. In the following century, in the *Speculum stultorum* of the Englishman Nigel Wireker, the genre would gain in fancifulness and in lightness. Certainly the satire is a minor genre, but it is not negligible when, in a civilization in which dogmatism is tending to invade everything, a satirist contributes to opening people's eyes and making them see the way of the world as it actually is.

More value is to be attached to the renaissance of a lyric poetry that was profane, often satirical, sometimes erotic, and readily concerned with pleasant country scenes. No doubt Ovid, and the elegiacal poets who followed him, are the patrons of that poetry, and "Solomon" too, author of the *Song of Songs*. But the form comes neither from Ovid nor from the Latin Bible. Those little lines—limpid, chiming, ringing from everywhere, have equivalents only in the religious lyric; not in the hymns, which were still constructed in a much more classical manner, but in the pieces meant for personal meditation, which were freer and bolder in their form, and in which Glyconic and Adonic lines and hemistichs of Sapphic or Asclepiadean lines or their rhythmic equivalents were combined. It is on this polymorphous lyric matter, so effective for the expression of all emotions, that the Horatian star exerted its influence. We recall

that in the schools and the celebrations at court the dialogue of
Horace and Lydia (*Od.* III 9 *Donec gratus eram* . . .), and the
Ode to the fountain Bandusia (*Od.* III 13) were sung. In the
long run, how could these poems, from another world but
officially celebrated and admired, have failed to bring about
the creation of something that would resemble them? By their
mere presence, they tirelessly reminded the hearer that the
human voice, in the "century" that we are discussing, was not
made only for singing in sanctuaries and on pilgrimages; they
reminded him that other sentiments too deserved finished expression. By the single fact that these poems existed, they gave
confidence to those few rare individuals who, with each generation, grew more capable of guessing that perhaps—although
for a time it had seemed nearly incredible—perhaps such works
might be possible again.

Of course no one needed Horace and the Latin poets to feel
the darts of love or to improvise rounds and chants for village
festivals. But without Horace and the Latin poets we may well
wonder whether these inchoate stammerings, these foaming
swells in the soul that often take place below the level of expression, would ever have resulted in art forms and the eventual
birth of modern poetry. At the very least it was necessary to
know that this progression was possible. Or rather, it was necessary that a model should present itself in answer to otherwise
undefined needs. The origins of the French and Provençal lyric,
or of the Minnesang, are even more obscure to us, and even
more disputed, than those of the *chansons de geste*. Certainly
it is less absurd to attribute a "popular" origin to songs of ten
or so verses than to epics that have thousands, and there is no
question of stating a doctrine here. I would only remind the
reader that when these great events took place, events so closely
linked to the history of metric forms—without an appropriate
line there is no poetry—the Horatian tradition was continuing in
a Latin poetry that was thoroughly alive and full of resources
and ingenuity.

TODAY

In modern times Horace has played a striking role, his influence leading in more or less the same direction as in the

medieval period. He made a powerful contribution to the flowering of a refined secular poetry in Italy, then in France and in all of Europe; but this time it was poetry in the various national languages. In France Ronsard and Du Bellay, in Italy Petrarch, in Spain Luis de León bear sufficient witness to him. He furnished the wisdom of our ancestors with a body of aphorisms that must sometimes have helped them in their lives. Entire Renaissance emblem books were based on these *sententiae.* In a Christian climate he has maintained an ideal of morality which it is peculiarly difficult for Christians to conceive of, for even stronger reasons than they would probably be able to invent, and which is essential to the equilibrium of European man. Finally, we are familiar with the salutary influence exercised by the *Ars poetica* on all that the moderns, including the Romantics, have written in verse: today, with a little perspective, we are better able to understand the perilous condition of poetry and how, lacking an *Art,* it is threatened by lack of rhythm and aphasia.

In France especially our literature owes it a great deal. Hugo and Musset were nourished by it; and then there are the Voltaire letters, La Fontaine, Théophile, Saint-Amant, and Boileau. There is a whole tradition there, and we would be very wrong to slight its intrinsic qualities and the continuous line that connects it with the very works we most spontaneously admire.

Today it requires a certain amount of application to take pleasure in Horace. Perhaps the best of us feel that before any effort of individual morality we must first, in the confusion in which we are struggling, make certain of some elementary evidence which should be generally accepted and could serve as a seat of a life in society: at least this appears to be what is being sought by our thinkers of today, who are all more or less metaphysicians or political men. Horace was neither one nor the other. Again: we no longer seek to be happy; we cultivate our anguish, and all equilibrium seems to us to be mediocrity. Finally, on the literary plane, our poets since Baudelaire have taken on exaggerated ambitions: we ask them for an explanation of the world, or for continual re-creation of a world: poetry has become "the only spiritual task." In that case, what kind of reception can we give to a drinking song or an *"Epistle* to his Gardener"? Perhaps too, our aesthetics are particularly ill suited to defining the importance of form in the genesis and effectiveness of poems: the ideal of many of our poets seems to be one of a form that is newly created each time, at each moment, with rapport to what they wish to express. We have come very far from the composition of Alcaic stanzas!

Sufficient to each day, to each century, is the affliction thereof; and in every century we do not all have the same work to do. It is well that some spirits who are free, or liberated from other tasks—literate men, aestheticians—should illustrate the treasures of the past as best they can, keep them living, and save them for the future; it is not the worst role a man may fulfill. Without denying any of our recent accomplishments, we will some day certainly find the way again to universal poetry, and even to light poetry. I think that it will be a very good sign; in a world grown more calm and healthy, it will be something resembling the happy release of tension that announces the spring.

There is no point in pretending that Horace will ever be a poet for young people. To appreciate his form and content, the reader must have much more maturity than is required by Vergil. A young man lives by nature in vastness, in God; he hardly sees other men and makes his life of himself. After some years, human anxiety has changed its object: God remains, certainly, but one would like to know for a fact that other men, those men who, in fact, have so much place in our life, also exist, and especially that one exists oneself. For here below it is of man that it is hardest to be sure. "What are the uses of friendship?" The young man will answer: "To exalt us together toward God! To help us serve a cause." The mature man will say: "To bear witness to each person that human beings exist, and that each of us truly exists." Then it is time for our poet. For the Christian particularly, Montaigne and Horace are not less necessary than Pascal and Vergil.

He was not an Epicurean: we have established this sufficiently; any more than he was a Cynic or Stoic. But I would find it easy to believe that, being what he was, he found the Epicurean climate the one in which he could breathe most freely. For the Epicureans, there was not a single God, that is, no necessary and demanding center to which the singular beings that we are must come to be absorbed and consumed. But there were gods, distinct as our friends are, with whom friendly links could be established. The stubborn nonintellectualism of the sect, absurd in certain regards, allowed the development, in those who were capable of it, of a particular attention to the concrete and the diverse. Perhaps Christians should not be shocked at this atheism or polytheism, which was normally translated on the moral plane as the rejection of all objectivism and of any fabricated garment. Does this not consist, quite simply, in turning oneself into the subject, and corresponding to the reality of a God who is above and beyond monotheism as well as polytheism?

It may seem strange that at the end of a literary study devoted to a poet, and so far-off a poet, one should feel oneself moved to carry the discussion to the moral plane, to ask questions about truth, and to judge. But it is apparently because the subject requires it: if today Horace has lost many of his readers, it is because he is still judged, as he was in the Middle Ages, as *lubricus et vagus*, selfish and superficially sensual, a man of ill company. Hence, it is just as well to ask these inevitable questions directly. Let us, furthermore, reread the *Satires* and the *Epistles*, and we will see clearly that he himself would not have resented such a challenge: it is a living man to whom we are speaking.

It is not suggested that Horace should be used as a model. But I see that each of us has great difficulty in living without little by little losing his humanity, since our laziness, the world's intellectual fashions, our particular obligations, our duties, even our vocations conspire to narrow us. Hence in order for us to keep at least a certain openness of imagination and heart, to remain worthy of the richness and diversity of being, we should have very different types of men as much present as possible in our friendship or our friendly thoughts. Horace is a man whose poetic genius and firmness of conscience permitted him to hold to a difficult position and make it illustrious. Let us not turn away from him, for around us we will not find many people who resemble him.

If our first movement does not carry us toward him, is this

an indication that he has nothing to say to us? Or is it rather an indication that, disaccustomed to what he can say to us, we would gain particular profit from listening to him? Our civilization disinterests us in the present in favor of chance speculations on the future. It turns our interest away from the persons whom we encounter daily or occasionally, and toward consideration of groups—races or classes—which are real, but with which we have a connection of a merely theoretical kind.

We perceive that the promoters of revolutions do not like up-heavals and convulsions. . . . To please them, there must be something on a global scale. The building of new worlds, periods of transition are ends in themselves for them. . . . And do you know why they keep vainly struggling with these eternal preparations? Because they lack real capacities, they have no talent. Man is born to live, not to prepare himself to live.

How can we not subscribe to these words of Pasternak (*Dr. Zhivago*)? Men more attached to the immediate present would perhaps be in less of a hurry to band together for "the last" of wars, or to inaugurate "singing tomorrows." We must again learn to feel the weight and density of life as it passes through our hands. We must realize that no day is wholly gray, wholly null, or existing only for another day. *Carpe diem.* Our life is made up of all our moments.

Antiquity and the Middle Ages seem to us to have been doctrinaire ages, in which redoubtable disputers and stubborn minds confronted each other; as good historians, we appreciate the resolution that Horace evidenced when he undertook to trace out his own road. But that enterprise did not isolate him; he remained sociable, present to those who surrounded him. His liberty was not a refusal of others: a free mind loves those who surround it as being different from itself, and believes that these differences—even if he cannot be sure that he entirely understands all their range—also have a meaning for him.

Horace, then, was neither Augustus, nor Maecenas, nor any of the political men among whom he lived. He did not wish to become like them, and he continued to take pleasure in them and to love them. Nor was he a rural proprietor like the others; he was very different from Ofellus and Cervius, who came to spend evenings with him. And how different he must have been from those charming little girls or those handsome boys with whom he exchanged pleasure, and whom he has preserved for thousands of years for us in a graceful gesture, a few happy, joyous moments, worthy of our species! A self-absorbed man? Yes, but always capable, whether with Davus or with Damasippus, to share bread and talk. Self-absorbed? But God grant that we may never become absorbed in objects of less value!

Decidedly, a dispute on Horace can only remain unresolved.

EACH of the three volumes of the edition of E. Burck (cf. *infra*,
p. 191) ends with a critical bibliography (nearly exhaustive
for the last thirty years) which is very intelligent and very
practical: it has an index through which the reader can find the
special studies on each piece and also the passages in larger
works in which it is particularly discussed. For the period before
1935, P. Faider, *Bibliotheca Horatiana*, Les études classiques,
IV, 1935, pp. 10–27, 351–66; M. Schanz-C. Hosius, *Gesch. d.
röm. Literatur*, vol. II, 4th ed. Munich, 1935, pp. 113–62. And
naturally the usual bibliographical tools: the *Jahresbericht* of C.
Bursian (the last report appeared in 1939, Suppl. CCLXVII,
pp. 1–174); *L'année philologique*; N. I. Herescu, *Bibliographie
de la littérature latine*, Paris, 1943.

I. EDITIONS

The text of Horace is, on the whole, very solidly established;
the manuscripts at our disposal, of which the oldest date from
the ninth century, seem to prolong two textual traditions established in antiquity as distinct from each other, though needless
to say they have not ceased to war with each other. Perhaps
yet a third tradition would have come down to us with a
manuscript *(Blandinius vetustissimus)*; it disappeared in a fire
in 1566, but the Flemish Humanist Jacques van Cruucke
(Cruquius) preserved a certain number of passages from it.
Once the data of these manuscripts are assembled (the essential
part of this work was done by O. Keller and A. Holder in their

edition of 1864–70), the editor is faced with a double task: to reinstate as precisely as possible the two or three versions in which we can find Horace's text toward the second and third centuries; and then to try to recognize, when there is a divergence between these reconstituted versions, the passage that in each case is most likely to come from the poet. The study of the manuscript tradition has recently made great progress thanks to the work of F. Klingner, which resulted in the editing of the *Bibliotheca Teubneriana* (3d ed., Leipzig, 1959; see especially "Über die Recensio der Horazhandschriften," *Hermes*, LXX, 1935, pp. 249–68, 361–403), and of M. Lenchantin de Gubernatis, resulting in the editing of the *Corpus Paravianum* (Turino, 1945; see especially "Sulla tradizione manoscritta di Orazio," *Athenaeum*, XV, 1937, pp. 129–79). F. Villeneuve's edition (Coll. des Universités de France, Paris, 1927–34) is not based upon such scientific methods, but it is inspired by an intelligent eclecticism and a very sure feeling for Horace's manner; it gives an excellent text, which is very abundantly and clearly documented and continuously clarified by a scrupulous translation.

For commentary, first place must be given to the edition of the *Satires* by P. Lejay (Paris, 1911) and to certain editions or commentaries on the *Epistle* to the Pisos (A. Rostagni, Turino, 1930; O. Immisch, Leipzig, 1932; W. Steidle, *Studien zur Ars poetica des Horaz*, Wurzburg, 1939). For the work as a whole, the French reader will use the scholarly edition of F. Plessis and P. Lejay (Paris, 1903) and the notes of F. Villeneuve's edition, which are particularly copious for the *Odes*. There is still much to be derived from the L. Mueller edition (Leipzig, 1891–1900). The most modern and elegant treatment is to be found in the latest version, edited by E. Burck (Berlin, 1955–57) of the constantly reworked and improved edition by A. Kiessling (1st ed. 1884–89) and then R. Heinze (from 1908 on).

II. GENERAL WORKS

From the diversity of the portraits that have been drawn of Horace, it is obvious that our poet, as inclined as he was to talk about himself, is yet very difficult to grasp. This comes from the diversity of his personality. Yet we can hope that in the long run progress in our objective knowledge will make it possible for us to be more just and more intelligent about him.

For anyone who interests himself in Horace today, the first step is to find a guide who is not too repugnant to him and who will put him in sympathy with at least some aspect of the poet's personality. The rest will come by itself, with more specialized study, as one meditates directly on the texts. I feel that a French reader cannot fail to find pleasure and profit in reading J. Marouzeau's "Horace dans la littérature française," *Rev. ét. latines*, XIII, 1935, pp. 274–95; P. Boyancé, "Grandeur d'Horace," *Bull. Assoc. G. Budé*, 1955, no. 4 (= *Lettres d'Humanité* XIV), pp. 48–64; and P. Grimal, *Horace*, Paris, 1958, which is as solid as it is brilliant and sheds fresh light on many problems.

To these should be added three fine studies by F. Klingner ("Gedanken über Horaz," *Die Antike*, V, 1929, pp. 23–44; "Horazische und moderne Lyrik," *ibid.*, VI, 1930, pp. 65–84; "Horaz," *ibid.*, XII, 1936, pp. 65–83; the first and third of these studies were reprinted in *Römische Geisteswelt*, 2d ed., Wiesbaden, 1953); also W. Wili's ample biography (*Horaz und die augusteische Kultur*, Basel, 1948). All of these are healthy and cordial studies; they reveal a Horace who is especially serious, patriotic, and preoccupied with moral problems. E. Turolla goes in the same direction, perhaps a little too far, in his "Il punto alto della personalità e della poesia Oraziana," *Maia*, VII, 1955, pp. 263–85, and "Unità ideologica e tematica nel primo libro delle epistole Oraziane," *Giorn. ital. d. filologia*, IV, 1951, pp. 289–306.

The erudition of the early part of this century resulted in syntheses that, although they are cast in a rather severe form, should not be neglected: R. Heinze, "Horazens Buch der Briefe," *Neue. Jahrb. f. d. kl. Altertum*, XLIII, 1919, pp. 305–16 (reprinted in E. Burck's edition, vol. III, pp. 367–80); R. Reitzenstein, "Horaz als Dichter," *ibid.*, XXV, 1922, pp. 24–42. In a rather academic genre, T. Zielinski's *Horace et la société romaine du temps d'Auguste*, Paris, 1938, may perhaps be read with pleasure.

The great work of E. Fraenkel, *Horace*, Oxford, 1957, is a collection of studies. It consists of a series of plumb lines dropped into Horace's *oeuvre*. This book is intellectually stimulating.

III. LIFE OF HORACE

On the status of Horace's father before his manumission, the negative conclusions of L. Halkin, "Le père d'Horace a-t-il été esclave public?," *L'antiquité classique*, IV, 1935, pp. 125–40, have seemed to me to be convincing.

The question has been raised of the ethnic origin of Horace's parents (W. H. Alexander, "The Enigma of Horace's Mother," *Class. Philology*, XXXVII, 1942, pp. 385–97; K. Mras, "Horaz als Mensch und als Dichter," *Wiener Studien*, LIV, 1936, pp. 70–85); this is because at the beginning of the first century Sylla's campaigns brought thousands of Asiatic slaves flooding into Italy, while it is hard to see how the slave population in Italy can yet have contained many individuals of Italian origin. But how can one believe that Horace could have jeered at Jews and abominated Syrians, as he did, if he had been one of them? One of the merits of the study by M. Bang, "Die Herkunft der römischen Sklaven" (*Röm. Mittheil.*, XXV, 1910, pp. 223–51; XXVII, 1912, pp. 189–221) is that it draws attention to the individual misfortunes, much more numerous than we think, which in Italy itself could push the child of a free family into slavery.

On Horace's horoscope, T. Nicklin, *Class. Review*, XXVIII, 1914, pp. 271–74; on Venusia, H. V. Canter, "Venusia and the Native Country of Horace," *Class. Journal*, XXVI, 1930–31, pp. 439–56; on young Horace and Epicurean circles, the evidence from the papyrus at Herculaneum has been presented by A. Körte in his "Augusteer bei Philodem," *Rhein. Museum*, XLV, 1890, pp. 172–77; on Horace's conduct at Philippi, L. Edelstein, "Horace, *Odes* II 7, 9–10," *Amer. Journal of Philology*, LXII, 1941, pp. 441–51.

On Horace's social position, two excellent articles: L. Ross Taylor, "Horace's Equestrian Career," *Amer. Journal of Philology*, XLVI, 1925, pp. 161–70; M. L. Gordon, "The Freedman's Son in Municipal Life," *Journal of Roman Studies*, XXI, 1931, pp. 65–77.

On friends of Horace: On Varius, J. P. Boucher, "L'oeuvre de L. Varius Rufus d'après Properce II, 34," *Rev. ét. anciennes,* LX, 1958, pp. 307–22. On the relations between Vergil and Horace, it is probably impossible to write a study of the whole situation; for Horace's "farewell" (*Ode* IV 12), cf. *infra,* p. 143. Maecenas: There is a fairly exact presentation of his relations with Horace by A. Noirfalise, "Horace et Mécène," *Les études classiques,* XVIII, 1950, pp. 289–303; after the very circumstantial but rather flat study by P. Lunderstedt, "De C. Maecenatis fragmentis," *Commentat. philol. Jenenses,* IX, 1, Leipzig, 1911, the position and literary tastes of Maecenas are very successfully evaluated by A. Kappelmacher in the article "Maecenas" of the *Realenzyklopädie,* XIV, 1928, 218–29. Propertius, friend, imitator, and, doubtless, finally rival of Horace: L. Herrmann, "Horace adversaire de Properce," *Rev. ét. anciennes,* XXXV, 1933, pp. 281–92; F. Solmsen, "Propertius and Horace," *Class. Philology,* XLIII, 1948, pp. 105–109 (the positive elements of their emulation); S. d'Elia, "Properzio e Orazio," *Ann. d. Fac. di Lettere di Napoli,* II, 1952, pp. 45–77; some penetrating studies by R. Lucot, "Vertumne et Mécène," *Pallas,* I, 1953, pp. 65–80; "Propertiana," *ibid.,* II, 1954, pp. 97–104; "Mécène et Properce," *Rev. ét. latines,* XXXV, 1957, pp. 195–204. On the Sabine farm, G. Lugli, *La villa d'Orazio nella valle del Licenza,* Rome, 1930; E. Galletier, "L'abbé Capmartin de Chaupy et la découverte de la villa d'Horace," *Les études classiques,* IV, 1935, pp. 74–92.

IV. SATIRES AND EPODES

The interpretation of the *Satires* requires research in several directions.

Horace's relations with popular philosophy and the Stoic-Cynic diatribe; this problem dominates the ample introduction of the Lejay edition (cf. *supra,* p. 191); in the same direction, A. Oltramare, *Les origines de la diatribe romaine,* Lausanne, 1926; A. Cartault, *Étude sur les satires d'Horace,* Paris, 1899, used the same approach to clarify many matters of composition and style.

Horace's position in the literary debates of his time was the subject, forty years ago, of an important debate: was he the

friend of the *neoteroi* (C. Jackson, "Molle atque Facetum . . .,"
Harvard Stud. in Class. Philology, XXV, 1914, pp. 117–37; B. L.
Ullman, "Horace, Catullus and Tigellius," *Class. Philology*, X,
1915, pp. 270–96), or their adversary (G. L. Hendrickson,
"Horace and Valerius Cato," *ibid.*, XI, 1916, pp. 249–69; XII,
1917, pp. 77–92, 329–50)? Much is still to be gained from reading these articles. Since then, the debate has been broadened to
take other texts of Horace into consideration; and now more
is known especially about the history of the doctrines and literary currents. Horace's debt to Catullus and the continuity of
the two poetics appear more and more evident (C. W. Men-
dell, "Catullan Echoes in the Odes of Horace," *Class. Philology*,
XXX, 1935, pp. 289–301; P. Gilbert, "Catulle et Horace,"
Latomus, I, 1937, pp. 88–93; J. Ferguson, "Catullus and
Horace," *Amer. Journal of Philology*, LXXVII, 1956, pp. 1–18).
Above all, the discovery of new texts by Callimachus has brought
to light a true unity of doctrine between Horace and the patron
of learned Alexandrianism (F. Wehrli, "Horaz und Kallimachos," *Museum Helveticum*, I, 1944, pp. 69–76). Yet agreement has not been reached among the philologists: according
to B. Otis ("Horace and the Elegists," *Trans. of the Amer.
Philol. Assoc.*, LXXVI, 1945, pp. 177–90), Horace's unquestionable aversion to the elegy must inevitably have put him in
opposition to the *neoteroi*. On the various Furiuses, cf. H.
Bardon, *La littérature latine inconnue*, I, Paris, 1952, pp. 179–81,
347–52. The authenticity of the first lines of *Satire* I 10 has been
defended by M. Rothstein, "Die Anfangsverse der Satire I, 10
des Horaz," *Hermes*, LXVIII, 1933, pp. 70–83 (cf. E. Fraenkel,
"Lucili quam sis mendosus," *ibid.*, pp. 392–99, which attributes
these lines to a contemporary of Horace's) and G. D'Anna,
"Oraziani i primi versi della decima Satira?" *Maia*, VII, 1955,
pp. 26–42.

For Horace, the Latin tradition of the satire went back to
Lucilius. Yet, the problem of the origins of that literary form,
that of the meaning (or the successive meanings) of the word
satura cannot be entirely indifferent to a reader of Horace; the
present state of the question and the bibliography can be found
in U. Knoche, *Die römische Satire*, 2d ed., Göttingen, 1957,
and in the Introduction of O. Weinreich, *Römische Satiren*,

Zurich, 1949. It would be extremely interesting to know the name given by Horace to what we call his *Satires*; but it seems impossible to determine with certainty between *Saturae* and *Sermones*; cf. G. L. Hendrickson, "Are the Letters of Horace Satires?" *Amer. Journal of Philology*, XVIII, 1897, pp. 313–24; B. L. Ullman, "Satura and Satire," *Class. Philology*, VIII, 1913, pp. 172–94; F. Marx, "Römische Volkslieder," *Rhein. Museum*, LXXVIII, 1929, pp. 398–426. On the tradition in Horace of the Varronian Menippea, cf. particularly O. Weinreich (*supra*). G. C. Fiske's *Lucilius and Horace* . . ., Univ. of Wisconsin Studies 7, 1920, is still very useful on everything concerning similarities of matter that can be established between the two works. But the interpretation of Lucilius has been entirely renovated by M. Puelma Piwonka in his *Lucilius und Kallimachos*, Frankfort, 1949; this book is thick, difficult, and debatable in more than one chapter, but it is animated by a powerful mind; and it sheds light on Lucilius' own links with the literary forms of Hellenism and gives us a better understanding than we have ever had of the profound unity of Horace's first works. In the same direction, H. Bardon ("Catulle et ses modèles poétiques de langue latine," *Latomus*, XVI, 1957, pp. 614–27) has written some penetrating pages on the affinities between Lucilius and Catullus: the taste for invective, for direct speech, and for personal confession.

On the language and metrics of the *Satires*, there is hardly anything but collections of facts, which are sometimes worthy of esteem; the following may be read with interest: G. Leich, *De Horatii in saturis sermone ludibundo*, Diss. Iéna, 1910 (on the parody); K. Büchner, "Die Trennung von Adjektiv und Substantiv durch die Versgrenze in Horazens Satiren," *Hermes*, LXXI, 1936, pp. 409–20; N. O. Nilsson, *Metrische Stildifferenzen in den Satiren des Horaz*, Uppsala, 1952; and naturally, A. Cartault, *supra*, p. 194.

In the collection of *Epodes* (here again we do not know what Horace called it: *Epodes* or *Iambics*), the philologists' interest has fallen by choice on the pieces inspired by civil matters, especially the sixteenth. There has been a very legitimate attempt to raise the evaluation of the seriousness and originality of that inspiration, notably by F. Klingner, "Gedanken . . ." (cf.

supra, p. 192). The question of the date is of vital importance here: the poem has a very different ring depending upon whether it is the first work of Horace, written in 41, or whether it is to be placed six or seven years later among the other epodes and satires. A very long controversy on the earlier date of the sixteenth *Epode* or the fourth *Bucolic* (written in 40) seems to me to have arrived at its epilogue in the studies of B. Snell, "Die 16. Epode von Horaz und Vergils 4. Ekloge," *Hermes*, LXXIII, 1938, pp. 237–42, and of C. Becker, "Virgils Eklogenbuch," *ibid.*, LXXXIII, 1955, pp. 314–49: the epode is posterior not only to the fourth *Bucolic* but to the publication (in 37) of the collection of *Bucolics*. E. Fraenkel in his *Horace* (cf. *supra*, p. 192) seems to have a very just appreciation of the character of this poem. The circumstances of the composition of *Epode* 9 appear to me to have been established by W. Tarn, "The Battle of Actium," *Journal of Roman Studies*, XXI, 1931, pp. 173–99: Horace was in Rome, and the epode was written on receipt of a dispatch sent by Octavius to Maecenas in the very course of the battle.

In F. Olivier, *Les Epodes d'Horace*, Lausanne, 1917, and F. Lasserre, *Les Epodes d'Archiloque*, Paris, 1950, may be found all that can be advanced in favor of a dependency between the two texts. In a word, not very much, if it is a question of commenting on the *Epodes* of Horace; but, at least if Archilochus is understood in the sense taken by A. Bonnard, "Poésie d'Archiloque" (in Archilochus, *Fragments*, Coll. des Universités de France, Paris, 1958, pp. xxx–lvi), it is impossible to deny a certain affinity between the two geniuses, combining as they both did individualism, a certain lyricism, and the spirit of satire. B. Kirn's dissertation *Zur literarischen Stellung von Horazens Jambenbuch*, Tübingen, 1935, gathers very practical documentation on the "sources" of each of the pieces.

It would be interesting to be able to date the various satires and epodes, if only relatively. I do not believe that it is possible to go beyond some basic statements: none of the pieces of *Satire* I seems to have been written after 35 (on that date, cf. J. Carcopino, "Notes biographiques sur M. Valerius Messala Corvinus . . .," *Rev. de philologie*, LXXII, 1946, pp. 96–117); they are so arranged in the book as to suggest a chronological

order corresponding to the social rise of the poet; the satires of
Book II are arranged in an architectural order with the two
halves of the book corresponding to each other, and they all
have to do with a situation which could have been that of the
year 30; the *Epodes* cannot have been written before 30. In R.
Latsch's thesis, *Die Chronologie der Satiren und Epoden auf
entwicklungsgeschichtlicher Grundlage*, Wurzburg, 1936, it can
be seen that hardly more can be said without begging the
question.

V. THE ODES

The rhythmic structure of the *Odes* has been the subject of
two very fine works: R. Heinze, "Die lyrischen Verse des Horaz,"
*Ber. über die Verhandl d. sächs. Gesellsch. d. Wissensch. zu.
Leipzig*, Philol.-hist. Klasse, LXX, 4, 1918, and K. Büchner,
"Zur Form und Entwicklung der horazischen Ode und zur Lex
Meinekiana," *ibid.*, XCI, 2, 1939. Büchner has the distinction
of having established positively that Horace conceived nearly all
his *Odes* in the mold of the four-line stanza (lex Meinekiana),
and from this he has drawn the *structura*, Diss. Berlin, 1929.

On details of expression, there are valuable studies by J.
Marouzeau, "L'art du nom propre chez Horace," *L'antiquité
classique*, IV, 1935, pp. 365–74; "Horace assembleur de mots,"
Emerita, IV, 1936, pp. 1–10; "Horace artiste de sons," *Mnemosyne*, IV, 1936, pp. 85–94; "Quelques éléments de poétique:
l'art horatien," in *Quelques aspects de la formation du latin
littéraire*, Paris, 1949, pp. 193–222. Also B. Axelson, "Zur Wort-
wahl des Odendichters Horaz," in *Unpoetische Wörter*, Lund,
1945, pp. 98–113, and the really remarkable study by F. Bömer,
"Beiträge zum Verständnis der augusteischen Dichtersprache,"
Gymnasium, LXIV, 1957, pp. 1–21 (the means used for great
poetry by Horace and Vergil).

On the composition of the books, P. Maury, *Horace et le
secret de Virgile*, Paris, 1945 (for the *Roman Odes*); W. Port,
"Die Anordnung in Gedichtbüchern augusteischer Zeit," *Philologus*, LXXXI, 1926, pp. 280–308, 427–68; T. Frank, "How
Horace Employed Alcaeus," *Class. Philology*, XXII, 1927, pp.
291–95 (on the first *Odes* of Book I).

The relationship of the *Odes* with Hellenistic poetry is demonstrated very convincingly by the fine book of G. Pasquali, *Orazio lirico*, Florence, 1920, which is as valuable for its interpretation of the civic odes as for that of the light odes; cf. also R. Reitzenstein, "Horaz und die Hellenistische Lyrik," *Neue Jahrb. f. d. klass. Altertum*, XXI, 1908, pp. 81–102.

On the civic inspiration of the *Odes*, one should read F. Klingner, "Gedanken . . ." (cf. *supra*, p. 192), but the best note has, I think, been struck by V. Pöschl in "Horaz und die Politik," *Sitzungber. d. Heidelberger Akad. d. Wissensch.*, Philos. histor. Kl., 1956, 4; without disputing the seriousness of that involvement, one must not do injury to the unity of Horace's poetry by forgetting how often it is often light. On Horace and Augustus, D. Norberg, "La divinité d'Auguste dans la poésie d'Horace," *Eranos*, XLIV, 1946, pp. 389–403 (excellent); L. Wickert, "Horaz und Augustus," *Würzburger Jahrb.*, II, 1947, pp. 158–72, vividly shows the complexity of Horace's attitude: most interesting observations in the realms of both exegesis of detail and the evolution of Horace's art.

R. Pichon, "Les mètres lyriques d'Horace," *Rev. de philologie*, XVII, 1893, pp. 132–40, and F. Muller-J. Fil., "De horatianis metris deque corum usu poetae animi habitui respondente," *Mnemosyne*, IIId Ser. vol. IV, 1936, pp. 114–28, have attempted, with some felicity, to define the ethos of the different meters by studying the literary themes for which they were most frequently used.

There is still much for the metrician to do. The studies of J. Irigoin, "La structure des vers éoliens," *L'antiquité classique*, XXV, 1956, pp. 5–19, and "Colon, vers et strophe dans la lyrique monodique grecque," *Rev. de philologie*, XXXI, 1957, pp. 234–38, give the Latinist precise information of great value on Horace's Greek models. For studies of verbal metrics (meter and accent, the word in the line), the tables drawn up by E. Zinn, *Der Wortakzent in den lyrischen Versen des Horaz*, Munich, 1940, are very useful. It is profitable to read M. Lenchantin de Gubernatis, "I metri eolici della lirica latina," *Athenaeum*, XII, 1934, pp. 239–54, and "Meletemeta metrica," *ibid.*, XXII–XXIII, 1944–45, pp. 72–97. On Horace and music, cf. G. Wille, *Die Bedeutung der Musik im Leben der Römer*, Diss. Tübingen, 1951.

On Horace's Pindaric intentions, cf. E. L. Highbarger, "The Pindaric Style of Horace," *Trans. of the Amer. Philol. Assoc.*, LXVI, 1935, pp. 222–55; F. Heinimann, "Die Einheit der horazischen Ode," *Museum Helveticum*, IX, 1952, pp. 193–203; but especially D. Norberg, "L'Olympionique, le poète et leur renom éternel . . . ," Uppsala Univers. *Arsskrift*, 1945, 6 (completed and confirmed rather than criticized by G. Carlsson, "L'Ode I 1 d'Horace, ses idées et sa composition," *Eranos* XLIV, 1946, pp. 404–20). Some interesting and often adventurous suggestions, are to be found in G. Daniels, *Die Strophengruppen in den Horazoden*, Diss. Königsberg, 1940, and G. Reincke, *De tripertita carminum Horatianorum* civism and yet indifference to public matters; F. Altheim, *Röm. Religionsgeschichte*, II, 2d ed., Baden-Baden, 1953, pp. 191–238, shows that the poets not only served Augustus' policies but may, in part, have inspired them. Certain somewhat disconcerting aspects of Horace's "imperial politics" have been fruitfully studied by A. Oltramare, "Auguste et les Parthes," *Rev. ét. latines*, XVI, 1938, pp. 121–38, and H. Haffter, "Die fünfte Römerode des Horaz," *Philologus*, XCIII, 1938, pp. 132–56. Over-all views, interesting and finely shaded, are to be found in H. Kempter, *Die römische Geschichte bei Horaz*, Diss. Munich, 1938.

Horace's religious attitude has been studied, often very subtly, by L. H. Allen, "Horace, Ode I 34–35," *Class. Review*, XXXII, 1918, pp. 29–30; and by L. A. Mackay, *id.*, *ibid.*, XLIII, 1929, pp. 10–12. We must decidedly reject the hypothesis of a conversion; cf. A. Delatte, "La conversion d'Horace (*Ode I 34*)," *L'antiquité classique*, IV, 1935, pp. 293–307. On some mythical themes, K. Barwick, "Horaz (*C I 2*) und Vergil," *Philologus*, XC, 1935, pp. 257–76; T. Zielinski, "Le messianisme d'Horace," *L'antiquité classique*, VIII, 1939, pp. 171–80.

Wilamowitz (*Sappho und Simonides*, Berlin, 1913, p. 309, n. 1) claimed that Horace had never had any understanding of the feminine soul; that he was totally mistaken in this can be seen from the penetrating analysis of *Odes* III 26–28 in F. Altheim (*op. cit.*, pp. 270–75).

On the morality to be found in the *Odes*, W. Kroll, "Horaz' Oden und die Philosophie," *Wiener Studien*, XXXVII, 1915, pp. 223–38, cites philosophical texts that can be paralleled to those of the *Odes*. There is a strange but very suggestive study by P. Gilbert, "Horace et l'Egypte. Aux sources du Carpe diem," *Latomus*, V, 1946, pp. 61–74. The truest perspective seems to me to be that of K. Büchner ("Altrömische und horazische Virtus," *Die Antike*, XV, 1939, pp. 145–64; "Horaz über die Gelassenheit, c. II 16," in *Humanitas Romana*, Heidelberg, 1957, pp. 176–202) and J. Fontaine ("Les racines de la sagesse horatienne," *L'Inform. littéraire*, XI, 1959, pp. 113–24).

VI. THE EPISTLES

The study by J. Sykutris, "Epistolographie," in the *Realenzyklopädie*, Suppl. V (1931), pp. 185–220, contains the most appropriate elements for the comprehension of Horace's creative originality. E. P. Morris, "The Form of the Epistle in Horace," *Yale Class. Studies*, II, 1931, pp. 79–114, insists too much, I think, on the conventional, not properly speaking, epistolary character of these poems.

Horace's moral personality is the core of this collection. One should read E. Courbaud, *Horace, sa vie et sa pensée à l'époque des Epîtres* . . . , Paris, 1914, for the very subtle analysis that he gives of each piece; his thesis of a progressive conversion on Horace's part and his attempt to establish a spiritual journey toward Stoicism seem to me to be a simplification of the facts. For the broad lines of the portrait I prefer A. La Penna, "Schizzo di una interpretazione di Orazio partendo dal primo libro delle Epistole," *Annali d. Scuola Norm. Sup. di Pisa*, XVIII, 1949, pp. 14–48: Horace's eclecticism is clearly seen, although the author makes it end in a discouragement, almost a nihilism, which is not apparent to me. Cf. also the studies of R. Heinze and E. Turolla cited above, p. 192.

The interpretation of *Epistle* 7 is essential to that of the whole book. I believe that E. Courbaud is wrong here, in spite of his scrupulousness, and so are all those (notably J. H. Gunning, "Der siebente Brief des Horaz und sein Verhältnis zu Maecenas," *Mnemosyne*, X, 1942, pp. 303–20) who have seen this letter as the expression of somewhat harsh demands; the proper note has been struck by K. Büchner, "Der siebente Brief des Horaz," *Hermes*, LXXV, 1940, pp. 64–80.

There is still much to be done toward better understanding of the *Epistles*. To a certain extent the philologists have turned their backs on them, because these scholars' habitual and surest methods (research into sources, comparison with analogous works, description of singularities of form in vocabulary and versification) seemingly do not allow them to obtain particularly brilliant results. Furthermore, it appears difficult to study the *Epistles* without forming in one's mind, at least as a hypothesis, a certain picture of Horace's personality; and for a scientific task this is a vexatious necessity. Perhaps the study should begin very modestly, with a literal exegesis which pays particular attention to the sense of each phrase, the movement of the thought, and the construction of the composition.

VII. GLORIOUS EPILOQUES

The Carmen saeculare On the history of secular traditions and the liturgical program of the festival of 17, M. P. Nilsson, "Saeculares ludi," *Realenzyklop.*, IId R. I (1920), 1696-1720; P. Wuilleumier, "Tarente et le Tarentum," *Rev. ét. latines*, X, 1932, pp. 127-46; J. Gagé, *Recherches sur les jeux séculaires romains*, Paris, 1934, and *Apollon romain*, Paris, 1955, pp. 583-637. On Horace's hymn, its inclusion in the festival, and its intentions, J. Vahlen, "Über das Säculargedicht des Horatius," *Sitzungsber. d. Preuss. Akad. d. Wissensch. in Berlin*, 1892, II, pp. 1005-21; W. Fowler, "The Carmen Saeculare of Horace and Its Performance . . . ," *Class. Quarterly*, IV, 1910, pp. 145-55; F. Altheim, "Almus Sol," in *Röm. Religionsgesch.*, II, 2d ed., Baden-Baden, 1953, pp. 239-53; the study of E. Fraenkel in his *Horace* (cf. *supra*, p. 192).

The Fourth Book of Odes The originality of the collection has been demonstrated very felicitously by D. Norberg, "Le quatrième livre des Odes d'Horace," *Emerita*, XX, 1952, pp. 95-107, and by E. Fraenkel, "Das Pindargedicht des Horaz," *Sitzungsber. d. Heidelberger Akad. d. Wissensch.*, Philos. histor. Kl., 1932-33, 2 and *Horace* (cf. *supra*, p. 192). *Ode* 7 is the subject of an admirable commentary by F. Altheim, *op. cit.*, pp. 265-70. Vergil is indeed the addressee of *Ode* IV 12, cf. C. M. Bowra, "Horace, *Odes* IV, 12," *Class. Review*, XLII, 1928, pp. 165-67.

The Letters on the Theater The group has been excellently situated in its place by A. La Penna, "Orazio, Augusto e la questione del teatro Latino," *Annali d. Scuola Norm. Sup. di Pisa*, XIX, 1950, pp. 143–54; on the problem of the theater in the Augustan age, there are very accurate views in E. Paratore, *Storia del teatro latino*, Milan, 1957; on the reservations expressed by Horace in the *Epistle* to Augustus, cf. F. Klingner, "Horazens Brief an Augustus," *Sitzungsber. d. Bayer. Akad. d. Wissensch. zu München*, Philos. his. Kl., 1950, 5.

The false problems accumulated from the search in Philodemus for the plan of the *Epistle* to the Pisos have been dissipated by P. Boyancé, "À propos de l'Art Poétique . . . ," *Rev. de philologie*, X, 1936, pp. 20–36, and by H. Dahlmann, "Varros Schrift de poematis und die hellenistisch-römische Poetik," *Abhandl. d. Akad. d. Wissensch. u. Literatur zu Mainz*, 1953, 3.

Since Horace dipped into many sources, all comparative studies are useful to know: with the Platonic tradition, C. Jensen, "Herakleides vom Pontos bei Philodem und Horaz," *Sitzungsber. d. Berliner Akad. d. Wissensch.*, 1936, pp. 292–320; with Panaitios and the doctrine of "propriety," R. Philippson, "Das Sittlichschöne bei Panaitios," *Philologus*, LXXXV, 1930, pp. 357–413; L. Labowsky, *Die Ethik des Panaitios. Untersuch. zur Gesch. des Decorum bei Cicero und Horaz*, Leipzig, 1934 (important for the distinction between the *pulcrum* and the *dulce*); with Roman traditions, M. A. Grant-G. C. Fiske, "Cicero's *Orator* and Horace's *Ars poetica*," *Harvard Stud. in Class. Philology*, XXXV, 1924, pp. 1–74; "Cicero's *de Oratore* and Horace's *Ars poetica*," *Univ. of Wisconsin Studies in Language and Literature*, XXVII, 1929.

F. Klingner ("Horazens Brief an die Pisonen," *Sitzungsber. d. sächs. Akad. d. Wissensch. in Leipzig*, Philol. hist. Kl., LXXXVIII, 3, 1936), has given a particularly refined and respectful analysis of the text. Horace's originality and his indebtedness to his forerunners are evaluated in the felicitous study of M. Delcourt, "L'esthétique d'Horace et les lettres grecques," *Mélanges Paul Thomas*, Bruges, 1930, pp. 187–200. For the editions of the *Epistle* to the Pisos and for commentaries, cf. *supra*, p. 191.

VIII. POSTERITY

It is perhaps not yet possible to write a coherent history of
Horace's later reputation. As far as antiquity and the Middle
Ages are concerned, a good number of studies, though indispensable, are conceived as a catalog of those texts in which
the echo of a passage from Horace is suspected of existing. But
word analogies do not always prove a borrowing, and a true
influence is not always betrayed by imitation or the reminiscence
of some particular passage. With these reservations in mind,
the reader will find the following works indispensable: M.
Hertz, *Analecta ad carminum horatianorum historiam*, I–V,
Breslau, 1876–82, and M. Manitius, *Analekten zur Gesch. des
Horaz im Mittelalter (bis 1300)*, Göttingen, 1893 (the work is
a continuation of Hertz's). On Ovid, A. Zingerle, *Ovidius und
sein Verhältniss zu den Vorgängern, pars IIIa*, Innsbruck, 1871;
on Seneca's tragedies (it is important to note that in spite of
the difference of meters, the *Satires* and *Epistles* also had their
influence here), and on Statius, *id.*, *Zu späteren lateinischen
Dichtern*, Innsbruck, 1873; J. Spika, *De imitatione Horatiana in
Senecae canticis chori*, Vienna, 1890; G. Lühr, *De P. Papinio
Statio in Silvis priorum poetarum . . . imitatore*, Brünsberg,
1880. Also to be read are G. B. Pighi, "Vestricio Spurinna,"
Aevum, XIX, 1945, pp. 114–41; A. Salvatore, "Qua ratione
Prudentius . . . Horatium Vergiliumque imitatus sit," *Annali
d. Facoltà di lettere di Napoli*, VI, 1956, pp. 119–40. The edition
of O. Keller and A. Holder (2d ed., Leipzig, 1899–1925) continuously accompanies Horace's text with indications of the
passages in which he seems to have been imitated.

Horace's fortunes must be placed in relationship with the
evolution of taste; such an attempt has been made by E. Fröbel,
Quid veteres de Horatii poematis judicaverint, Diss. Iéna, 1911.
But for the first and second centuries a clarification of the facts
is to be sought in the reading of general works, especially H.
Bardon, *Les empereurs et les lettres latines d'Auguste à Hadrien*,
Paris, 1940, and R. Marache, *La critique littéraire de langue
latine et le développement du goût archaïsant au IIᵉ siècle de
notre ère*, Rennes, 1952.

Horace's scholiasts do not, any more than Vergil's, add very much to our knowledge of the man or his work; but they help us to have an idea of the history of the scholarly and scientific exegesis of our poet from the third century (Porphyrio) to well into the Middle Ages; cf. particularly, H. Färber, "Die Termini der Poetik in den Odenüberschriften der Horazoden," *Philologus*, XCII, 1937, pp. 349–74.

There is no reason whatever to believe, with P. von Winterfeld (*Rhein. Museum*, LX, 1905, pp. 31–37), that between 550 and 850 Horace's work had completely disappeared, even materially, in Continental Europe, surviving only in Ireland; it is even possible that the scholia of a certain number of our manuscripts go back to work executed in the seventh century in the region of Metz; cf. H. J. Botschuyver, "Quelques remarques sur les scholies parisiennes λφω d'Horace," *Latomus*, III, 1939, pp. 25–51; on the distribution of Horace manuscripts in medieval Europe, cf. H. Buttenwieser, "Popular Authors of the Middle Ages . . . ," *Speculum*, XVII, 1942, pp. 50–55.

There is much to be derived from the Indices (s. v. *Horaz*) of the *Gesch. der latein. Literatur des Mittelalters* (up to 1200 only) of M. Manitius, Munich, 1911–31. For poets the reader will then turn to F. J. Raby, *A History of Christian Latin Poetry from the Beginnings to the Close of the Middle Ages*, 2d ed., Oxford, 1953; *A History of Secular Latin Poetry in the Middle Ages*, 2d ed., Oxford, 1957, 2 vols. A somewhat summary perspective view is to be found in A. Monteverdi, "Orazio nel medio evo," *Studi Medievali*, IX, 1936, pp. 162–80. On the influence of Horace in the *Gesta Danorum* of Saxo (about 1220), F. Blatt, in "L'oeuvre d'un humaniste médiéval," *Mélanges Marouzeau*, Paris, 1948, pp. 29–41, offers some extremely interesting views on the significance of that fidelity to ancient sources, and particularly to Horace. His views conform to those of R. Bezzola, *Les origines et la formation de la littérature courtoise en Occident . . .* , Paris, 1944: an effort to develop in the culture, and in connection with the political authorities, some components that did not belong strictly to the church.

For the musical setting of a certain number of *Odes*, cf. S. Corbin, "Comment on chantait les classiques latins au Moyen âge," *Mélanges P.-M. Masson*, I, Paris, 1955, pp. 107–13. I have not been able to read F. Liuzzi, *La poesia oraziana nella tradizione musicale del medio evo*, Rome, 1938. On the role of Horace in the formation of the hymnographers, the very important text of Reginald of Canterbury (about 1050) was published by J. Hammer, "A Monastic Panegyrist of Horace," *Philological Quarterly*, XI, 1932, pp. 303–10.

For Horace's influence in modern times, the reader can orient himself with *Orazio nella letteratura mondiale*, Rome, 1936. Results and method: the greatest profit will be derived from reading R. Lebègue, "Horace en France pendant la Renaissance," *Humanisme et Renaissance*, III, 1936, pp. 141–64, 289–308, 384–412. J. Marmier took his inspiration from this work for his *Horace en France au XVIIᵉ siècle* and *Influences horatiennes sur le romantisme, Lamartine, Hugo, Musset et leur temps*, Theses Paris (typescript), 1955. See also J. Marouzeau, cf. *supra*, p. 192; G. Curcio, *Q. Orazio Flacco studiato in Italia dal secolo XIII al XVIII*, Catane, 1913.

E. Stemplinger, "Horaz im Urteil der Jahrhunderte," *Das Erbe der Alten*, II, 5, 1921, assembles critical appreciations of Horace: both an anthology and a collection of nonsense, it is a handy source of curious texts.

Let me quote here two texts of Nietzsche:

No other poet up to the present time has given me to know the aesthetic delight, and the wonder, that I have always felt on reading one of Horace's odes. There are languages in which it would be impossible even to hope for such success. That mosaic of words, in which each element, by its sonorities, by its position, by the images that it evokes, causes its peculiar virtues to radiate to left, to right, and over the whole work, that minimum of volume and number of signs, the maximum energy of signs thus obtained— all of that is Roman, and, in my opinion, distinguished beyond equal. In comparison, all other poetry seems vulgar, a simple sentimental babbling. [*Werke*, X, p. 343]

And elsewhere:

If all goes well, the moment comes when the man who wishes to make progress in morality and in reason will return more readily to recollections of Socrates than to the Bible, and when he will recognize in Montaigne and in Horace those who are better able than any other to open his way before him, and to introduce him to that wise man, the most simple of all, in whom all forms of wisdom are united. [*Werke*, IV, p. 248]

Index